CIPS Study M

Level 3

Certificate in Purchasing and Supply

COURSE BOOK

Understanding the Purchasing Environment

© Profex Publishing Limited, 2010

Printed and distributed by the Chartered Institute of Purchasing & Supply

Easton House, Easton on the Hill, Stamford, Lincolnshire PE9 3NZ

Tel: +44 (0) 1780 756 777

Fax: +44 (0) 1780 751 610

Email: info@cips.org

Website: www.cips.org

First edition August 2009
Reprinted with minor amendments October 2010

Contents

Page

Preface   *v*

The Exam   *vii*

How to Use Your Study Pack   *xi*

1   Introduction to the Purchasing Environment   1

What is the purchasing environment?; why analyse the purchasing environment?;
the PESTLE framework; other tools of analysis

2   Business Sectors   19

Sectors of the economy; private and public sectors; private sector organisations;
public sector organisations; the third sector

3   Markets   39

How markets work; perfect competition; monopoly; monopolistic (imperfect) competition; oligopoly;
competitive forces; international markets

4   Stakeholders   63

Stakeholders in purchasing; why are stakeholders important?; stakeholder
analysis and management; stakeholder conflict and co-operation

5   Political Factors   73

The political environment; local politics; national politics; government policy and funding;
international politics and policies

6   Economic Factors   85

The economic environment; the national economy; the business cycle;
international economics; exchange rates; the economics of international sourcing

7   Social Factors   101

The socio-cultural environment; cultural factors; demographic and socio-economic factors;
corporate social responsibility (CSR) and ethics; socio-cultural factors in international supply chains

8   Technological Factors   115

The technological environment; technological development; developments in ICT; e-sourcing and e-
procurement

9   Environmental Factors   131

The natural environment; current environmental concerns; pressure for environmental responsibility;
environmental policy; the contribution of purchasing to 'green' business

10   Legal Factors   145

The sources of English law; contracts and the sale of goods; employment law; equal opportunity;
health and safety at work; other law affecting purchasing

11   Financial Concepts   161

Why should purchasers understand finance?; the regulatory framework; sources of finance;
costs and cost analysis

12   Financial Analysis   177
       The balance sheet; the profit and loss account; ratio analysis; profitability ratios; liquidity
       ratios; efficiency ratios

13   Mock Exam   193

14   Mock Exam: Suggested Solutions   199

Subject Index   **207**

Preface

Welcome to your new Study Pack.

For each subject you have to study, your Study Pack consists of three elements.

- A **Course Book** (the current volume). This provides detailed coverage of all topics specified in the unit content.

- A small-format volume of **Passnotes**. For each learning objective, these highlight and summarise the key points of knowledge and understanding that should underpin an exam answer. Use your Passnotes in the days and weeks leading up to the exam.

- An extensive range of **online resources**. These include a **Quick Start Guide** (a rapid 40-page overview of the subject), practice questions of exam standard (with full suggested solutions), notes on recent technical developments in the subject area, and recent news items (ideal for enhancing your solutions in the exam). These can all be downloaded from the study resources area at www.cips.org. You will need to log in with your membership details to access this information.

For a full explanation of how to use your new Study Pack, turn now to page xi. And good luck in your exams!

A note on style

Throughout your Study Packs you will find that we use the masculine form of personal pronouns. This convention is adopted purely for the sake of stylistic convenience – we just don't like saying 'he/she' all the time. Please don't think this reflects any kind of bias or prejudice.

October 2010

The Exam

The format of the paper

The time allowed is three hours. The examination is in two sections.

Section A – case study scenario, with two compulsory application questions based on the case study, each worth 25 marks.

Section B – questions to test knowledge and understanding. Candidates will be required to answer two questions from a choice of four, each worth 25 marks.

The unit content

The unit content is reproduced below, together with reference to the chapter in this Course Book where each topic is covered.

Unit characteristics

This unit is designed to develop an understanding of the impact of the external national and international business environment upon the purchasing function in a range of different organisations and sectors.

Purchasing has a critical role to play in ensuring value for money is achieved in both profit making and non-profit making organisations. In addition to understanding the macro/micro environment, purchasing professionals must have a commercial and financial awareness relating to ensuring best value is achieved.

By the end of this unit students should be able to recognise the implications of the purchasing environment for a variety of organisations, in a variety of sectors, and have an awareness of business and commercial issues associated with achieving best value in the purchasing function.

Statements of practice

On completion of this unit, students will be able to:

*   Explain how different organisations and sectors interact in the business environment, both nationally and internationally
*   Describe the different types of market structures in which organisations operate
*   Outline the importance of understanding and meeting stakeholder expectations in the purchasing environment
*   Explain how analysing the external environment can assist in making informed purchasing decisions
*   Demonstrate an understanding of the importance of analysing financial information relating to the external environment

Learning objectives and indicative content

Chapter

1.0   Understanding different purchasing contexts
(Weighting 40%)

1.1   Describe the different types of organisational structures and sectors
involved in purchasing goods and services

• Public sector	2
• Private sector	2
• Small, medium enterprise	2
• Third sector	2
• Primary sector, manufacturing sector, retail sector, service sector	2

1.2   Explain the effects of different market conditions on the following:

• Perfect competition	3
• Imperfect competition: monopolistic competition, monopolies	3
• Oligopolies	3

1.3   Discuss how different market forms affect the degree of competition in a
market and how this impacts on how purchasing operates in the market

• Sole suppliers: monopolies	3
• Large supplier base giving competitive advantage	3
• Restricted supply markets	3

1.4   Identify the different stakeholder groups involved in the public and private
sector purchasing functions, and understand the concept of stakeholder
co-operation.

• Employees; customers; suppliers; shareholders; local government; local businesses; charities; political parties; pressure groups	4
• Stakeholder co-operation	4

2.0 Understanding the local, national and international external factors impacting upon purchasing
(Weighting 40%)

2.1 Explain the impact of political factors affecting purchasing locally, nationally and internationally:

- Political initiatives and drivers: changes in public and private sectors   **5**
- Private finance initiatives (PFI), Public private partnerships (PPP) and Design/build/finance/operate (DBFO)   **5**
- Government policy and funding   **5**
- Political drivers   **5**
- International politics and policies   **5**
- Trade sanctions   **5**
- Political directives

2.2 Identify economic factors affecting purchasing locally, nationally and internationally, including:

- Interest rates   **6**
- Exchange rates   **6**
- Investment programmes   **6**
- The business cycle – boom and bust   **6**
- International economics   **6**

2.3 Explain how social factors can affect purchasing locally, nationally and internationally

- Culture   **7**
- Demographics   **7**
- Local practices   **7**
- Language   **7**
- Behaviour   **7**
- Communications   **7**
- Ethics   **7**
- Local working practices and working hours   **7**

2.4 Identify and explain how technological factors can affect purchasing at local levels, nationally and internationally

- Technology as a way of opening up new markets 8
- New communication technologies 8
- Government initiatives with technology 8
- Evolving nature and scope of e-procurement 8
- Different paces of technology development nationally and internationally, in developed and developing economies 8
- E-sourcing 8

2.5 Identify environmental factors affecting purchasing at local levels, nationally and internationally and explain their potential impact.

- Environmental policy 9
- Pollution, removal of rain forests, ie issues relating to environmentally friendly practices 9
- Reducing and disposing of waste in the purchasing function 9
- Legislation on emissions 9
- Kyoto agreement and its impact upon commercial operations 9

2.6 Explain and provide examples of the main sources of English law.

- Statute law 10
- Common law 10
- European law 10

3.0 Understanding financial tools for analysing the external purchasing environment
(Weighting 20%)

3.1 Identify the legal obligations relating to financial reporting of public, private and not-for-profit organisations

- UK legal requirement to put accounts into the public domain 11

3.2 Use a range of basic ratio analysis tools for assessing financial data on suppliers and competitors active in the purchasing environment including:

- Gross profit ratio 12
- Net profit ratio 12
- Current ratio 12
- Acid test ratio 12

How to Use Your Study Pack

Familiarisation

At this point you should begin to familiarise yourself with the package of benefits you have purchased.

- Go to www.cips.org and log on. Then go to Study and Qualify/Study Resources. Browse through the free content relating to this subject.
- Download the Quick Start Guide and print it out. Open up a ring binder and make the Quick Start Guide your first item in there.
- Now glance briefly through the Course Book (the text you're reading right now!) and the Passnotes.

Organising your study

'Organising' is the key word: unless you are a very exceptional student, you will find a haphazard approach is insufficient, particularly if you are having to combine study with the demands of a full-time job.

A good starting point is to timetable your studies, in broad terms, between now and the date of the examination. How many subjects are you attempting? How many chapters are there in the Course Book for each subject? Now do the sums: how many days/weeks do you have for each chapter to be studied?

Remember:

- Not every week can be regarded as a study week – you may be going on holiday, for example, or there may be weeks when the demands of your job are particularly heavy. If these can be foreseen, you should allow for them in your timetabling.
- You also need a period leading up to the exam in which you will revise and practise what you have learned.

Once you have done the calculations, make a week-by-week timetable for yourself for each paper, allowing for study and revision of the entire unit content between now and the date of the exams.

Getting started

Aim to find a quiet and undisturbed location for your study, and plan as far as possible to use the same period each day. Getting into a routine helps avoid wasting time. Make sure you have all the materials you need before you begin – keep interruptions to a minimum.

Begin by reading through your Quick Start Guide. This should take no more than a couple of hours, even reading slowly. By the time you have finished this you will have a reasonable grounding in the subject area. You will build on this by working through the Course Book.

Using the Course Book

You should refer to the Course Book to the extent that you need it.

- If you are a newcomer to the subject, you will probably need to read through the Course Book quite thoroughly. This will be the case for most students.
- If some areas are already familiar to you – either through earlier studies or through your practical work experience – you may choose to skip sections of the Course Book.

The content of the Course Book

This Course Book has been designed to give detailed coverage of every topic in the unit content. As you will see from pages vii–x, each topic mentioned in the unit content is dealt with in a chapter of the Course Book. For the most part the order of the Course Book follows the order of the unit content closely, though departures from this principle have occasionally been made in the interest of a logical learning order.

Each chapter begins with a reference to the learning objectives and unit content to be covered in the chapter. Each chapter is divided into sections, listed in the introduction to the chapter, and for the most part being actual captions from the unit content.

All of this enables you to monitor your progress through the unit content very easily and provides reassurance that you are tackling every subject that is examinable.

Each chapter contains the following features.

- Introduction, setting out the main topics to be covered
- Clear coverage of each topic in a concise and approachable format
- A chapter summary
- Self-test questions

The study phase

For each chapter you should begin by glancing at the main headings (listed at the start of the chapter). Then read fairly rapidly through the body of the text to absorb the main points. If it's there in the text, you can be sure it's there for a reason, so try not to skip unless the topic is one you are familiar with already.

Then return to the beginning of the chapter to start a more careful reading. You may want to take brief notes as you go along, but bear in mind that you already have your Quick Start Guide and Passnotes – there is no point in duplicating what you can find there.

Test your recall and understanding of the material by attempting the self-test questions. These are accompanied by cross-references to paragraphs where you can check your answers and refresh your memory.

Practising what you have learned

Once you think you have learned enough about the subject, or about a particular topic within the overall subject area, it's good to practise. Access the study resources at www.cips.org, and download a practice question on the relevant area. Alternatively, download a past exam question. Attempt a solution yourself before looking at our suggested solution or the Senior Assessor's comments.

Make notes of any mistakes you made, or any areas where your answer could be improved. If there is anything you can't understand, you are welcome to email us for clarification (course.books@cips.org).

The revision phase

Your approach to revision should be methodical and you should aim to tackle each main area of the unit content in turn. Begin by re-reading your Quick Start Guide. This gives an overview that will help to focus your more detailed study. Then re-read your notes and/or the separate Passnotes accompanying this Course Book. Then return to question practice. Review your own solutions to the practice questions you have had time to attempt. If there are gaps, try to find time to attempt some more questions, or at least to review the suggested solutions.

Additional reading

Your Study Pack provides you with the key information needed for each module but CIPS strongly advocates reading as widely as possible to augment and reinforce your understanding. CIPS produces an official reading list of books, which can be downloaded from the bookshop area of the CIPS website.

To help you, we have identified one essential textbook for each subject. We recommend that you read this for additional information.

The essential textbook for this unit is *The Business Environment*, by Ian Worthington and Chris Britton, published by Pearson (ISBN: 978–0273–716754).

CHAPTER 1

Introduction to the Purchasing Environment

Chapter headings

1   What is the purchasing environment?

2   Why analyse the purchasing environment?

3   The PESTLE framework

4   Other tools of analysis

Introduction

In this chapter, we start by setting the scene for all that follows. We start by defining the purchasing environment, and explaining why it is an important area of study. We then go on to survey the main model used to categorise and analyse environmental factors (the PESTLE model); sources of information for such an analysis; and ways in which an environmental analysis can be used by managers to make decisions for an organisation or purchasing function.

This material is designed to give you an overview of the syllabus which seems to be assumed in the way the learning objectives are structured. The syllabus doesn't mention the PESTLE model, for example – but the learning objectives specifically address Political, Economic, Socio-cultural, Technological, Legal and Environmental (PESTLE) factors. So even though this chapter doesn't directly cover any particular learning objective, it will be helpful!

Exam questions can be set on quite detailed areas of the syllabus – such as developments in one aspect of the environment or another – and it is easy to get bogged down in the technicalities and develop a compartmentalised view. However, an exam question might equally well ask you to survey and analyse the environment as a whole – so it is important to retain an overview, and to get a sense for how the different aspects of the environment interrelate. This chapter should give you an integrated, introductory-level view. Later chapters will focus on specific areas in greater detail, and with more technical terminology.

1   What is the purchasing environment?

Micro and macro environments

1.1   The 'purchasing environment' is the 'macro' environment or context within which purchasing activity takes place.

1.2   The environment of a given purchasing function can be seen as a series of concentric circles: Figure 1.1.

- The internal environment of the organisation includes its various functions and personnel; its style or 'culture'; its objectives and plans; systems and technology; rules and procedures and so on.

- The immediate operating or micro environment of the organisation includes the customers, suppliers and competitors who directly impact on its operations.
- The general or macro environment incorporates wider factors in the market and society in which the organisation operates: industry structure, the national economy, law, politics, culture, technological development and natural resources.

Figure 1.1: *The purchasing environment*

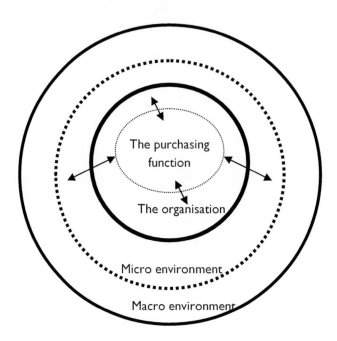

1.3 Purchasing activity will be strongly *influenced* by factors in all three 'tiers' of the environment: from internal purchasing procedures, to supplier changes, to national contract law or international commodity prices. In turn, a purchasing function has a measure of *influence* or control *over*:

- The *internal* environment (most obviously, by managing the flow of materials into and through the organisation) and
- The *micro* environment (most obviously, by seeking to manage supplier behaviour).

1.4 The 'macro' environment, however, is *not* generally within the organisation's control – however much it may seek to predict, manage or even influence events – and it is this part of the environment that is really referred to when we use the term 'purchasing environment'.

1.5 Throughout this Course Book we will explore a range of macro environmental factors and consider how they influence purchasing decisions.

Local, national and international environments

1.6 As well as distinguishing between 'micro' and 'macro' environments, it is possible to classify environmental factors according to their *scale:* that is, whether they affect a local, national, international or global sphere. Here are some examples.

- Local factors might include Council byelaws and planning regulations that affect the activities of an organisation within its local area.

- National factors might include the business law and government policy affecting a company within the UK (or other country of operation).

- International factors (affecting more than one nation) might include exchange rates for the currencies of two or more nations, which affect trading between those nations, and the formation of trading blocs such as the European Union (EU).

- Global factors (affecting all nations) might include industrialisation, technological development or global warming.

1.7 A given purchasing organisation will be subject to the law, regulation, social customs and technological limitations of the country in which it operates: its national environment. However, it is increasingly likely also to be subject to the same kinds of factors as they apply in *other* countries, or *across* national boundaries. This will certainly be the case in any of the following situations.

- The organisation has subsidiaries, or works with customers or suppliers, in other countries.

- Its country of operation is part of an international political or economic 'bloc' (such as the EU), where international laws, trading agreements and shared social policies apply to all members.

- Its activities are subject to genuinely international or global influences, such as international law, global commodity prices or climate change.

1.8 **Globalisation** itself is one of the major current trends in the purchasing environment (alongside technological development, which will be discussed in Chapter 8). It has been driven by factors such as the following.

- Improvements in transport technology, creating the 'shrinking' of distance for the physical movement of goods

- Improvements in information and communication technology or ICT (including the e-commerce potential of the internet), abolishing distance for the purposes of communication

- Reduction in the financial and administrative barriers to imports and exports (eg through the formation of trading blocs and agreements such as the European Economic Area)

- Convergence in cultural values and consumer tastes (due to increased travel and global media), creating markets for global brands such as Coca Cola or McDonald's

- The business benefits of international trade: access to larger markets, economies of scale, the ability to outsource activities to low-cost-labour economies and so on.

1.9 In this Course Book, much of our detailed discussion will necessarily focus on the UK or EU environment, but we will remind you of the international context where relevant to the syllabus.

The stakeholder environment

1.10 Stakeholders are individuals and groups who have an interest or 'stake' in an organisation, project or activity – whether because they are participants or investors in it, or because it affects them significantly in some way. Key stakeholders in purchasing activity, for example, may include: purchasing staff; senior management; other functions relying on the timely supply of materials; the organisation's suppliers and potential suppliers; customers relying on product quality and timely delivery; regulatory and industry bodies; and, arguably, the wider community which benefits from ethical and sustainable purchasing. We will discuss these issues in detail in Chapter 4.

1.11 Stakeholders form an important part of the purchasing environment.

- They may seek to influence the organisation, if they perceive that their interests are threatened. Some stakeholder groups will have more power than others. Staff and/or suppliers may negotiate for better terms, for example, or activists may threaten a boycott if the organisation uses environmentally-unsound or labour-exploiting suppliers.

- There is strong public and regulatory pressure for business organisations to be 'socially responsible': taking into account the wider social and environmental impacts of their activities on a range of stakeholders.

- Organisations themselves increasingly follow (and publicise) ethical frameworks, acknowledging their responsibility not to trample on stakeholders' interests – whether or not they have an influential 'voice' in the matter.

1.12 Since stakeholders can be within the organisation or purchasing department, within its immediate trading networks and/or in its wider field of operations, the 'stakeholder environment' effectively cuts through the boundaries between the internal, micro and macro environments: Figure 1.2.

Figure 1.2: *The stakeholder environment*

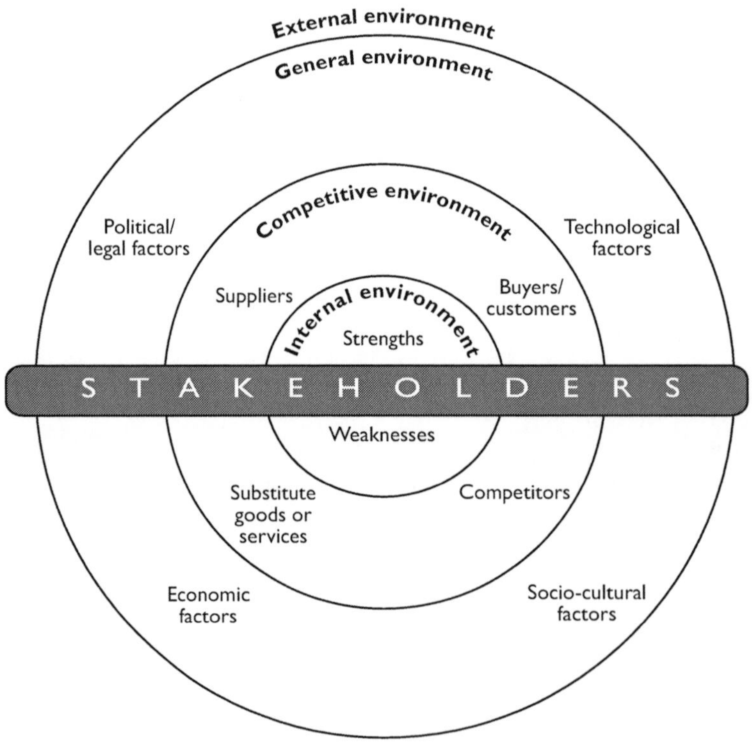

Adapted from Dobson & Starkey (1993) and Boddy (2002)

4

2 *Why analyse the purchasing environment?*

The organisation as an open system

2.1 If you're going to study this topic effectively, it helps to know why it's important – and how the knowledge and tools you acquire will help you in a purchasing job. Why do purchasing managers analyse the purchasing environment, and monitor changes to it over time, and take it into account in making their decisions? The answer lies partly in the definition of a **system.**

2.2 A system is 'an entity which consists of interdependent parts'.

- A **closed system** is one which operates entirely separately from its environment, needing nothing from it and contributing nothing to it.

- An **open system** is a system which is connected to, and interacts with, its environment. It receives various 'inputs' from its environment and converts these into 'outputs' to the environment. Feedback information (Did we get the result we wanted? Does something need to be changed?) enables the system to change its behaviour in order to stay stable in a changing environment.

2.3 An organisation can be seen as an open system: Figure 1.3

Figure 1.3: *The organisation as an open system*

2.4 The open systems model emphasises the importance of taking the environment into account. Firstly, because an organisation *depends* on its environment as the source of its inputs; the market for its outputs; and a key source of feedback information to measure and adjust its performance. And secondly, because an organisation also *impacts* on its environment, in the process of taking in inputs and creating outputs (both products, such as goods and services, and 'by products' such as waste, pollution or local employment).

2.5 The purchasing function is particularly important in this context, because buyers – by means of their contacts with the external supply market – span the boundary between the organisation and its environment (as shown in Figure 1.1). The marketing function performs a similar role by means of its contacts with external customers.

2.6 The environment will therefore exert a strong influence on an organisation's strategy, activity and performance, in various ways.

- It presents *threats* (such as restrictive legislation, competitor initiatives, technology obsolescence or industrial action by trade unions, say) and *opportunities* (such as growth in market demand, technological improvements or more skilled workers entering the labour pool). These affect the organisation's ability to compete in its market and fulfil its objectives. Environmental threats and opportunities are key factors in the formation of business strategies and plans.

- It is the source of *resources* needed by the organisation (labour, materials and supplies, plant and machinery, energy, finance, information and so on). Environmental factors determine to what extent these resources are, or are not, available in the right quantity, at the right time and at the right price.

- It contains *stakeholders* who may seek, or have the right, to influence the activities of the organisation. An organisation must comply with laws and regulations, for example, in order to avoid legal and financial penalties, but it may also have to negotiate with employees, suppliers and customers – or bow to public opinion which might jeopardise its market or reputation.

2.7 So purchasing officers, among other managers, must analyse and understand the environmental factors affecting their organisation. But that's only the beginning – because those factors are also constantly *changing*.

Environmental change

2.8 Change in the environment often creates a need (or opportunity) for change in an organisation's plans and activities. A purchasing function, for example, may need to respond to any or all of the following factors.

- Emerging economic opportunities and threats, such as the opening up of new supply markets, falling/rising prices for critical supplies, or competitors tying up the best sources of supply

- Changes in social values, preferences and expectations, which may give rise to demand for new or modified products (eg recyclable materials) or business processes (eg purchasing over the internet) or higher expectations on the part of suppliers and other stakeholders (eg for 'fair trade' dealings)

- Environmental ('green') considerations, including the increasing scarcity of resources – and changes in consumer perceptions. A purchasing function may have to develop plans for sustainable sourcing, eco-friendly materials, pollution and waste management, for example.

- Technological developments: supporting new products and business methods, while rendering others obsolete

- The move from a national to an international and ultimately (perhaps) to a global economy, changing corporate structures, communication systems and supply chain strategies

- Constant amendments and additions to the law and regulation of business activities by the EU, national governments and other agencies. One major example is the recently revised regulations on public sector procurement – but much of the law affecting purchasing is also constantly altered by decisions made in the courts.

We will see many more examples as we proceed through this Course Book.

The nature of environmental change

2.9 The precise nature, direction and pace of environmental change will depend on the organisation, its industry and its market. What major changes or trends can you see impacting major supermarkets, say, or local grocery stores? What about banks, travel and tourism operators, or car manufacturers? What about your own work organisation?

2.10 What we can say is that most business environments are getting both more *complex* (more interrelated factors to take into account) and more *dynamic* (faster and more wide-reaching change) – forcing organisations to adapt.

2.11 Strategy gurus Johnson & Scholes *(Exploring Corporate Strategy)* argue that the main problem posed for organisations by their environments is uncertainty, arising from complexity and dynamism.

- In a complex environment, there are a variety of influences which may impact on the organisation. These may be interrelated, so that change in one factor causes change in another. A high degree of knowledge is needed to cope with the environment.

- In a dynamic environment, change is driven by significant and powerful forces. A dynamic economy, for example, is one which is growing rapidly due to forces such as expanding global demand, the increased use of information technology or deregulation.

2.12 Organisations will need to assess the degree of uncertainty in their environments, and identify trends or directions of change, in order to measure and manage risk. Businesses often use historical data (what has happened in the past) in order to plan for the future (by building on past experience, or extrapolating past trends into the future). This is effective in stable or slow-changing environments – but dynamic or fast-changing environments require a more discontinuous, future-oriented perspective: What is likely to happen? What *might* happen? What threats and opportunities may emerge? How might things be different in five or ten years time?

2.13 Complex and dynamic environments require a new set of core competencies from organisations: the ability to be flexible or adaptable, and to respond swiftly (and without trauma) to constant and perhaps unforeseeable change.

- Organisations may need to adapt their processes and structures so that they can change direction swiftly if they need to. This may mean using versatile (multi-skilled) or cross-functional teams, which can be flexibly allocated to different tasks. It may mean improving communication in the organisation, so that environmental information (including shifts in customer demand) flows swiftly up to the top-level decision makers – and so that response plans and decisions flow swiftly back down for implementation.

- Organisations may need to develop strategies on a short time-horizon, rather than planning 5 or 10 years ahead, in order to stay sensitive and responsive to changing needs. Environmental scanning will become an important part of strategic management, ensuring that the organisation is aware of emerging threats and opportunities. Organisational strategy and change may be implemented in small steps or increments, allowing for review and adjustment at each stage.

- Organisations may need to improve their risk analysis and contingency planning, in order to minimise the risks of uncertainty, and to be prepared (as far as possible) for unpredictable changes.

2.14 Another term you might hear in relation to environmental change is 'turbulence'. Turbulence is the degree of volatility or instability in an environment, making it liable to sudden, unpredictable and potentially massive changes. Turbulence may arise from factors such as: changing governments or political instability, civil unrest or warfare; panic on the financial markets at the threat of recession, arising from the US mortgage lending crisis (as has been seen in 2008 and 2009); the collapse of the value of particular currencies (eg the Asian crisis of 1997); or changes in a regional balance of power due to the economic growth of particular nations (eg the emergence of Pacific Rim manufacturing).

2.15 In addition, you should be aware of the potential for single unpredictable or 'catastrophic' events to disrupt business (and supply chains). This would be a great focus of exam questions. What was the effect of the SARS virus outbreak on the travel industry, for example, and how could organisations such as airlines respond? What risks might be faced by buyers with key suppliers in areas prone to earthquakes or tsunamis? How might they make contingency plans for the risks, or respond to the risk event if it happens? What would be the effect on different types of businesses of the collapse of share prices and investor/consumer confidence as a result of the 2008/2009 financial crisis?

2.16 Get used to asking such questions of just about any headline you see in the quality press. What's going on here? What effect might this have on organisations of different types? How might this affect their supply chains, or disrupt supply, or raise (or lower) the price of materials?

Environmental analysis

2.17 Johnson & Scholes suggest that in order for an organisation to interact effectively with its environment, it must first analyse it systematically. An adapted version of their framework for environmental analysis is shown in Figure 1.4.

Figure 1.4: *Steps in environmental analysis*

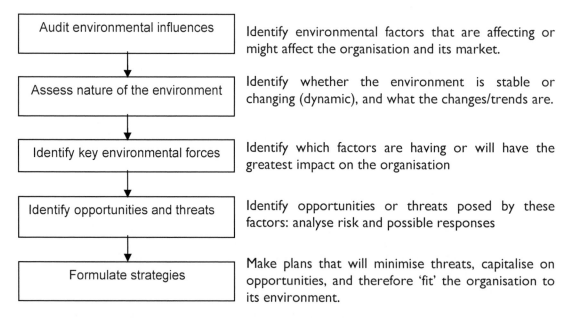

Audit environmental influences	Identify environmental factors that are affecting or might affect the organisation and its market.
Assess nature of the environment	Identify whether the environment is stable or changing (dynamic), and what the changes/trends are.
Identify key environmental forces	Identify which factors are having or will have the greatest impact on the organisation
Identify opportunities and threats	Identify opportunities or threats posed by these factors: analyse risk and possible responses
Formulate strategies	Make plans that will minimise threats, capitalise on opportunities, and therefore 'fit' the organisation to its environment.

2.18 In the following sections of this chapter we will look briefly at some of the tools used in this process.

Environmental monitoring

2.19 As well as environmental analysis for formal strategic planning, most large organisations would carry out some form of environmental monitoring. This involves continually gathering and analysing intelligence from sources such as professional, industry and trade journals and their websites; conferences and exhibitions; published reports and online databases (such as Mintel); published statistical sources such as *Social Trends* and the *Economic & Labour Market Review*; and so on. (If you are interested, you might like to browse National Statistics Online, at http://www.statistics.gov.uk.)

2.20 The organisation may also retain specialist consultants or advisers who have knowledge, experience and contacts relevant to a particular aspect of the environment – such as technology, law or social trends – or who specialise in the discipline of environmental analysis and risk management.

2.21 However, one of the key roles of *any* manager (as identified by Henry Mintzberg) is that of 'Monitor': scanning the environment for information about changes, trends, threats and opportunities. This is one of the reasons for networking within your profession (other people are a great source of information), as well as reading quality newspapers and professional journals, and searching the internet with your eyes open!

2.22 In this Course Book we will highlight and explain the key environmental factors and trends commonly monitored by organisations – which should be a sufficient basis for exam answers. We'll keep our coverage up-to-date with major changes, as far as possible, via the additional student resources posted on the CIPS website. Even so, given the nature of this paper, we strongly recommend that you browse through *Supply Management* and quality newspapers (and their online versions), and start a file of notes or cuttings on environmental issues and changes affecting purchasing in different types of organisations – including your own. (The examiner always appreciates the illustration of theory with real-life examples.)

2.23 We will now get an overview of some of the main tools used to analyse the purchasing environment in its various aspects.

3 The PESTLE framework

Acronyms for environmental analysis

3.1 A popular tool for analysing the macro environment is described by the acronym PEST (and more comprehensive variants), which sets out the main categories of environmental factors which impact on organisations.

3.2 It is well worth remembering these categories: if you are asked in the exam to comment on the purchasing environment as a whole, they provide a good 'checklist' around which to build a systematic and well-structured answer. You can use whichever version is most readily applicable, depending on whether there are strong environmental and ethical elements to discuss: the syllabus doesn't specify, although it uses the 'PESTLE' version as the framework for its indicative content.

Political/legal	*Socio-cultural*	*Political*	*Socio-cultural*
Economic	*Legal*	*Economic*	*Technological*
Socio-cultural	*Economic*	*Socio-cultural*	*Economic*
Technological	*Political*	*Technological*	*Environmental*
	Technological	*Legal*	*Political*
		Environmental	*Legal*
			Ethical

Political factors

3.3   The political environment (covered in Chapter 5) embraces factors such as: the policies of national governments and wider political bodies such as the EU; State support for industry (eg regional grants or industry subsidies, or assistance to small firms); the strength or weakness of trade unions; the influence of lobbying groups and public opinion on government policy; and the stability of governing regimes and other forms of political risk (particularly in international markets).

3.4   Sources of political information include: published government policy; direct contact with government or trade union representatives and lobbyists; media analysis of the political scene; published, online or specially commissioned surveys and reports; and specialist consultancies dealing in political risk analysis.

Economic factors

3.5   The macro-economic environment (covered in Chapter 6) embraces the general level of activity and growth in the economic system, and the effect of economic 'boom and bust' cycles. This is related to more detailed economic factors such as a government's fiscal (tax) and monetary (money supply) policy; interest and foreign exchange rates; inflation; consumer spending; labour costs and unemployment levels; international trade agreements and so on.

3.6   Making informed judgements and assumptions about future macro-economic events is crucially important for planning business strategy. Think about the effects on purchasing of import taxes or exchange rate fluctuations, raising the cost of supplies; or rising UK labour costs, making it more attractive to source labour-intensive supplies from low-labour-cost countries; or quota limits on imports, restricting supply. (In a recent example, the EU imposed quotas on clothing imports from China – leaving UK retailers short of stock to meet demand, and scrambling to find alternative sources of supply.)

3.7   Organisations also operate within the more immediate economic environment of a business sector, industry and market. The first section of the syllabus explores how different organisations and sectors interact in the business environment (covered in Chapter 2), and how competition works in different markets (Chapter 3). The third section looks more specifically at how an organisation can investigate key stakeholders in the market, by analysing the financial position of suppliers and competitors (Chapters 11 and 12).

3.8   Sources of economic data include: published government forecasts, reports and statistics; media analysis; industry projections and reports; and industry conferences and contacts.

Socio-cultural factors

3.9   The socio-cultural environment (covered in Chapter 7) embraces 'people' aspects of the society in which the organisation operates and from which it draws its suppliers, customers and workers. Socio-cultural factors include: demographic characteristics (age, gender and geographical distribution, population density and movements, educational and occupational trends); cultural norms, values and customs; lifestyle and fashion trends; and so on. These factors reflect the needs and expectations of the organisation's target market and customers, and will obviously be taken into account when developing marketing plans. However, they also reflect other stakeholder groups: shaping relationships with suppliers from different cultures, say, and affecting the availability of the skilled labour needed by the organisation.

3.10   Sources of socio-cultural data include: published demographic surveys and reports (eg the *Economic and Labour Market Review*); media and specialist analysis of trends; market research programmes and consultancies and/or access to their published research reports; stakeholder feedback (eg customer, supplier or employee surveys); and general 'scanning' of the environment.

Technological factors

3.11   The technological environment (covered in Chapter 8) embraces the technological sophistication of the organisation's national or international markets, and developments in the particular fields that are relevant to the organisation. Technology becomes more important every day, as innovations and developments have the following effects.

- Increasing the speed and power of information gathering, processing and communication (via information and communications technology or ICT) – supporting streamlined, automated, 'paperless' purchasing processes, for example

- Enabling 24/7 global business activity, via the World Wide Web – supporting international and global purchasing

- Enabling new products (such as music downloads and digital cameras) and new business processes (such as e-commerce and computer-assisted design and manufacture) – to which purchasing must adapt

- Shortening the shelf life of products (or 'product lifecycles'), due to the increasing pace of modification and obsolescence – creating pressure for product innovation, with fast, flexible supply chains to support it

- Changing industry structures and activities. (Think about the impact of digital cameras on photographic services, for example, or the impact of the internet on entertainment/travel booking agencies – and the implications for purchasing in both industries.)

- Creating 'virtual' teams and organisations, in which people share data and work together linked mainly by ICT, regardless of their physical location.

3.12   Information on the technology environment is available from: technology surveys; specialist journals; media analysis; trade conferences and exhibitions; technology-based consultancies and providers (eg R&D companies, software and systems developers, robotics companies and so on).

Environmental factors

3.13   The natural environment (covered in Chapter 9) embraces factors such as: legislation, international obligations (such as the Kyoto agreement on climate change) and government targets in regard to environmental protection and sustainability; consumer and pressure-group demand for eco-friendly products and business processes; issues of pollution, waste management, disposal and recycling; the depletion of non-renewable natural resources; the protection of habitats and biodiversity from urbanisation and industry; the reduction of carbon emissions; the risk of natural forces (such as weather) affecting supply; and so on.

3.14   All these factors will impact on purchasing activity in areas such as: materials specification; supplier selection and management (to ensure good environmental practice); logistics (eg transport) and reverse logistics (eg returns and recycling) planning; and compliance and risk management. Specific industries and firms will also have particular concerns: you might like to think what 'green' issues might be a priority for a car manufacturer, an airline, a brand of canned tuna or a hospital, say; or what kinds of supply are most likely to be subject to weather risk.

Legal factors

3.15   The legal environment (covered in Chapter 10) includes the operation of the justice system (the law and how it is enforced) and the organisation's contractual relationships with various parties (including suppliers, customers and employees). There is a wide range of national and trans-national (eg EU) law and regulation on issues such as: commercial contracts; the rights of employers and employees; health and safety at work; consumer protection; environmental protection; data protection; public sector procurement; and so on. In addition to principles laid down by statute, there are principles developed by judges' decisions in the courts, which determine how the law is interpreted. Compliance with relevant legal provisions is essential both to demonstrate ethical behaviour (an important objective for many organisations) – and to avoid penalties and sanctions for *not* doing so.

3.16   Information on legal provisions and changes is well-publicised, and regularly scrutinised by specialist advisers. However, purchasing professionals will need to keep up to date with developments in their own areas of interest: *Supply Management*, for example, offers regular briefings and updates on relevant law and cases.

Ethical factors

3.17   The ethical environment, if you choose to add it to the mix, embraces a range of issues to do with corporate social responsibility and business ethics: what constitutes 'right conduct' for an organisation in its context. This overlaps with the legal and ecological environments, since compliance and environmental protection are generally regarded as ethical responsibilities. However, it also includes industry/professional Codes of Practice and stakeholder pressure in areas such as: fair trading and the ethical treatment of suppliers; the fair and humane treatment of employees (over and above legal minimum requirements); supporting local communities (with investment and employment); and selecting and managing suppliers so that *they* comply with good practice in these areas.

3.18   Industry associations and professional bodies such as CIPS often publish Codes of Ethics to provide guidelines in these areas. Many organisations also develop their own objectives for corporate citizenship or corporate social responsibility, and codes of ethics or codes of practice to support them. Debate in the media, attitude/feedback surveys, and the activities of pressure groups are also good sources of information about the ethical concerns of the wider stakeholder environment.

Using a PESTLE analysis

3.19   Having gathered and classified information on critical factors, changes and trends, using the PESTLE framework, managers can consider the implications for their organisation.   A broad example of the kind of analysis that can be conducted, to support planning and decision-making, is shown in Table 1.1. Obviously, more specific factors or changes would raise more specific questions.

Table 1.1 *PESTLE analysis*

Factor	Description	Analysis
Political	Government influence on your industry	What are the likely implications of a change in government policy?
Economic	Growth trends; patterns of employment, income, interest/exchange/tax rates etc.	How might changes affect future demand for your products/services, or future supply and cost of resources/labour?
Socio-cultural	Changing composition, attitudes, values, consumption patterns and education of the population	How might changes affect the demands and expectations of customers, suppliers and other stakeholders, or skill availability?
Techno-logical	Changing tools for design/manufacturing, information and communications etc.	Are there opportunities for development – or risks of obsolescence? Are competitors adapting more quickly?
Legal	Law and regulation on business, employment, information etc.	How will the organisation need to adapt its policies and practices in order to comply with forthcoming measures?
Ecological	Resources, sustainability, pollution/impact management, weather, 'green' pressures	Which factors may cause supply or logistical problems, compliance issues, market pressure or risk to reputation?

4   *Other tools of analysis*

4.1   Having audited the environment and gathered information on factors which might affect its activities and plans, the organisation needs to take action accordingly.

- Prioritise factors for problem-solving: that is, identify which are likely to have the greatest impact
- Identify whether and to what extent the factors represent opportunities or threats, to which the organisation must respond in order to stay competitive.

Two simple tools can be used for these purposes: the impact assessment grid and SWOT analysis.

Impact assessment

4.2   The Chief Examiner for the old *Purchasing Environment* paper highlighted this technique for evaluating environmental information, so although it is not specifically mentioned in the syllabus, it is worth looking at briefly. An impact (or risk) assessment grid is a two-by-two grid on which factors, changes or events can be plotted according to (a) the likelihood of their happening and (b) the seriousness of their effect if they do happen: Figure 1.5.

Figure 1.5: *Impact assessment grid*

		Impact/effect on organisation	
		Low	*High*
Likelihood of occurrence	*Low*	**A**	**C**
	High	**B**	**D**

4.3   Taking the segments of the grid one by one:

- Segment A will contain events which are not likely to happen and would have little effect if they did: say, a power failure at all suppliers' factories at once, when they all have emergency back-up generators. Given the low level of impact, the organisation can safely *ignore* such factors as low-priority.

- Segment B will contain events which are relatively likely to occur, but will not have a major effect: say, an exchange rate fluctuation, if the organisation is not heavily exposed in this area. The appropriate response is to *monitor* such factors, in case the situation changes and the impact may be greater than expected.

- Segment C will contain events which are not likely to happen, but will have a big impact if they do: say, the sinking of a ship with a cargo of critical supplies. The appropriate response is to draw up a *contingency plan* to minimise the impact, in case the event occurs: perhaps having a back-up source of supply, and insurance.

- Segment D will contain events which are both likely to happen and serious in their impact: say, a major new tax on your product, or the discovery of a new technology that will alter products and processes in an industry. The appropriate response is to *respond* to the perceived threat or opportunity, including it in strategic analysis and planning.

SWOT analysis

4.4   Strengths, Weaknesses, Opportunities and Threats analysis is a strategic planning technique, used to assess the internal resources of the organisation (or a function such as purchasing) to cope with and/or capitalise on factors in its environment.

4.5   Strengths and weaknesses are *internal* aspects of the business that enhance or limit its ability to compete, change and thrive. Internal appraisal may cover aspects such as the following.

- Physical and financial resources: plant and machinery, availability of raw materials, owned assets, revenue-earning potential, profitability

- The product/service portfolio, and its competitive strength (eg brand positioning and market share)
- Human resources: management expertise, staff skills, labour flexibility
- The efficiency and effectiveness of functions and operations (eg production, marketing, purchasing and supply)
- The efficiency and effectiveness of systems (eg for quality control, inventory management, communication, information processing)
- Organisation structure: adaptability, efficiency, co-ordination, teamwork
- Distinctive competencies: things the organisation does better than its competitors.

4.6 Opportunities and threats are factors in the *external environment* that may emerge to impact on the business. What potential do they offer to either enhance or erode competitive advantage or profitability?

4.7 Internal and external factors can be mapped in a SWOT grid as follows: Figure 1.6.

Figure 1.6: *SWOT analysis*

Internal	**Strengths** New technology Quality management systems Stable, high-quality staff Market leading brands	**Weaknesses** Low new product development Poor financial controls Non-renewable resources
External	**Opportunities** E-commerce Consumer values re quality Tax breaks for regional development	**Threats** Environmental protection law Fashion trends Ageing demographic

4.8 SWOT is used to identify areas where strategic responses are required in order for the organisation to maintain or enhance its position in relation to the environment.

- Plan to build on strengths and/or minimise weaknesses – in order to be able to capitalise on the identified opportunities (or create new ones) and to cope better with the identified threats.
- Plan to convert threats into opportunities – by developing the strengths (and contingency plans) to counter them more effectively than competitors, and by being prepared to learn from them.

Financial analysis

4.9 A variety of financial tools is available for analysing the external purchasing environment: specifically, the financial stability and strength of suppliers (in order to minimise the risk of their unexpectedly going bust and disrupting supply) and competitors (in order to identify their ability to invest in competitive pricing, innovation and promotion). Information for this analysis is available in the published financial statements of public, private and not-for-profit organisations.

4.10 Examples of the kind of thing you might be looking for include signs that an organisation:

- Is not making much profit, which suggests that it is operating inefficiently (revenue is too low or costs are too high) – and that it may run out of finance to continue or develop the business

- Is not managing its cashflow (the balance and timing of cash coming in and going out), making it difficult to meet its short-term debts and expenses

- Has more loan capital (borrowed from lenders) than share capital (invested by owners), incurring high finance costs (interest payments) and the obligation to repay the loan. This is known as 'high gearing'.

Any of these signs may suggest a risk of financial instability in a supplier, or a weakness in a competitor. The opposite signals (high profits, plenty of liquid assets to cover debts, 'low' gearing) would suggest a strong and financially stable organisation.

4.11 **Ratio analysis** examines the relationship between sets of financial factors, expressed as a ratio or percentage. It defines performance indicators for organisations which can be *measured* using available financial data, and *compared* with performance in previous years (to highlight trends) or with other organisations (to highlight competitive strengths and weaknesses).

- Profitability ratios (including the gross and net profit percentage) measure the extent to which a firm has traded profitably.

- Liquidity ratios (including the current ratio, acid test ratio and gearing ratio) measure the extent to which a firm is able to meet its liabilities or debts, both in the short term and in the medium-to-long term.

- Efficiency ratios (such as the asset ratios and stock turnover ratios) measure the efficiency with which a firm utilises its assets.

- Investment ratios (such as earnings per share) measure the attractiveness of a firm to potential investors.

4.12 We will explore the use of financial statements, and the key profitability and liquidity ratios mentioned in the syllabus, in Chapters 11 and 12.

Chapter summary

Key learning points include the following.

- The purchasing environment is the macro or wider environment or context within which purchasing takes place. It includes external factors which are largely outside the organisation's direct control. These may be local, national, international or global.

- Stakeholders are individuals and groups who have a legitimate interest or stake in the organisation's activities. They are a feature of the internal, micro and macro environments of the organisation, and an important influence on its policies.

- The organisation can be seen as an open system, connected to and interacting with its environment: taking in inputs and influences from the environment and creating outputs to the environment. The environment will therefore exert a strong influence on organisation strategy and activity, as a source of market threats/opportunities, resources and stakeholder influence.

- Environmental factors are subject to constant change, so organisations must monitor their environments in order to respond effectively (and if possible, proactively) to changing opportunities and threats.

- The PESTLE framework is used to categorise macro environment factors as: Political, Economic, Socio-cultural, Technological, Legal and Environmental. (An extra 'E' for Ethical factors may also be added.)

- Other tools of analysis include: impact/risk assessment (to prioritise environmental factors affecting the organisation); Strengths, Weaknesses, Opportunities, Threats analysis (to identify threats that need to be neutralised and opportunities that can be capitalised on); and financial analysis (to analyse the financial strength and stability of the organisation and its suppliers and competitors).

Self-test questions

Numbers in brackets refer to paragraphs where you can check your answers

1   Distinguish between the micro and macro environments. (1.2–1.4)

2   List three factors driving globalisation. (1.8)

3   Why are stakeholders important in the purchasing environment? (1.11)

4   Describe an open system, and suggest its relevance to the study of the purchasing environment. (2.4–2.5)

5   Give three examples of environmental change affecting purchasing. (2.8)

6   How can a purchasing manager contribute to environmental monitoring? (2.19–2.21)

7   What does 'STEEPLE' stand for? (3.2)

8   Give two examples of each of the STEEPLE factors. (3.3, 3.5, 3.9, 3.11, 3.13, 3.15, 3.17)

9   Explain each of the segments in (a) an impact assessment grid, and (b) a SWOT analysis grid. (4.3, 4.5–4.7)

10   Why would an organisation want to carry out financial analysis of the external purchasing environment? (4.9)

Further reading

From your 'Essential Reading' list, you might look at Worthington & Britton (*The Business Environment:* 5th edition, 2006, FT Prentice Hall):

- *Chapter 1: Business Organisations: the External Environment.* This chapter covers the organisation as an open system, the different 'tiers' of the external environment; and the PESTLE model. The short closing section 'Central Themes' provides a useful overview of some key issues to bear in mind – and the Case Studies provide helpful examples which you may be able to use in the exam.

- *Chapter 18: Monitoring Change.* This chapter elaborates on the need for environmental analysis and scanning, and on techniques which can be used (including PESTLE, impact analysis and SWOT). Worth a skim through, to appreciate the importance of monitoring change, although many of the techniques used are beyond the scope of your syllabus.

CHAPTER 2

Business Sectors

Learning objectives and indicative content

1.1   Describe the different types of organisational structures and sectors involved in purchasing goods and services

- Public sector
- Private sector
- Small, medium enterprise
- Third sector
- Primary sector, manufacturing sector, retail sector, service sector

Chapter headings

1   Sectors of the economy

2   Private and public sectors

3   Private sector organisations

4   Public sector organisations

5   The third sector

Introduction

The immediate operating environment of an organisation consists of three main structures: economic sectors, industry sectors and markets.

Sectors are simply ways of grouping organisations. Economic sectors are grouped by ownership: public or private. Industry sectors may be grouped by industry type (resource extraction, production or service provision), area of activity (eg retail, manufacturing, construction, media and publishing and so on), size (eg the small business sector) or primary objective (profit-making or non-profit-making).

In this chapter, we will look at various ways of defining key sectors of the economy. We start with different industry types, including the special conditions relating to the provision of services. We then explore the nature of the public and private sectors, the types of organisation operating within them, and the different purchasing objectives and challenges of each. Small and medium enterprises or SMEs are considered as a special category of private sector organisation. Finally, we note that both public and private sector organisations may not have profit as their primary objective, and we discuss the nature of the third sector (not-for-profit, voluntary and non-government organisations).

In Chapter 3, we will go on to look at markets: the 'places' in the business environment where buyers and sellers interact.

1   *Sectors of the economy*

Introduction

1.1   There are various ways of classifying organisations involved in purchasing goods and services.

- By *activity*: extraction of raw materials, generation of energy, manufacturing, retail, health care, information technology, media and so on. Organisations performing different activities are likely to have different objectives, technologies and practices, in order to meet the particular challenges of their task and environment.

- By *structure and ownership*, including issues of incorporation (the legal structure of the organisation), ownership, control and funding. On this basis, the economy is often divided into the private sector (eg business companies), public sector (eg government, health authorities, police and defence forces), voluntary sector (eg churches and charities) and subscription-paid sector (eg clubs, societies and associations).

- By *primary objective*. Profit-oriented organisations (common in the private sector) aim to generate profits for their owners, or return on investment. Not-for-profit organisations (common in the public, voluntary and subscription sectors) aim to provide public, social or charitable services, protect stakeholder interests or fulfil the purposes of their members – without aiming to make a profit from doing so. Any 'surplus' of funds is reinvested in the organisation's activity.

- By *size*: special categories are often given, for example, to **small and medium enterprises** (SMEs) at one end of the scale and **multinational corporations** (MNCs) at the other.

1.2   We will look at some of these distinctions and their relevance for purchasing.

The primary, secondary and tertiary sectors

1.3   It is common to distinguish between three major industry sectors, according to the type of process they perform.

- *Primary industries* are concerned with extracting natural resources or producing raw materials. This sector includes oil and mineral extraction (mining), agriculture and forestry.

- *Secondary industries* are engaged in transforming raw materials into end components, assemblies or finished products. This sector includes the manufacturing, engineering and construction industries, for example.

- *Tertiary industries* are those engaged in the development and provision of services. This sector includes professional services, financial services, transport, hospitality and so on.

1.4   This classification is neither clear cut nor exhaustive. Agriculture these days has some of the features of secondary industry, for example, and is often classified as such. The retail, energy and IT sectors do not fit clearly into any one category and are sometimes regarded as sectors in their own right. Nor is it helpful to separate the three types of activity when thinking about supply chains. The purchasing function in a manufacturing organisation, say, might have to buy across a number of categories: raw materials, manufactured goods (such as components, or computers, tools, machinery and office furniture) and services (such as IT consultancy, insurance and transport).

1.5 It should not be surprising, however, to find that purchasing priorities and practices do differ from one sector to another. Clearly, the organisational characteristics and operational challenges of an oil drilling company are likely to be very different from those of a management consultancy – and these differences are likely to be apparent at least to some extent within the purchasing function.

Purchasing in a primary industry

1.6 For example, in an *extractive industry* such as mining, purchasing expenditure will be very high, because of the need for large, specialised heavy-duty machinery: this usually gives purchasing a relatively high-level role. There is less likely to be a continuous demand for supplies than in a manufacturing company, so purchasing's focus may be less on swift response times, and more on ongoing support and service from suppliers. There may be particular transport and storage problems involved in supplying remote and difficult locations.

Purchasing in a secondary industry

1.7 The essence of a *manufacturing industry* is to purchase raw materials and/or manufactured components, for conversion into finished goods. Because there is a continuous need for inputs to the production line, the most important task is to ensure that production teams have materials of the right quality available in the right place at the right time in the right quantity, achieving all this at the right price: the traditional 'five rights' of purchasing. There may also be a need to manage long-term, high-value (capital) investment in plant and machinery. Purchasing is a relatively advanced function in many manufacturing companies, and the purchasing role typically extends through almost the whole spectrum of organisational activities, from new product development to customer delivery.

Purchasing in the retail sector

1.8 In the *retail sector*, buyers are purchasing goods for sale onwards to customers – with little or no work done on them by the organisation itself. Issues such as quality control, keeping stock levels down and managing relationships with suppliers will still be important, but the focus of purchasing will be on selecting products that will appeal to external customers: much closer to marketing activity. Buyers will often be involved in market research and monitoring sales performance, in order to adjust their selection. If the organisation sells 'own-brand' products (like Marks & Spencer, say), it may order goods made to its specification, as in other purchasing contexts – but most retail buyers will focus more on product selection and availability: securing supply of ready-to-sell goods at a price that will allow them to be sold on at a profit.

Purchasing in the services sector

1.9 In the *services sector,* the link between inputs, processing and outputs is even less clear. The major input of many service companies is staff time and expertise, generally sourced by the human resources (HR) function, rather than purchasing – although with the trend towards outsourcing of service functions, purchasing may have a more important role. Service organisations also purchase office equipment and supplies, IT systems and support, motor vehicles, office maintenance services, advertising services and so on, but these sorts of items are often sourced by general managers or the users of the items: purchasing may occupy a merely administrative or support role in the organisation. Physical supply may be more important in some circumstances, however: services may be based on the use of hard assets such as property (as in a hotel or fast food restaurant), vehicles (as in an airline or logistics company) or machinery (as in a computer bureau or printing factory).

Industry sectors within the overall economy

1.10 As with many developed economies, the UK's employment and wealth generation depends very largely on the activities of service companies. In the past decade the importance of the service sector has outstripped that of manufacturing in terms of contribution to the country's gross domestic product or GDP: that is, the total value of goods and services produced by the country in a given year.

1.11 The relative importance of the three industry sectors in a country's economy varies according to the country's *economic development*, defined by the availability of resources, skills, capital (or finance) and advanced technology.

- In countries with little wealth and technology, most people will be employed in the primary sector, mainly in agriculture or fishery. These are known as 'developing' economies: you might think of nations such as Ghana, Nigeria or Bolivia, for example.

- Greater availability of finance and technology supports the development of manufacturing. 'Advanced developing' countries such as India and China therefore divide employment and production between the primary and secondary sectors.

- In 'developed' economies, such as the UK, Western Europe and the USA, the highest proportion of employment – and of the total value produced by the economy – is in the tertiary sector.

1.12 Why does economic development support a growing tertiary sector? For one thing, it makes possible a higher GDP, which is the index of a country's overall 'wealth'. Businesses are able to invest in labour-saving technologies, reducing the number of workers required in the primary and secondary sectors. Meanwhile, greater prosperity allows better education, higher wages, higher disposable incomes and more leisure time. And this in turn creates both growing demand for services – such as leisure, tourism, hospitality and financial services – and growing numbers of skilled people available to supply them. As the tertiary sector grows, the primary and secondary sectors contract, both in employment terms and as a proportion of the total GDP.

Services

1.13 A service may be defined as 'any activity or benefit that one party can offer to another that is essentially intangible and does not result in ownership of anything. Its production may or may not be tied to a physical product' (Kotler).

1.14 Carla S Lallatin categorises the services most commonly used by organisations as follows.

- Personal (eg editing, translation)
- Professional (eg consultancy, legal, medical, insurance)
- Support (eg administrative, financial, IT management, procurement, logistics, waste management, catering, security)
- Personnel (eg recruitment and selection, training and development, welfare)
- Construction (eg building repair, alteration and maintenance).

1.15 One impact of the growth of the service sector is the corresponding growth in *outsourcing*: the practice of buying services from specialist external suppliers instead of performing them in-house. For example, many companies that used to employ their own cleaning staff now pay cleaning companies to perform their tasks on a contract basis. This has enlarged the role of purchasing functions, which may have the responsibility of selecting and managing a larger number of external service providers.

1.16 In addition to the relative growth of the service sector, it is worth noting that purchasing services – as opposed to physical products – poses some unique challenges.

- *Intangibility*: a service cannot be seen, touched, measured, weighed or otherwise 'inspected' before it is purchased, or when assessing satisfaction after purchase. The buyer will have to look for other evidence of its attributes and quality, such as promised or agreed service levels, price, convenience and the staff who provide the service.

- *Inseparability*: services are produced and consumed at the same time. The efficiency and effectiveness of the processes and people involved in 'producing' the service are crucial to the buyer's experience of it, and will be crucial to the buyer's selection and evaluation of the service.

- *Heterogeneity* or variability. Because of inseparability, the service will be influenced by many factors such as the mood of the buyer/supplier, the weather and other circumstances. This makes it difficult to 'standardise' services so that buyers can be sure what they will get, or that they will get the same thing every time.

- *Perishability*: a service cannot be 'stored' for later use, so supply is difficult to control. Buyers will have to plan ahead so that the service is available when it is needed.

- *Ownership*: services do not result in the transfer of ownership of anything. This makes it difficult to define when a contract for services has been properly fulfilled. (Baily *et al* use the example of an architect who submits a design which meets all the client's stated criteria – but which the client simply doesn't 'like'.) Buyers will have to define their requirements very clearly, in detailed service specifications, service level agreements and an agreed basis for charges: an area often fraught with difficulties!

1.17 These kinds of challenges present a strong argument for purchasing to be involved in sourcing services – rather than users, who may lack expertise in demand forecasting, negotiation, specification, contracting and ongoing supplier management.

2 *Private and public sectors*

Introduction

2.1 As we saw at the beginning of the chapter, another major classification of the purchasing environment distinguishes between private and public sector organisations. Let's start by stating the main differences between them.

2.2 In the *private sector*:

- Organisations are owned by their investors (owner/proprietors or shareholders), and controlled by directors or managers on their behalf

- Activity is funded by a combination of investment, revenue (from the sale of goods or services) and debt

- The primary purpose is the achievement of commercial objectives: generally, maximising profits for their owners, or for reinvestment in the business. Managerial decisions are assessed on the extent to which they contribute to organisational profit or shareholder wealth.

- Competition is a key factor. Several, or many, firms may offer goods or services of a particular type, with consumers free to choose between their offerings: consumer choice ensures that quality and efficiency are maintained at an acceptable level.

- The core 'constituency' served by firms is shareholders, customers and employees, all of whom are involved with the firm by choice. Firms can and must, therefore, focus their activity on meeting the needs of these few key stakeholders.

2.3   In the *public sector:*

- Organisations are owned by the government on behalf of the State, which represents the public

- Activity is financed by the state, mainly via taxation – as well as any revenue the organisation's activities may generate

- The primary purpose is achieving defined service levels: providing efficient and effective services to the public, often within defined budgetary constraints and sustainability strategies

- There has traditionally been little or no competition, although, since the 1970s, successive UK governments have sought to introduce some market disciplines (eg competitive tendering). In the absence of consumer choice, quality and efficiency are imposed by mechanisms such as regulation, customer charters, performance targets and competition for funding allocations.

- The 'constituency' of concerned stakeholders is wider and more diverse, including government, taxpayers, funding bodies, those who consume services – and society as a whole. There is a far greater need for accountability and stakeholder consultation in managing the organisation.

Why have a private and public sector?

2.4   Looking at the big picture, economic activity can't produce *everything* that might conceivably be wanted or needed by consumers, because the resources to do so (the 'factors of production': land, natural resources, labour, capital and knowledge) are limited. Some mechanism is required to decide how these resources should be used, and what goods and services should be produced.

2.5   A **market economy** operates on the basis of supply and demand: people will purchase goods and services to satisfy their wants and needs, at a price they are able and willing to pay. Commercial organisations have to offer goods and services which are in demand, at prices which maintain that demand, in order to compete with others in the market. In other words, consumer choice decides which goods and services are produced, and at what price they can be sold. This has been the basis of the private sector, ever since commerce began with barter and trade in medieval rural economies.

2.6 However, some goods and services are perceived as essential for the wellbeing of individuals and society – such as health, education, utilities and security services – even if commercial organisations don't want to produce them, because consumers are unwilling or unable to pay the market price. In such circumstances (ie when the market mechanism of supply and demand 'fails') government must step in to control production, funded via taxation and public borrowing, so that basic goods and services are available to everyone on a free or subsidised basis. This is the basis of the public sector. In its extreme form (a *centrally planned economy)*, the government would control all factors of production: all business would be publically owned or 'nationalised'.

2.7 A **mixed economy** is one in which there is neither complete capitalist control nor complete government control of resources. Instead, the state controls essential public services and basic industries which cannot raise adequate capital investment from private sources, while at the same time supporting private enterprise and the open market in other fields.

2.8 The functions of the public sector in a mixed economy are therefore as follows.

- To provide essential goods and services which might not be provided by the private sector, owing to 'market failure'
- To redistribute wealth, via taxation, in order to provide financial support for non-wage earners such as the sick, pensioners and the unemployed
- To regulate private sector activity in the public interest, eg in the case of bodies such as the Competition Commission or the Health and Safety Executive
- To 'bail out' private enterprises, where necessary in the public interest. There have been several high profile examples in the recent 'credit crunch': UK regulators being forced to vouch for the viability of Britain's biggest home loan provider, HBOS, among fears it was facing collapse – on the same day that the US central bank had to agree to pump $US85 billion into American International Group (AIG) to prevent the failure of the world's biggest insurance company.

2.9 The balance of a mixed economy – and therefore the relative size of the public or private sector – will depend partly on political factors. Communist or socialist governments (as in Cuba, China, Sweden or Norway) are more likely to support a large public sector, with government expenditure representing a higher proportion of the GDP. Capitalist societies with right-wing governments are more likely to reduce the public sector (eg by privatisation of public services and industries). In highly committed 'free enterprise' economies, such as Japan and the USA, few services are provided by the state.

Private and public sector purchasing

2.10 A glance through standard purchasing textbooks is enough to show that private sector organisations are regarded as the main sphere of purchasing operations. Although there are some sound reasons for this, it would be wrong to see public sector operations as a trivial addition to 'mainstream' economic activity: the spending power of such enterprises can be enormous! Despite programmes of privatisation, the sheer range of public sector service provision is staggering: roads, law and order, education, health services, emergency services, and much more.

2.11 Private and public sector organisations and environments are different in some key respects, as we noted above. The key implications for purchasing management have been catalogued by Gary J Zenz, whose analysis forms the basis of Table 2.1 with our own points added.

Table 2.1 *Differences between public and private sector purchasing*

Area of difference	Private sector	Public sector
Objectives	Usually, to increase profit	Usually, to achieve defined service levels
Responsibility	Buyers are responsible to directors, who in turn are responsible to shareholders	Buyers are responsible ultimately to the general public
Stakeholders	Purchasing has a defined group of stakeholders to take into account.	Purchasing has to provide value to a wider range of primary and secondary stakeholders.
Activity/process	Organisational capabilities and resources used to produce goods/services	Add value through supply of outsourced or purchased products/services. (Tend not to purchase for manufacture.)
Legal restrictions	Activities are regulated by company law, employment law, product liability law etc	Most of this applies equally to public sector, but additional regulations are present too (eg EU procurement directives)
Competition	There is usually strong competition between many different firms	There is usually no competition
Value for money	Maintain lowest cost for competitive strategy, customer value and profit maximisation.	Maintain or improve service levels within value/cost parameters.
Diversity of items	Specialised stock list for defined product/service portfolio.	Wide diversity of items/resources required to provide diverse services (eg local government authority).
Publicity	Confidentiality applies in dealings between suppliers and buyers	Confidentiality is limited because of public interest in disclosure
Budgetary limits	Investment is constrained only by availability of attractive opportunities; funding can be found if prospects are good	Investment is constrained by externally imposed spending limits
Information exchange	Private sector buyers do not exchange information with other firms, because of confidentiality and competition	Public sector buyers are willing to exchange notes and use shared e-purchasing platforms, consolidate purchases etc.
Procurement policies and procedures	Tend to be organisation-specific. Private sector buyers can cut red tape when speed of action is necessary	Tend to follow legislative directives. Public sector buyers are often constrained to follow established procedures
Supplier relationships	Emphasis on long-term partnership development where possible, to support value chain.	Compulsory competitive tendering: priority to cost minimisation and efficiency, at the expense of partnership development.

2.12 The differences between public and private sector purchasing should not be overemphasised, however. Differences in objectives, organisational constraints and so on may not necessarily lead to differences in *procedure*. Public sector buyers may not be seeking to maximise profit, for example, but they will still be concerned to achieve value for money. Public sector buyers may not seek competitive advantage, but they will still aim to ensure the quality of inputs in order to support the quality of outputs (to fulfil the terms of a customer charter, say). Meanwhile, private sector buyers may not have non-economic goals as their primary objective, but they are increasingly being challenged to consider the interests of wider stakeholders in society (through pressure for corporate social responsibility).

2.13 An article in *Procurement Professional* journal recently noted that: 'Key issues for the procurement profession... are as relevant for the public sector as they are for the private sector... Work is currently underway in public sectors around the world to address these issues, centred on:

- Developing standards for the assessment and ongoing development of public procurement professionals
- The greater application of strategic sourcing principles to public procurement
- The introduction of e-procurement systems.'

3 *Private sector organisations*

Introduction

3.1 Private sector organisations may be formed or 'constituted' in various different ways.

- An individual may carry on a business as a **sole trader**.
- A group of individuals may carry on a business together by legal agreement, as a **partnership**.
- A potentially very large number of people may carry on a business according to specific legal requirements for 'incorporation' as a **company**.

We will look at each of these types of organisation in turn.

Sole tradership

3.2 A sole tradership may be an appropriate business type for a tradesperson, say, or a shopkeeper or freelance designer. There is no legal distinction between the individual person and the business entity: the individual supplies all the capital for the business, and is personally liable for its debts. (This is *not* the case for a company, as we will see later...)

3.3 The advantages and disadvantages of sole tradership can be summarised as follows.

Advantages	Disadvantages
Few costs or legal requirements to establish the business	The proprietor is personally liable for the business's debts
No public accountability (though financial records are required for tax purposes)	It may be difficult to get finance for the business (eg a loan by personal guarantee)
The proprietor controls all decisions for the business – and enjoys all the profits	Resources are limited to what the proprietor can personally generate

Partnership

3.4   Many sole traders find that a logical way of expanding without the formalities of incorporation is to take on one or more partners, who contribute capital and expertise to the business, and who share the managerial and financial responsibilities. A partnership is defined in UK law (Partnership Act 1890) as 'the relation which subsists between persons carrying on a business in common with a view of profit'. There must be at least two to a standard maximum of 20 partners, for a commercial partnership. (A professional practice, such as a firm of accountants or solicitors, can have any number of partners.)

3.5   Like a sole tradership (and *unlike* a company), a partnership does not have a separate legal identity from its members. This means, for example, that:

*   Partners jointly own the assets of the partnership and are personally liable for its debts

*   Partners are entitled to participate in management and act as agents of the firm (unlike in a company, where owners/shareholders do not necessarily have this status)

*   A change of partners terminates the old firm and begins a new one (unlike in a company, where shares can be transferred from one person to another).

3.6   The advantages and disadvantages of partnerships may be summarised as follows.

Advantages	Disadvantages
Partners contribute capital and expertise	Decision-making has to be shared/negotiated
Partners share managerial and financial responsibilities and liability	Profits have to be shared among the partners
With greater asset backing, it is often easier to raise loans than for a sole trader	Partners are generally personally liable 'without limit' for the partnership's debts
Suits professions, as members are prohibited from practising as limited companies	

Limited company

3.7   By far the most common trading vehicle in the private sector is the *limited company*. A limited company is an 'incorporated' body: that is, it is considered a separate legal entity from its individual owners (shareholders).

*   The company can own assets, enter into contracts and incur liabilities in its own name.

*   If the company incurs a debt, payment will come from the assets owned by the company. The individual owners cannot be asked to contribute to the payment from their personal funds: their liability is *limited* to the amount they have invested in the company – usually by buying shares. (Hence, a 'limited company'.)

3.8   A company may be registered as a *public limited company* ('*plc*') or as a *private limited company* ('*Ltd*'). The key differences are as follows.

*   A *public* limited company may offer its shares to the general public. (A relatively small number of public companies – known as listed companies – trade their shares on The Stock Exchange.) This is not the case for a *private* limited

company, whose shareholders are generally directors of the company, or connected to it in some way. This means that PLCs are able to raise significantly larger sums of capital than private limited companies.

- A *public* limited company must have a minimum authorised share capital (the value of shares the company is allowed to issue) of £50,000, with allotted shares of at least that value, and a minimum of two members and two directors. There are no minimum capital requirements for a private limited company, and the minimum number of directors is just one.

- A *public* limited company is subject to detailed company law requirements in regard to shares, directors, annual general meetings, accounting and so on. For *private* limited companies, there is much less red tape!

3.9 The advantages and disadvantages of incorporation may be summarised as follows.

Advantages	Disadvantages
Limited liability protects owners from personal liability for contracts and debts	Expense and red tape of incorporation, and the constraint of a written constitution
Shares are a stable source of finance: the amount of capital is unaffected by trading, and is not subject (like loans) to finance costs	Subject to regulation eg re public disclosure (in financial reports and accounts etc)
Directors provide the expertise the business needs, without 'diluting' ownership	Share trading can result in unwanted change of ownership

3.10 In the UK, limited companies are set up by filing a Memorandum of Association and Articles of Association with the Registrar of Companies, who issues the Certificate of Incorporation.

- The **Memorandum of Association** defines the constitution and set up of the company. It must include the name of the company, the location of its registered office, its objects/business, a statement of limited liability, and the amount of authorised share capital.

- The **Articles of Association** define the company's internal administration, rules and procedures: how shares will be issued and managed, the rights of shareholders, requirements for shareholder meetings, the powers and remuneration of directors, payment of dividends, and division of assets if the business is wound up.

The small and medium firm sector

3.11 From your own experience, you will have gathered that private sector organisations vary widely by size: from one-person operations to small businesses to vast global conglomerates. According to a 2005 European Union definition (used for grant-aid purposes):

- A 'micro' enterprise is one which has fewer than 10 employees and an annual turnover of less than 2 million euros.

- A 'small' enterprise is one which has 10–49 employees and an annual turnover of less than 10 million euros.

- A 'medium-sized' enterprise is one which has 50–249 employees and an annual turnover of less than 50 million euros.

- A 'large-scale' enterprise employs more than 250 employees, with an annual turnover of more than 50 million euros.

3.12 Particular attention has been given to small and medium enterprises (SMEs) in recent years, because (a) they are a significant contributor to economic activity (by the above definition, some 99% of enterprises in the EU in 2005, providing around 65 million jobs), and (b) because they require financial and guidance support in order to overcome lack of economic strength in competition with larger players.

3.13 Worthington and Britton *(The Business Environment)* ascribe the resurgence in the importance of the small-firm sector in the UK to a range of factors.

- The shift from manufacturing to service industry: many services are dominated by small firms

- Increasing consumer demand for more specialised and customised (as opposed to mass produced) products, to which small firms are better able to respond

- The growth of outsourcing, where non-core activities are contracted to small specialist firms

- Reorganisation and job cutting to reduce costs, creating 'downsized' organisations

- Government policy, with initiatives designed to support SMEs in creating economic activity and jobs

- More accessible technology, allowing small firms to reach global markets (via ICT) and eroding larger firms' technological edge and economies of scale

3.14 SMEs may have an advantage over large firms in clearly defined, small markets: it would not be worth large firms entering markets where there is no scope for cost-effective mass production. Such an advantage may apply in a geographically localised market, say, or in a 'niche' market for specialist, customised or premium-quality products. In addition, the entrepreneurial nature and speed of communication in small enterprises makes them particularly well suited to innovation and invention, and they may have an advantage over larger, less flexible firms in fast-changing, high-technology markets.

3.15 On the other hand, SMEs are at a disadvantage in areas such as: raising loan and share capital (because they are a greater risk); managing cashflow (being harder hard hit by late payment or non-payments); ability to take financial risks (including investment in research and development); and dealing with bureaucratic requirements.

3.16 Large organisations are able to take advantage of economies of scale.

- Technical economies, which arise in the production process. Large undertakings can afford larger and more specialised machinery, for example, and can take advantage of the cost-efficiency of mass production.

- Commercial economies, such as purchasing economies (eg through bulk purchase discounts)

- Financial economies, such as obtaining loan finance at attractive rates of interest – or being able to raise large amounts of capital via the sale of shares to the public (as a public limited company).

A firm in an industry with a large consumer market may have to grow to a certain size in order to benefit from such economies of scale, and thus to be cost-competitive with larger players.

3.17 UK government support has focused on the problems and disadvantages of SMEs, in these areas, with initiatives designed to:

- Encourage on-time payment of bills by PLCs and public sector bodies
- Relax rules and regulations applicable to SMEs
- Reduce the tax burden (eg levels of corporation tax) on small business
- Provide grants to assist SMEs in rural areas or areas of industrial decline (eg the EU SME Initiative and the Enterprise Fund)
- Provide information, advice and support (eg through the Small Business Service and Business Link network).

3.18 From the above discussion, you may be able to identify particular challenges for the purchasing function in SMEs.

3.19 A purchaser in an SME will work within a limited expenditure budget and tight cost controls; will need to manage cashflow closely (eg securing long credit terms from suppliers); and may have to develop a supply chain which can respond to innovation, short product lifecycles and small-quantity, fast-turnaround requirements.

3.20 A purchaser buying *from* an SME will need to take into account the firm's limited capacity to handle volume; its potential financial stability (if it hits problems in the midst of a supply contract); and its cashflow issues (the ethical response to which would be to pay invoices in full on time!).

Regulation of the private sector

3.21 We will look at the law affecting companies in Chapter 10, but it is worth noting that there are various ways in which the activities of private sector organisations are regulated or controlled, in order to protect the interests of their stakeholders.

- *Law and regulations* affect the conduct of private sector businesses in a number of areas: restricting practices that tend to stifle competition; protecting the rights of employees and consumers; requiring financial accountability and public disclosure; restricting the types of products that firms can supply (eg dangerous goods) and the ways they manufacture (eg damaging the environment) and promote their goods (eg advertising to children); and so on. Compliance is overseen by various regulatory bodies, such as the Competition Commission, the Advertising Standards Authority and the Health and Safety Executive.
- *Privatised firms* (such as British Telecom and British Gas), which used to be in public ownership but were sold into private hands, are subject to a regulatory regime in order to protect consumers in the absence of a genuinely competitive market. Bodies such as Ofcom (telecommunications) and Ofgem (energy supply) are mainly concerned with limiting price rises.

3.22 While there has been a move towards deregulation and/or voluntary self-regulation by industries, governments generally recognise that *some* intervention in the private sector is desirable in order to protect consumer rights; promote competition; assist firms to prosper; and protect the national interest (eg by protecting domestic companies from unfair competition from imports).

3.23　In addition to formal regulation, remember that the behaviour of firms is also intended to be constrained by:

- *The market:* that is, by supply and demand, and the power of consumer choice. Organisations will seek to avoid conduct which might lose them customers.

- *Corporate ethics and corporate social responsibility.* There has been considerable public pressure in recent decades for firms to become 'good corporate citizens': to protect the environment, maintain employment, trade fairly, contribute to communities and generally protect the interests of wider stakeholders. Many firms now set objectives and submit to voluntary self-regulation in these areas.

4　*Public sector organisations*

Types of organisations in the public sector

4.1　There are several different types of public sector organisation.

4.2　**Government departments** (eg the Departments of Defence, Health, HM Treasury and the Foreign and Commonwealth Office) carry out the work of central government. They are financed by taxation revenue, although they also include trading organisations such as the Stationery Office.

4.3　**Local government authorities** (eg County Councils, District Councils and Metropolitan District Councils) carry out the work of local service administration, financed by revenue raised predominantly from local sources.

4.4　**Quasi-Autonomous National Government Organisations** (QUANGOs) are set up by the government as independent (non-departmental) bodies, which are nevertheless dependent on the government for their existence. UK examples include the Environment Agency, the Competition Commission and the new Equality and Human Rights Commission. (In the US, QUANGO stands for Quasi-Autonomous *Non* Governmental Organisation, and you may see this version used in some text books.)

4.5　**Public corporations** (eg the BBC) are state-owned industrial and commercial undertakings. They are run by a board accountable to the Secretary of State of a sponsoring government department, with which they agree their strategic objectives, performance targets and funding. These public enterprises are an important part of the public sector, contributing significantly to national output, employment and investment. British Coal, British Energy, the Post Office and British Steel were among them in the UK, for example, but such industries have been progressively privatised (sold into private ownership) since the 1980s.

4.6　**Municipal enterprises** are providers of goods and services (eg leisure services, museums, parks), run by local government authorities – often in competition with the private sector. Increasingly, local councils are creating separate companies or trusts to deliver such services, allowing partnership with private investors and providers.

Financing the public sector

4.7　All sources of public sector funding derive ultimately from the taxpayer. Funds are collected in various different forms: direct taxes (taxes on income, such as the corporation tax paid by companies and the income tax paid by individuals); indirect taxes (ie taxes on expenditure, such as value added tax and excise duties); and local taxes (such as council tax and business rates).

4.8 In the UK, most of this income is collected by central government (although some of it, such as council tax, is collected by local authorities). It is the task of government, and specifically the Treasury department, to distribute the income for use in the areas prioritised by government policy. Where funds are collected locally, they are also spent locally, on services such as policing, rubbish collection, road maintenance and so on.

Regulation of the public sector

4.9 There are a number of regulatory bodies operating in the public sector: eg Ofsted for educational standards and the General Medical Council for health care. The purpose of these regulators is to protect public welfare and national interest, to ensure compliance with institutionalised standards – and to ensure that taxpayers' money is well spent!

4.10 Regulators may be responsible for any or all of the following issues.

- Highlighting and advising on best practice, quality standards and service levels
- Reviewing and evaluating government strategies
- Receiving reports and returns on performance, and publishing evidence-based findings
- Monitoring and auditing organisational activity for compliance to standards
- Helping customers to make informed choices and, where necessary, complaints
- Communicating and promoting the work of the sector to the public.

4.11 As in the private sector, the impact of regulation on public sector procurement is, broadly, to ensure that materials, goods and services comply with defined standards and specifications; that they comply with defined service levels (eg if outsourced to third party providers); and to ensure that all processes are compliant with health and safety standards (eg in regard to manual handling or transport of dangerous goods) and environmental standards (eg in regard to waste disposal, recycling and sustainability).

4.12 Public sector *procurement* is specifically subject to additional regulation.

- Review by the **National Audit Office** (central government and public bodies) and the **Audit Commission** (local government authorities), whose job is to review public spending, efficiency and standards and publish reports and recommendations
- **EU procurement directives**, now enacted in UK law as the Public Contracts Regulations 2006 and the Public Utilities Regulations 2006. These regulations are designed to open up new supply markets to the public sector; to ensure free movement of goods and services within the EU; to ensure that public sector purchasing decisions are based on value for money, through competitive tendering; and to ensure that public sector bodies award contracts efficiently and without discrimination. The regulations, which apply to purchases by public authorities (above a certain financial threshold), contain detailed requirements for fair and open competitive tendering procedures, in which buyers are generally obliged to award contracts on the basis of lowest price *or* value for money.

5 *The third sector*

Types of organisation in the third sector

5.1 As we noted earlier, the primary objective of most public sector organisations is the achievement of service levels, rather than generating profits. A number of organisations in the private sector are also operated on a not-for-profit (NFP) basis, including: charities, churches, private schools and hospitals, political parties, museums, clubs and associations, interest/pressure groups, trade unions and professional bodies such as CIPS. These are often identified separately as the 'third' sector of the economy.

5.2 Organisations in this sector have typically been set up to achieve a defined objective (eg for a charitable purpose) rather than to maximise profit. They usually derive their income from donations, legacies (money left to the organisation in someone's will), sponsorships and government grants and subsidies, although they may also have a trading arm to generate revenue (as in the case of Oxfam shops, say). They may be owned by their members (as in a club or association) or by a trust (as in a charity), and managed by a board of trustees or directors.

5.3 NFP organisations are sometimes subdivided into further sectors, according to their membership and funding.

- In the **voluntary sector** (eg churches, charities and interest groups), the organisations are generally controlled by a few individuals (eg trustees), but operate by voluntary contributions of funding (eg donations and grants, plus sales of product where relevant) and participation (volunteer labour). The funds are used to maintain the work.
- In the **subscription paid sector** (eg clubs, trade unions and professional bodies), the organisations are owned by the people who pay subscriptions to be members.

5.4 Obviously, the range of not-for-profit organisations is very wide, and they may have a range of different purposes.

- Raising public awareness of a cause or issue (eg pressure and interest groups)
- Political lobbying and advocacy on behalf of a cause, issue or group
- Raising funds to carry out activities (perhaps using commercial operations to generate profits, in addition to requesting grants, donations or subscriptions)
- Providing material aid and services to the public or specific beneficiaries (eg homeless or aged care charities, wildlife protection and conservation groups)
- Providing services to members (eg trade unions, professional bodies, sports clubs)
- Mobilising and involving members of the public in community projects, for mutual benefit (eg Volunteer Service Overseas).

5.5 As with public sector organisations, the range of a NFP organisation's stakeholders can therefore be wide, including: contributors (staff, volunteers, members, donors); funding bodies (sponsors, funding authorities); beneficiaries of the services or activities; the media (since activities are often 'in the public interest'); and regulatory bodies (such as the Charities Commission). This means that there will be multiple influences on organisational policy and decision-making.

Purchasing in the third sector

5.6   The term 'non-profit' or 'not-for-profit' should not be interpreted as implying a disregard for commercial disciplines. On the contrary, such disciplines may be more important than in the private commercial sector, because of the scarcity of funds; pressure to devote as much as possible of their income to beneficiaries; or (in the case of public sector educational institutions and hospitals) expenditure limits set by funding authorities.

5.7   Purchasing professionals therefore have a key role to play. NFP organisations may need to source inputs for a very wide range of activities, some of which pose particular logistical challenges (eg foreign aid work). Some have very large procurement budgets. The regulatory framework under which they operate often calls for particularly specialised purchasing skills.

5.8   A significant factor affecting NFP buyers is that they are performing a stewardship function. That is to say, they are spending money that has been derived not from the organisation's own trading efforts, but from someone else's donations or taxes. In fact, funding will often come from persons or organisations not themselves benefiting from the services provided. For this reason, purchasers in this sector are more closely regulated, with a strong emphasis on accountability and stewardship.

5.9   Johnson & Scholes argue that this may cause a focus on resource efficiency at the expense of service effectiveness. In other words, there is a danger that such organisations will be less concerned to identify and satisfy the needs of their 'customers' – and more concerned with demonstrating absence of waste in their use of sponsors' funds.

Regulation of the third sector

5.10 As we noted above, there is a strong emphasis on accountability and stewardship in regulating the third sector. The Charities Commission, for example, is the regulatory body for UK charities. Its objectives are as follows.

- To ensure that charities meet the legal requirements for being a charity (in order to register with the Commission), and are equipped to operate properly and within the law
- To check that charities are run for public benefit, and not for private advantage
- To ensure that charities are independent and that their trustees take their decisions free of control or undue influence from outside agencies
- To detect and remedy serious mismanagement or deliberate abuse by or within charities. The Commission has the power to audit charities, investigate complaints, and – in the case of mismanagement or abuse – to intervene to protect the charity's assets.

Chapter summary

Key learning points include the following.

- Organisations can be categorised by activity (industry sectors), structure and ownership (public, private), primary objective (profit and not-for-profit) or size (eg small medium enterprises).

- It is common to distinguish three major industry sectors: primary (extracting or producing raw materials), secondary (converting raw materials into products) and tertiary (developing and providing services). Different activities pose different purchasing challenges.

- The tertiary or service sector represents a major contributor to employment and gross domestic product in developed nations. As resources, skills, capital and technology become available, with economic development, the tertiary sector grows. There are particular challenges to purchasing in service organisations – and to purchasing services.

- The private and public sectors differ in factors such as ownership, funding, primary objective, competition and stakeholder constituency. This creates some differences in purchasing objectives and constraints – although these should not be overemphasised.

- The main functions of the public sector in a mixed economy are to provide essential goods and services in areas of market failure; to regulate the private sector; and to redistribute wealth.

- Private sector organisations include sole traders, partnerships and limited companies (both public and private). Many enterprises are now classed as small medium enterprises (SMEs), which face particular challenges and receive public sector support.

- Public sector organisations include: central government departments, local government authorities, QUANGOs, public corporations and municipal enterprises.

- The third (not-for-profit) sector includes charities, churches, political parties, interest and pressure groups, clubs and associations. They may have a range of purposes and activities. The main challenges for purchasing will be limited funds and accountability in the use of those funds.

Self-test questions

Numbers in brackets refer to paragraphs where you can check your answers

1 Give two examples each of primary, secondary and tertiary industries. (1.3)

2 Describe the distinctive features of retail purchasing. (1.8)

3 Explain why economic development supports a growing tertiary sector. (1.12)

4 What are the key differences between the public and private sectors? (2.2, 2.3)

5 Why does an economy need a public sector? (2.4–2.8)

6 Compare the advantages of sole tradership, partnership and incorporation. (3.3, 3.6, 3.9)

7 What is the difference between a public and a private limited company? (3.8)

8 In what areas might an SME be (a) at an advantage and (b) at a disadvantage in relation to larger firms? (3.14–3.16)

9 Explain how public sector organisations are funded. (4.2–4.3)

10 List five possible objectives of a not-for-profit organisation. (5.4)

Further reading

From your 'Essential Reading' list, you might look at Worthington & Britton (*The Business Environment:* 5th edition, 2006, FT Prentice Hall), Part 3: FIRMS.

- *Chapter 8: Legal Structures:* the nature of private and public sector organisations in the UK (and Europe).

- *Chapter 9: Size Structure of Firms:* the implications of organisational size and growth.

- *Chapter 10: Industrial Structure:* different business activities and sectors

Unless you are particularly interested, you can probably read relatively quickly through most of this material, as much of it lies outside the scope (or beyond the depth) of the syllabus – and we have already covered the essentials. Focus on the mini-case and case study features, which are a good source of illustrative examples for the exam.

CHAPTER 3

Markets

Learning objectives and indicative content

1.2   Explain the effects of different market conditions on the following:

- Perfect competition
- Imperfect competition: monopolistic competition, monopolies
- Oligopolies

1.3   Discuss how different market forms affect the degree of competition in a market and how this impacts on how purchasing operates in the market

- Sole suppliers: monopolies
- Large supplier base giving competitive advantage
- Restricted supply markets

Chapter headings

1   How markets work

2   Perfect competition

3   Monopoly

4   Monopolistic (imperfect) competition

5   Oligopoly

6   Competitive forces

7   International markets

Introduction

In this chapter, we introduce another element of the purchasing environment: markets. Markets are the 'places' where buyers and sellers of a product or service are brought together to interact. (We'll explain what we mean by 'places' first.)

Buyers and sellers together create a particular dynamic: the forces of supply (how much sellers want to, or can, produce) and demand (how much buyers want to, or can, consume). We start the chapter by exploring supply and demand, and how they make markets work.

We then go on to consider another important aspect of markets: competition. Buyer spending power (and therefore demand) and production resources (and therefore supply) are limited, so if there is more than one buyer or seller in a market, they will have to compete for a share of the value available. Different market conditions create different types and degrees of competition: from perfect competition at one end of the scale to no competition at all (monopoly) at the other, with imperfect competition in between (including 'oligopoly', a particular favourite of the examiner). We will explore each option in detail.

Finally, we examine the forces that influence the amount and intensity of competition in an industry, using a well known framework: Porter's Five Forces model. And we add some brief comments on international markets, in preparation for considering the international dimensions of environmental factors, in subsequent chapters.

1 How markets work

What is a market?

1.1 A market is a place where buyers and sellers of a product are brought together to trade. This may be a physical location where they interact face to face (like a supermarket or car showroom) – but it may equally well be 'cyber space' (as in online share trading, online stores and auction sites such as e-Bay) or a network of contacts with intermediaries (eg share brokers or export agencies) so that buyer and seller never deal directly with each other. In each case, the main features of a market are the exchange of goods or services and payment in some form.

1.2 **Product markets** are the markets in which a firm sells its products and services to consumers. **Supply (or factor) markets** are the markets in which a firm purchases the resources it needs for production (eg materials and labour). The purchasing function therefore deals primarily in various supply markets.

1.3 As we saw briefly in Chapter 2, a **market economy** (or **free market system**) is one in which basic economic choices (what to produce, how, for whom and at what price) are made through the market – by consumer choice – without state intervention. There are two key economic concepts that will be helpful for you to understand the market environment.

- The so-called **market mechanism** is the relationship between demand and supply, and the way in which price affects both. This isn't featured explicitly in your syllabus, but it is important underpinning knowledge – and is covered in detail in the Recommended Reading. We give you a very quick tour of the topic here.

- The concept of **market structure** refers to the degree of competition that exists in the market for a product. This topic *is* featured explicitly in your syllabus, and we will give it detailed coverage.

The market mechanism: demand and supply

1.4 *Demand* is the quantity of goods that consumers are willing and able to buy. It varies with price: in general, as the price of a good goes up, demand goes down – because some people will cut down on their purchases, or switch to cheaper substitutes.

1.5 However, this depends on other factors such as the following.

- The price of **substitute goods**. If substitute goods become cheaper, demand for our first-choice product will go down even if its price stays the same, because people will switch. (Think of rented DVDs as a substitute for cinema tickets, say.)

- The price of **complementary goods** (goods which are consumed together with another good: as petrol is with cars, say). If the price of a complement (petrol) goes down, demand for our product (cars) will go up even if its price stays the same, because the total 'package' will be cheaper.

- **Disposable income**: that is, how much money consumers have to spend. An increase (or fall) in disposable incomes will lead to an increase (or fall) in demand for most goods, even if their prices stay the same.

- **Consumer preferences** and attitudes. Fashions and promotional campaigns may increase (or decrease) demand for a product, regardless of price. Think i-Pod.

1.6 It may help to see a very basic diagram of the relationship between price and demand, called a 'demand curve'. As prices rise, demand falls, as shown by a movement *along* the downward demand curve: Figure 3.1 (a). However, changes in the other determining factors lead to a *shift of the demand curve itself:* at *any* given price, demand may fall or rise: Figure 3.1 (b).

Figure 3.1 (a):

Price affects demand: movement along the curve

Figure 3.1(b):

Other factors affect demand: movement of the curve

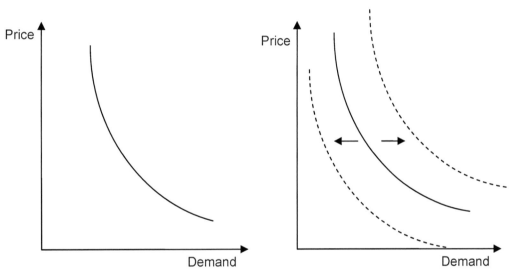

1.7 *Supply* is the amount that firms are willing and able to sell. This too varies with price: in general, as the market price of a good rises, supply also rises – because higher prices mean greater profitability, increasing the willingness of firms to produce more.

1.8 However, again, this depends on other factors.

- Production costs. If the producer's costs rise, its profits (selling the product at the market price) will be eroded, and it will tend to produce less in order to maintain profitability. Similarly, if production costs are lower, the producer will be able to produce more.

- Technology. Improved technology enables firms to produce more at the same cost (ie more profitably) and thus increases the amount they are willing to supply at a given market price.

- The number of suppliers in the market. New suppliers mean more supply, while a supplier leaving the market will decrease supply.

- Expectations. If a firm is confident about the economic future, or about demand for a product, it will be willing to invest more in production capacity, or increase supply in expectation of future demand.

1.9 Again, it may help to see a very basic diagram of the relationship between price and quantity of supply, called a 'supply curve'. As prices rise, supply also rises, as shown by a movement *along* the upward supply curve: Figure 3.2 (a). However, changes in the other determining factors lead to a *shift of the supply curve itself*: at *any* given market price, producers may raise or lower supply: Figure 3.2 (b).

Figure 3.2 (a):

Price affects supply: movement along the curve

Figure 3.2(b):

Other factors affect supply: movement of the curve

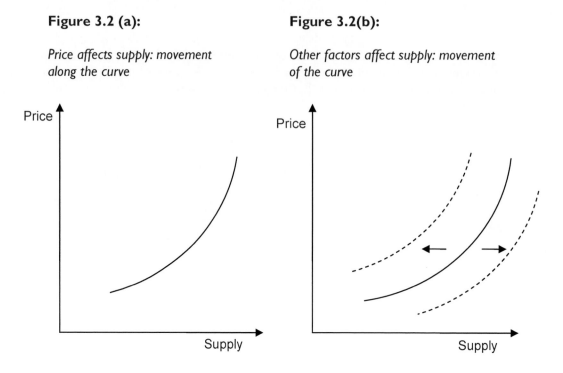

1.10 There is one price (called the **equilibrium price**) at which producers wish to sell the same amount as consumers wish to buy: in other words, the market 'clears' (without either surplus supply or unsatisfied demand). Say that, at a certain price, supply exceeds demand. Goods will pile up in the shops – and the price will start to fall. Falling prices act as a signal to suppliers to cut back on supply – at the same time as increasing demand again. The market eventually stabilises at a price at which the supply of a good matches demand for that good: Figure 3.3. Both parties are relatively satisfied, so there is (for the moment) no need for further adjustment.

Figure 3.3: *Equilibrium price*

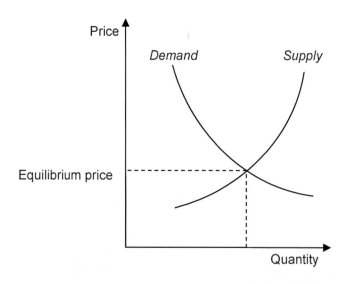

1.11   So by consuming a product at a given level at a given price, consumers are effectively determining the resources that will be devoted to production of that product: price is the economy's mechanism for allocating resources.

Market structure

1.12   The term 'market structure' refers to different *forms of competition* that might be found in a market. Customer spending power (in product markets) and resources or factors of production (in factor markets) are inevitably limited. This means that if there is more than one player in a market, they will have to compete for a share of the market. The nature and intensity of that competition will influence the behaviour and performance of the players in the market – and their purchasing strategies.

1.13   There are four basic market structures.

- **Perfect competition** is a theoretical construct, which is never really achieved in practice – but is useful for analysing the effects of competition. It represents a set of conditions in which no supplier (among many) has the market power to influence the price of a good: there will be only one price for the good, determined by total market supply and demand.

- **Monopoly** is another theoretical construct at the opposite end of the scale: a situation in which no competition exists at all, because a single producer supplies the whole market. This producer has ultimate market power, and can (unless regulated) decide what it will charge for the good.

- **Monopolistic competition** is a form of 'imperfect' competition. It describes a situation where there is competition between a large number of suppliers producing goods which are slightly different (or differentiated) in some way: in specification, or packaging, or consumer perception, say. These differences may allow suppliers to set slightly varying prices for a good.

- **Oligopoly** is another form of 'imperfect' competition. It describes a situation where there is competition between a small number of large suppliers of differentiated goods. Such suppliers have considerable market power to set prices, but will be reluctant to engage in unilateral price rises (risk of losing market share) or cuts (risk of creating a price war): instead, they will usually work together to keep prices stable.

1.14   These structures can be seen as a continuum from very competitive markets to markets in which there is no competition at all: Figure 3.4.

Figure 3.4: *The competitive spectrum*

Decreasing degree of competition	**Perfect competition** Many producers with no market power
	Monopolistic competition Many producers with little market power
	Oligopoly A few producers with high market power
	Monopoly Only one producer with absolute market power

1.15   We will now look at each of these structures in more detail.

2   *Perfect competition*

Market conditions creating a perfectly competitive market

2.1   As we noted above, perfect competition is an 'ideal' situation in which no player in the market has market power to influence the price of a good. The market conditions which need to be fulfilled to bring this situation about are as follows.

- There are many buyers and sellers: each is so small relative to the total market that its actions cannot affect the market. For example, there is no buyer able to buy such large quantities that it could influence the market price.
- The goods being marketed are 'homogeneous': in other words, identical.
- 'Perfect information' about the market is available to all parties.
- There is no 'economic friction': the same market factors (eg risk, storage and transport costs) affect all parties equally.
- There are no 'barriers to entry or exit': firms can choose to enter or leave the market without cost. (We will discuss this further below.)
- There is 'perfect mobility': producers can use resources for any purpose, and consumers can purchase from any supplier, without incurring switching costs.

2.2   What this essentially means is that no supplier or buyer will have power to influence the price of the good in the market. If one supplier tries to charge a higher price than the others, everyone will know (because of perfect information) – and there will be no barrier to consumers simply switching to another supplier (because the goods are identical and all other factors are equal). All firms will have to toe the line of market price, which will be determined by supply and demand in the total market: they are said to be *price takers* – accepting the 'going rate' for the good.

2.3   Market price will generally settle at a level which allows suppliers to make 'normal profits': that is, sufficient revenue to cover their costs, plus a margin of profit sufficient for them to stay in business. If a firm earns less than this, in the absence of barriers to exit, it will simply leave the market. If a firm earns more than this ('abnormal profits'), everyone will know: in the absence of barriers to entry, other firms will enter the market seeking to share in the supra-normal profits that are available – and with more competition and higher supply, prices will fall, returning profits to the normal level.

Barriers to entry and exit

2.4   *Barriers to entry* are factors which reduce the attractiveness or profitability of a market to potential new competitors from outside, and therefore reduce the likelihood that they will enter the market. In perfect competition, no such barriers exist – but in oligopoly and monopoly markets, firms will have an interest in *erecting* such barriers (if they do not already exist) in order to protect their power and profits.

2.5   The main barriers to entry include the following.

- Economies of scale and other cost advantages for established competitors (eg bulk purchasing/production economies, fewer marketing costs, no learning curve, preferential access to necessary inputs), allowing them to squeeze out new entrants with a price war if necessary
- High capital investment requirements in order to enter the market

- Product differentiation and brand identity: hard-to-imitate offerings with costly-to-counter market profile and customer loyalty. Established competitors can afford to spend heavily on advertising, the cost of which will be spread over a large number of units sold: newer, smaller entrants may struggle to advertise at levels required to create awareness and woo customers from existing players.

- Switching costs (eg time, inconvenience, unfamiliarity with the new product, perhaps cost of getting out of existing contracts) and customer loyalty to existing brands, hindering new product trial and adoption by the market

- Existing players' control over supply and distribution channels (perhaps on a selective or exclusive basis which would hinder competitors)

- Existing players' control over a natural resource for which no close substitutes exist (eg ownership of or access to minerals or forests)

- Restricted labour or skill supply (eg the provision of accountancy and legal services being restricted to members of appropriate professional bodies)

- Government policy and legislative barriers: for example, laws protecting established players' intellectual property (eg design patents and copyrights) or physical property (such as mineral or fishing rights).

2.6 *Barriers to exit* are factors which make it difficult for an existing supplier to *leave* an industry, if it proves unattractive or unprofitable. Here are some barriers to exit.

- A lack of assets with significant break-up, re-sale or re-use value, so that the firm will not be able to realise any value from them (other than by continuing to use them)

- The cost of redundancy payments, if workers have to be laid off as a result of the closure or change of activity

- Effects on other divisions or activities maintained by the firm: loss of morale and/or strategic direction due to the divestment, loss of complementary products (which may have an impact on the sale of other items in the product range), loss of managerial talent (if not transferred to other divisions)

- Reputational damage, as a result of factory closures, product withdrawals and so on – which may impact on the firm's other product lines

- Corporate social responsibility and/or government pressure to maintain employment and the production of essential goods and services (even if they are unprofitable).

Are there any perfectly competitive markets?

2.7 There are some markets which arguably come close to being perfectly competitive. The stock markets and foreign exchange markets are examples: there are many operators in the market; each company's shares and each country's currency are identical; there is an emphasis on transparency and information is transmitted very quickly to all market participants; and transaction costs are similar for all operators. However, some operators (eg large pension funds or insurance companies) do have market power; and there are barriers to entry (eg in the form of minimum authorised share capital).

The implications of perfect competition for purchasing

2.8 Perfect competition means that there will be literally nothing to choose between one supplier and another. Buyers have perfect information about all suppliers' prices, and since all offerings are identical, they are perfectly free to switch suppliers to secure the market rate: any supplier who charges above the market price, or seeks abnormal profit margins, will quickly have to come into line in order to stay competitive. Buyers may also seek to play suppliers against each other to secure prices below market rate: it doesn't matter if a supplier is driven out of business, because there are plenty of others – and no costs of exit for the supplier.

2.9 Even where a market is slightly less than perfect, there will be the same incentive for suppliers to compete on price, and this will be to buyers' advantage: given identical offerings, and low switching costs, buyers have the market power to 'shop around'.

2.10 From the buyer's viewpoint, the *downside* of perfect competition is that there may be many buyers as well as many sellers. Small buyers will lack market power to influence suppliers on price: if they don't like the terms of business, suppliers will know they can sell their goods to plenty of other buyers instead.

3 Monopoly

Features of a monopoly

3.1 In its 'ideal' form, a monopoly exists when one producer supplies the whole market. The conditions for a monopoly are as follows.

- Only one supplier of the good exists. It may be a single organisation, or a group of producers acting together to control supply (eg a cartel such as the Organisation of Petroleum Exporting Countries, or OPEC).
- There are barriers to entry, preventing other firms from entering the market (eg high set-up costs, high customer loyalty to the existing producer, or the existing producer monopolising sources of supply and distribution channels).
- There are no close substitutes for the good being produced (which would enable buyers to switch).

3.2 If these conditions are met, the monopolist essentially controls supply, and has absolute power to determine the price of the good in its market: it is said to be a *price maker*. It is this feature which can lead to consumers being over-charged, which is why monopoly markets are usually regulated, as we will see.

3.3 Control over supply and price enables monopolists to achieve and sustain abnormal profits, because there are no competitors to increase supply (lowering prices and therefore eroding profits).

Price discrimination

3.4 A monopolist may be able to operate *price discrimination:* charging different prices for the same good in different markets or market segments. So, for example, the same train ticket may be more expensive in peak commuter hours than in off-peak hours – or if booked in person rather than online. Consumers with higher disposable income will be willing to pay more for the same good or service than less affluent consumers (perhaps even perceiving that the higher price tag means better quality).

3.5 In order for price discrimination to be possible, the firm must be able to identify different market segments with different demand conditions, so that different prices are tolerated by each. The higher price will be charged to the market where the demand is relatively 'inelastic' (that is, where demand is not sensitive to price changes) and the lower price where it is relatively 'elastic' (where demand is sensitive to price).

There must also be no possibility of resale by one consumer to another, so people charged the lower price can't go out and resell the good to those being charged the higher price, possibly undercutting the original provider.

3.6 You might think of price discrimination as 'discriminatory' in a bad sense, exploiting some consumers by charging them more for the same good. However, it has some benefits for both the supplier and the consumer.

- It allows efficient resource usage: lower prices can be used to stimulate sales in 'off-peak' periods, to shift unused stock (or fill last-minute vacancies) – and hence to smooth out fluctuations in demand.

- It takes into account affordability for different groups of consumers, allowing less affluent groups equal access to goods and services, and charging more to groups who are able and willing to pay more.

Regulation of monopoly

3.7 UK law defines a monopoly, for the purposes of regulation, as a situation in which one firm or group of firms acting together (a cartel) supplies or purchases 25% or more of all goods or services of a particular type in the UK, or in a part of the UK. This is obviously not a *pure* monopoly, but represents considerable power to dictate terms in a market.

3.8 UK legislation (including the Competition Act 1998 and Fair Trading Act 1973) is designed to regulate monopolies – and mergers which would result in monopolies – in the public interest. A monopoly may be considered to endanger the public interest if its effect is: to hinder effective competition; to damage consumer interests (eg by unfairly raising prices or reducing quality); to limit development; or to distort the distribution of industry and employment. If the Office of Fair Trading finds evidence of harmful conduct by a monopoly, it may seek assurances that the organisation(s) will alter anti-competitive business practices – or may refer the matter to the Competition Commission.

3.9 Similar provisions apply in European law: Article 82 of the Treaty of Rome prohibits abuse of a monopoly position by an organisation within the EU. In this case a 'monopoly position' is defined not in terms of market share, but relative economic strength: the ability of a company to 'behave to an appreciable extent independently of its competitors, customers and ultimately of its consumers'. Software giant Microsoft, for example, has been repeatedly investigated (and fined) by the European Commission for abusing its dominant market position to freeze out competing products.

3.10 So is there such a thing as a pure monopoly? Perhaps the purest examples of monopoly in the UK were the old nationalised utilities like British Gas – but they have now been privatised, and the market is open to competition (although it has been slow to develop, with significant barriers to entry).

The implications of monopoly for purchasing

3.11 The main concern for buyers will be a *monopoly supplier's* absolute power in the market: there will be no opportunity for the buyer to take its business elsewhere, so the monopolist will be able to dictate terms and conditions of trade. The only alternatives will be to seek substitute goods or services which would serve the same purpose, *or* to seek new supply markets, perhaps internationally: this may even be a helpful spur to strategic thinking and innovation!

3.12 Prices will generally be higher in the absence of competition, and the buyer will not be able to exert pressure to reduce prices – nor to improve quality or service levels: its business is likely to represent only a small part of the supplier's revenue. However, monopolists enjoy *economies of scale:* that is, cost savings due to their large size. Large-scale operations make greater use of advanced machinery and efficient mass production techniques; are able to access finance more cheaply; are able to benefit from bulk discounts on purchases; and so on. Some of these cost savings *may* be passed on to buyers in the form of reasonable prices – although this may have to be achieved by regulation. Regulation limits the prices that monopolists are allowed to charge, in the case of privatised industries in the UK, for example.

3.13 Another issue of concern is that buyers may be unable to specify their exact supply requirements, since the monopoly supplier has little incentive to tailor its product range to the needs of a large number of potential buyers. There may be little or no choice, customisation or innovation – and this might be a serious problem for buyers whose own competitive market is highly specialised or fast-changing. Again, however, this is not *necessarily* the case: monopolists may have more resources to invest in customisation, flexibility and innovation, with the incentive of even higher profits.

3.14 You should also be able to think of the issues raised by the reverse set of circumstances: the position of suppliers faced with a *monopoly buyer,* with absolute bargaining power. There will be considerable risk for suppliers forced to adapt their technology, processes and offerings to the needs of a single customer: if they lose the monopoly's custom, there may be few immediate alternative markets. Suppliers may be driven out of business when large customers, on whom they are highly dependent, squeeze their prices beyond the point of sustainability, or terminate the supply relationship.

4 *Monopolistic (imperfect) competition*

Features of monopolistic competition

4.1 'Monopolistic competition' is not to be confused with 'monopoly'! It is a form of imperfect competition, brought about where the following market conditions apply.

- There are many suppliers (though not as many as in perfect competition)
- Goods are *not* homogeneous: each supplier produces a good which is slightly differentiated from its competitors. (This means that each supplier is a monopoly for its own 'version' of a good – hence 'monopolistic' – but faces competition in the market for the good in general. Apple is a monopoly producer of i-Pods, but there are many types of personal music players on the market.)
- There are barriers to entry (such as customer loyalty and brand strength), but not sufficient to prevent other firms from entering the market in the long term.

4.2 Products may be different in their technical specifications or performance, or differentiation may be added to the total offering: better after-sales service, say, or longer warranty periods. The difference may also lie in the perception of consumers, rather than in the product itself: product 'positioning' is the name given in marketing to consumers' perception of a product's values and attributes in comparison to competitors. Consumers can be encouraged to develop a preference for, and ultimately a loyalty to, a product through distinctive branding, packaging and promotion – even if the product itself is identical to its competitors. (Why is an i-Pod different from another functionally similar MP3 player, for example?)

4.3   Differentiation gives firms a degree of market power, as (unlike in a perfectly competitive market, where goods are identical) consumers may develop a preference for certain features and products, allowing suppliers to charge a little above market price without losing all their customers. In fact, it may be possible to *increase* demand for a product by raising prices slightly, where consumers perceive this to be a sign of high-quality or high-status goods. Similarly, a firm which lowers its prices slightly will not necessarily benefit from increased demand, because many consumers will remain loyal to their preferred brand.

4.4   With the ability to sustain slightly above-market prices, firms may be able to make modest super-normal profits in the short term – although in the long run, super-normal profits will still attract new competitors, which will bring profits back into line.

4.5   It could be argued that imperfect competition is wasteful of resources, compared to perfect competition, because of the investment in promotion and other forms of differentiation. However, this can be seen as the price society has to pay for choice.

4.6   Monopolistic competition is very common: you should be able to think of many examples, from clothes to cereals to cars.

Implications of monopolistic competition for purchasing

4.7   These are probably the market conditions you will face most commonly in your professional work as a purchaser. They create a more complicated market than either of the theoretical extremes, in that suppliers will compete along a range of different dimensions: not just price, but non-price criteria such as quality, variety, flexibility, speed of delivery, service and so on. Buyers will need to have a clear idea of what price and non-price criteria are most important for a given purchase category in a given set of circumstances, in order to select the right suppliers for their needs.

4.8   The balance of power between buyers and sellers will also be more complex: buyers will have the power to switch brands, but not without cost (researching other suitable suppliers, losing their 'preferred' brand and so on). There may be room for negotiation of mutually satisfying purchase contracts and relationships, achieving a balance between the needs of both sides.

5   *Oligopoly*

Features of oligopoly

5.1   An oligopoly is a situation in which a small number of large producers dominate a market in which products are differentiated. This may sound like monopolistic competition, only with fewer players – but the number of players makes a significant difference. With so few firms in the market, each having a significant share of the total market, actions by any one will have direct consequences for all the others. No firm in the market can take decisions independently of the others, because of the likelihood that competitors will respond.

5.2   This creates a distinctive tactical climate.

- There is little *price competition* in the market. Firms have similar market knowledge, so their cost structures and prices will be broadly similar. Moreover, a firm will be reluctant to lower prices unilaterally, because competitors will simply do the same to protect their market share – creating price wars in which the whole industry will lose out. And it will be reluctant to *raise* prices unilaterally, because if competitors *don't* do the same, it may lose market share.

- Competition often takes *non-price forms*: product differentiation supported by branding, advertising, promotions (special offers) and added-value benefits (eg sales and after-sales service, loyalty reward programmes and so on). Think about how the major supermarket or petrol station chains try to stimulate sales and customer loyalty, for example.

- Market prices tend to be set by non-competitive means, in order to maintain price stability and avoid damaging price wars. One approach is that a dominant firm takes the lead in setting the market price, and smaller firms follow suit: this is called *price leadership*. Another approach is for firms in the market to agree between them what prices will be: this is called 'collusion'. (We will discuss it further below.)

- Firms often maintain high barriers to new competitors entering the market, in order to preserve the *status quo* and their market share: for example, by strong branding, controlling channels of supply and distribution, and preventing newcomers from joining cartels.

5.3   Oligopolists have a great deal of market power, by virtue of their size. Super-normal profits are therefore achievable, depending on the strength of competitors and the level of prices that are sustainable in the market.

5.4   There are many examples of oligopoly markets, including the tobacco, brewing, confectionery and toy industries – in all of which, the top three to five firms in the industry have a market share over 85%.

Collusion in oligopoly markets

5.5   There is a temptation for the few firms in an oligopolistic market to join forces to keep out new competitors and fix prices. This can be done by various forms of collusion.

5.6   A **price cartel** or **price ring** is formed when a group of oligopoly firms join forces to agree – and therefore control – output quotas (the amount that will be produced) and market prices. Each participant can increase its profits, if all major competitors charge the same price: potentially, the same price as a monopoly might be able to charge.

5.7   In order for a cartel to be successful, it must include most or all of the major producers/distributors (in order to avoid price competition). There must not be close substitutes for the product (in order to avoid customers' switching in response to high prices), and demand cannot be too price sensitive (so that demand will not fall so much, in response to high prices, that the producers' income will be reduced rather than raised). In addition, the participants must be able to agree on their share of the total supply to the market (which dictates their proportion of the revenue/profits available): this is sometimes the hardest hurdle of all!

5.8   The best known cartel is OPEC, which controls most of the oil production in the world. However, EU treaty provisions, the UK Competition Act and the Enterprise Act 2002 now outlaw cartels. In a well-known 2003 case, for example, a group of ten businesses was found to have illegally entered price-fixing agreements in relation to the sale of replica football kit, around the time of the Euro 2000 Championship (the 'duplicate kit cartel').

5.9   There are also various forms of *informal price collusion*, including the following.

- Systems of 'recommended retail prices', with sellers discouraged from selling at lower or differentiated prices.

- Price leadership by one firm, which is then followed by others in the market.

5.10   Informal collusion is also outlawed in most countries, because its effect is to reduce or distort competition between firms, to the detriment of consumers. Even so, it goes on: collusion includes not just explicit agreements but implicit 'understandings' and even competitors watching each others' pricing decisions and following suit. These kinds of behaviour can be difficult to control.

5.11   Apart from collusive agreements being against the best interests of the consumer, and subject to law and public scrutiny (with the risk of financial penalties and reputational damage), they are also tricky for the participants. This is because of the temptation for cartel members to break ranks for short-term profit-taking. Nevertheless, the market is best served in the long run by price stability, so competition is usually focused on non-price differentiation and promotion.

Implications of oligopoly for purchasing

5.12   Because of the non-homogeneity of goods in the market, buyers will (as with monopolistic competition) have a degree of product choice. Because of the oligopoly's avoidance of price competition, particular emphasis will have to be placed on getting the best possible value for money through a combination of non-price factors: if buyers cannot negotiate on price, they will need to use whatever buyer power they have to secure the best possible service, support and other added value benefits.

5.13   In an oligopoly supply market, suppliers have strong market power by virtue of their size and small number – and any type of formal or informal collusion will add to their bargaining strength and reduce that of buyers. As with a monopoly, oligopoly suppliers can therefore charge high prices – but will benefit from economies of scale which they *may* choose to pass on to buyers. Buyers may seek to enhance their bargaining power in various ways: by developing their negotiating skills; perhaps by consolidating their purchases; or by banding together in a buying consortium with other purchasing organisations, so that they can offer a larger volume of business to a given supplier.

5.14   For a supplier dealing with an oligopoly *buyer*, the position will be reversed. The buyer will represent a potentially large volume of business (although it may divide its demand among a large number of suppliers), allowing the supplier economies of scale and standardisation. On the other hand, bargaining power will lie with the buyer, enabling it to force prices down and raise quality/service (in the interests of its own competitive advantage).

5.15   Oligopoly is a favourite topic of the examiner for this paper. Make sure you have got to grips with our coverage in detail.

Round-up of market structures

5.16   Here is a summary and comparison of the key features of the four market structures: Table 3.1.

Table 3.1: *Comparison of market structures*

⟵──────────────── *Decreasing competition* ────────────⟶

Perfect competition	Monopolistic competition	Oligopoly	Monopoly
Very many small suppliers	Many slightly larger suppliers	Few large suppliers	One supplier
No market power	Little market power	High market power	Absolute market power
Homogeneous goods: suppliers' products are interchangeable	Differentiated goods: suppliers' products are close substitutes	Differentiated goods: degree of substitution variable	No substitutes
One market price: suppliers are 'price takers'	Price competition	Seeking of price stability by price leadership or collusion	Price set by one 'price maker': potential for price discrimination
Normal profits	Small abnormal profits, short term	Abnormal profits, depending on competition	Abnormal profits
No advertising or branding (everyone knows all goods identical)	Heavy advertising and branding > differentiation	Much advertising and branding > non-price competition	Not much advertising or branding required (no competition)
No barriers to entry	No barriers to entry in the long run	Barriers to entry	Barriers to entry

6 *Competitive forces*

6.1 Some of the key texts on competition and competitive advantage were written in the 1980s by Professor Michael Porter. He suggested that 'competition in an industry is rooted in its underlying economics' (as we have already seen) and that 'competitive forces exist that go well beyond the established combatants in a particular industry'. Porter developed a framework which argues that the extent of competition in an industry – and therefore its attractiveness or potential profitability to any given player within it – depends on the interaction of five forces in the organisation's industry environment.

Porter's Five Forces Model

6.2 Although the *five forces model,* as it is called, is not mentioned explicitly in your syllabus, it is an important tool for understanding markets – and occupies a section in your Recommended Reading textbook. We will therefore summarise its main features here.

6.3 Five forces determine the extent of competition in an industry: Figure 3.5.

Figure 3.5: *Porter's five forces model*

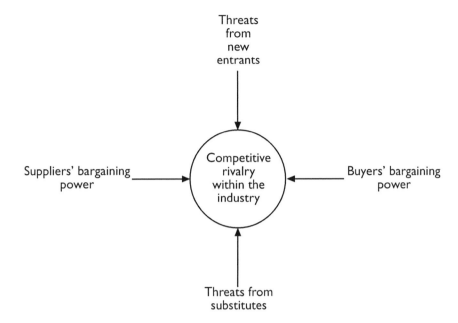

6.4   **Potential new entrants** to an industry may make it more competitive by: expanding supply (without necessarily increasing market demand); striving to penetrate the market and build market share, perhaps by innovating or competing aggressively; and increasing costs, as they bid for factors of production. It is therefore in the interests of existing competitors to deter new entrants! The strength of the threat from new entrants will vary from industry to industry, according to the strength of barriers to entry (discussed earlier) – and the response of existing competitors to any new entrant. (If existing players typically respond to new competitors by competing aggressively on price, a prospective entrant might think twice about whether entry will be profitable…)

6.5   **Substitute products** are alternative products that serve the same purpose (eg postal services, courier services, fax machines, e-mail), making it easy for buyers to switch, and therefore limiting the price that a company can charge for its products. There is a particular risk in that a company may not see a substitute coming, if it results from innovation. Where there are plenty of substitutes available, demand for a product is likely to be relatively price sensitive: buyers are more likely to switch in response to price rises (or price cuts by competitors). Improved price or value positioning in substitute products is therefore a significant threat.

6.6   **Buyer power** may make an industry more competitive by enabling buyers (customers) to: force down prices; bargain for higher quality or improved services; or play competing providers against each other. Porter suggested that buyers are particularly powerful in the following situations.

•   They are limited in number and/or large in size, relative to supplying firms.

•   Their spend is a high proportion of suppliers' revenue (but not a high proportion of their own spend, since this will make them dependent on the supplier).

•   Products/services are undifferentiated, or there are substitute products, making it easy to switch suppliers.

- There is potential for 'backward integration' (ie buyers can own or control their suppliers: a book publisher taking over a printing company, say).

6.7 **Supplier power** (as we saw in the case of oligopolists and monopolists) is generally exercised to raise prices, squeezing buyers' profits (especially if they are unable to recover their cost increases by raising their own prices). Suppliers are particularly powerful in the following situations.

- They are limited in number and/or large in size, relative to buying firms.
- There are few substitute products and/or the supplier's product (and/or service) is highly differentiated.
- The volume purchased by the buyer/industry is not important to the supplier.
- The supplier's product is an important component in the buyer's business.
- The switching cost for buyers is high (eg because of investment in the relationship with a particular supplier, or contract penalties for switching).
- There is potential for 'forward integration' (ie suppliers can own or control their buyers: a clothing manufacturer opening retail stores, say).

6.8 The **intensity of rivalry** among current competitors may range, as we have seen, from collusion between competitors (in order to maintain and share the profits available in the industry) to the other extreme of aggressive competitive strategies such as innovation, price wars and promotional battles, where one firm's gain is another firm's loss. Rivalry is likely to be more intense in the following situations.

- There are many equally-balanced competitors.
- There is a slow rate of industry growth. (If the 'pie' isn't getting larger, the only way firms can grow will be to compete for a bigger 'slice'.)
- There is a lack of product/service differentiation.
- There are high fixed costs of production, since firms need higher revenue to cover them and make a profit.
- There are high barriers to exit, so it is less costly to compete harder than to withdraw from the industry.

6.9 You might like to think about the mobile phone industry, for example, or the soft drinks industry (the famous 'Cola wars' between Pepsi and Coke). What makes competition in these industries so intense – and on what basis do the major players seek to compete (a) with potential new entrants and (b) with each other?

Industry structure

6.10 Porter also classified industry structures according to the amount and type of competition within them.

- **Fragmented industries** are 'populated by a large number of small and medium-sized companies' and characterised by 'the absence of market leaders with the power to shape industry events'. You should be able to see how this corresponds to the market structure of perfect or monopolistic competition. An example of a fragmented industry in the UK might be hairdressing (since there are few large chains of salons).
- **Concentrated industries** are dominated by a small number of large competitors, which are able to exercise a significant influence over the market. You should be able to see how this corresponds to the market structure of oligopoly.

6.11 Industries may become fragmented over time, if their markets are attractive to smaller firms (as we saw in Chapter 2, when we looked at the reasons for the growth in SMEs). This may be the case if barriers to entry are low, or there are few economies of scale to be exploited by larger firms; if innovation and flexibility are required in response to changing or fluctuating demand; if 'local' contacts, differentiation and reputation are important; or if the market itself is fragmented into small segments of customers with distinct tastes or needs (separate niche markets not worth the while of a large organisation to pursue). You might like to think about which of these conditions apply to the increasing fragmentation of the media/publishing industry, for example, with the availability of satellite/digital TV, web-based publishing and so on.

6.12 On the other hand, industries may become (or remain) concentrated, if conditions favour fewer, larger players: there are high barriers to entry, high costs of staying in business and competing, and/or good economies of scale available (where it is cheaper to purchase, produce, distribute and market goods in bulk). There may be consolidation of smaller competitors into fewer, larger ones, through mergers and acquisitions (although the larger resulting groups or chains may retain the distinctive features and markets of their component parts, eg by retaining different brands). A standardised product or service offering may become preferred to smaller, more customised competitors, enabling customers' needs to be fulfilled by fewer firms: think about large fast food chains and supermarkets, for example.

6.13 Porter also noted the existence of **emerging industries**: new or re-formed industries which have not yet settled into established patterns of competition. These may be created by technological innovation (eg creating electronic publishing and music industries) or social change (eg creating eco-friendly industries such as reverse logistics and waste storage/recycling).

6.14 Emerging industries pose distinctive problems for organisations active within them, because of early barriers to entry (technology development, access to materials, problems obtaining funding, problems establishing a market) and uncertainty about the market and competition. Internal capabilities may have to be developed (including purchasing, in contexts where supply markets may not yet be established) and external environmental factors may be unfamiliar.

6.15 Emerging markets may also require a different approach to competition. If a company is first into an emerging market (eg discovering and patenting a new technology), it may choose *not* to maintain barriers to entry, in order to establish a monopoly, but to *encourage* competition (eg by licensing the technology to competitors), in order to co-opt other firms in building the profile and size of the market.

Monitoring competitors

6.16 Although they are not explicitly mentioned in the syllabus (even under the listing of stakeholder groups), competitors are an important part of the external micro (market and industry) environment of purchasing.

- An organisation's strategies and products will, to an extent, be influenced by the need to gain or maintain an advantage over competitors in the market. Managers will attempt to predict what competitors will do, in order proactively to counter threats (or exploit opportunities) arising from their plans. So, for example, purchasers may need to monitor competitors' materials costs and quality, in order for their own purchasing and products to stay competitive.

- Competitors may be used as benchmarks for key competencies that are valued by the market. The organisation may measure its customer service, quality management or procurement efficiency, say, against the standards set by key competitors or market leaders.

- Competitors may seek advantage by controlling supply and distribution channels, eg by forming preferential relationships with suppliers or distributors, or negotiating exclusive supply/distribution contracts. An organisation's purchasers are therefore in direct competition with competitors' purchasers, especially where supplies are limited or scarce.

6.17 **Competitor analysis** is therefore a key component of environmental analysis. It involves analysing competitors' goals, capabilities (strengths and weaknesses), strategies (on what basis is it aiming to compete: price, product differentiation, niche markets?) and likely response to environmental threats and opportunities. Purchasers may, for example, need to look at competitors' relationships with key suppliers; whether they have (or may be able to obtain) control over sources of key or scarce supplies; how well they are able to control or reduce purchasing costs (enabling greater profitability and/or price competition); and so on.

Regulation of competition

6.18 We have said a little bit about the regulation of competition in our discussion of oligopolistic collusion and monopoly conditions. We will return to this topic in a little more detail in Chapter 10 on the legal environment. For the moment, just note that the state can, through legislation and other means, significantly influence the nature of relationships between a firm and members of its micro/competitive environment: controlling prices and competitive practices (such as cartels); giving new producers access to previously concentrated markets; regulating quality, testing and environmental standards (and in some industries, the adoption of new products, eg pharmaceuticals); offering grants, tax incentives and other subsidies to encourage competition and innovation; and so on.

7 *International markets*

Why trade internationally?

7.1 It should be obvious that markets – places where buyers and sellers interact – can be international as well as local or national. Even if a firm does not operate in an international *product* market (ie producing goods for export to other countries), it is quite likely, these days, to operate in an international *supply* market (ie purchasing and importing supplies from other countries).

7.2 We can consider the growth of international trade from two viewpoints: the viewpoint of a country as a whole (a macro-economic viewpoint), and the viewpoint of an individual firm (or purchasing department).

7.3 *Countries* involve themselves in international trade for two main reasons.

- Countries differ in the natural resources they control and the areas of skill and expertise they have developed. Like individual people, countries can benefit from their differences by reaching agreement that each will do whatever it does best and provide what it can produce most efficiently. A country which does not have oil, say, is obliged to buy from a country which has a surplus of oil for export. A country with high labour costs may import manufactured goods from countries such as China which have the capacity to produce them at lower cost.

- If countries can specialise (to an extent) in the production of certain goods or the provision of certain services, it may be able to produce them on a larger scale – and thus benefit from economies of scale. The Japanese domination of the market in electronic goods in recent years is one example of this effect. International trade enables different countries to reap the benefits of specialisation, while still ensuring that a variety of goods and services is available.

7.4   The theory that international trade is for the mutual benefit of the partners involved is known as the **theory of comparative advantage.** A country can increase its national income – and potentially improve the standard of living of its population – by specialising in the manufacture of those products, or provision of those services, in which it has the highest productivity or comparative advantage over other nations. (Think about the transformation of the Indian economy, as a result of specialisation in call centre services, say, supported by global ICT links.) Because each nation is able to use its resources to best effect, and nations effectively 'pool' their best resources, the theory suggests that the overall result of international trade is to raise overall economic prosperity and well-being.

7.5   Other advantages are claimed for international trade.

- The stimulation of local economic activity helps to create employment, leading to greater prosperity, educational development and other standard-of-living benefits. Smaller developing nations particularly benefit from the wider scope of markets, since their domestic economy may have represented too small a market to allow development and resulting economies of scale.

- The siting of operations in developing countries may bring investment in technology, infrastructure, education and skill development which the host country could not afford on its own. It may also bring about improvements in human rights and labour conditions, whenever foreign investors and buyers operate ethical (CSR) policies and monitoring.

- Global consumers benefit from more product/service choice and competitive pricing.

- It has been argued that international trade is a primary mechanism for positive international relations and a deterrent to conflict.

7.6   *Individual firms* may wish to enter international product or supply markets for any of the following reasons.

- The domestic market is mature or 'saturated' with their products, with no room for growth, so they need to open up new markets overseas, to maintain sales growth (or, it is sometimes argued, to offload stock which has become obsolete in the domestic market).

- Particular materials or resources are not available (or have become scarce and costly) in the domestic supply market.

- Domestic suppliers have become complacent or uncompetitive on price, compared to overseas suppliers (who may have readier access to resources, lower labour costs or less stringent regulatory regimes): one of the main reasons for international sourcing is its potential cost savings.

- Exchange rates support the exporting of UK-produced goods (by making their price competitive in the overseas market) or the importing of overseas-produced supplies (by making their price competitive with the domestic supply market). We will explain how this works in Chapter 6.

- Technological advances, particularly in information and communication technology, reduces the cost and risk of sourcing internationally: it is easier to gather information, monitor and manage suppliers, track deliveries and so on.

Barriers to international trade

7.7 Now for the downside: the reasons why not every company markets or sources internationally – and why the decision to source internationally (of most relevance to purchasers) must be taken with care!

- Costs of identifying, evaluating and developing new product and supply markets, in situations where information may be difficult to obtain

- Differences in culture, legal systems and infrastructure development, which may cause incompatibility, misunderstanding or conflict. (On the marketing side, consumers may have different perceptions, tastes and values, and may not have access to a wide range of advertising media. On the supply side, suppliers may have different technical, quality or ethical standards, for example.)

- Differences in language and resulting costs of translation (and risks of mis-translation. There are some very funny examples of brand names translating badly: like the Vauxhall Nova car – 'No va' meaning 'doesn't go' in Spanish.)

- Transport risks, costs and delays, caused by distance and infrastructure differences

- Currency management issues and exchange rate risk (which will be discussed in detail in Chapter 6)

- Market risks, posed by factors such as political instability or policy change, industrial unrest or natural factors (eg drought or flood)

7.8 In addition, governments may place restrictions on international trade, in order to protect their country's producers from competition from imports: a policy called 'protectionism'. Such restrictions include: import quotas (limiting the volume of specified goods allowed into the country); tariffs (taxes placed on imported goods); and subsidies to domestic producers (to make them more competitive).

7.9 Although the trend is now to reduce trade restrictions, they can perform a useful function: protecting strategic industries (in order to preserve the economies which depend on them); protecting emerging industries (in order to encourage development); and improving a country's 'balance of payments' (the ratio of its exports to imports).

Globalisation

7.10 Globalisation may be defined as 'the increasing integration of internationally dispersed economic activity' (Boddy).

7.11 This integration may involve the globalisation of *markets*. It has been argued that with worldwide access to media, travel and communications, there has been a convergence of consumer needs and wants: major brands (such as Coca Cola or McDonald's) can be sold worldwide, without much modification for particular geographic markets. This opened up new markets and offered economies of scale – but these advantages have proved hard to grasp for some brands, which lost (or failed to gain) market share against locally-adapted brands which catered to specific national and regional cultures, tastes and conditions. (Marks & Spencer, for example, has had a mixed history with its international stores.)

7.12 A parallel development has been the globalisation of *production*. High domestic labour costs, for labour-intensive operations, has enabled intense competition from cheaper imports originating in countries with lower-cost labour. (Think about industries such as electronic goods, clothing, footwear and toy manufacture, for example.) This has stimulated the growth of outsourcing, as developed countries have outsourced the production of finished goods and components, and the delivery of service, to countries such as Taiwan, China, South Korea, Singapore, Sri Lanka and India. The media is now full of examples of companies 'offshoring' their administrative work and telephone enquires (eg major banks) and product assembly (eg Hitachi, Compaq, Mattel).

7.13 The main drivers for any given industry to become globalised (based on Yip, *Total Global Strategy*) include the following: Table 3.2.

Table 3.2: *Drivers for globalisation of an industry*

Factor	Examples
Market factors	• Convergence of customer needs, creating demand for products and services to be available on a worldwide basis
	• Globalised marketing firms becoming global customers – seeking suppliers who can also operate on a worldwide basis
	• Transferable marketing, with the development of global communication and distribution channels (including the internet).
Cost factors	• Economies of scale available through the large potential volume of global sales
	• Sourcing efficiencies, as firms are able to select the lowest-cost supplier from anywhere in the world
	• Product development costs: where development costs are high, firms will need to extend the earning potential of products by selling into international markets
Government factors	• Trade policies, which have tended to support free markets between nations (reducing protectionist barriers to trade)
	• Harmonisation of technical standards, which has enabled the sourcing of standardised components, compatible systems etc
	• Host government policies, aimed at encouraging global operators to base themselves in their countries, eg via tax incentives
Competitive factors	• Companies faced with global competition will have to consider becoming global themselves, in order to stay competitive
Technology factors	Developments in ICT support and enable:
	• 'Virtual organisation': sourcing expertise and collaboration regardless of location (eg off-shored administrative centres)
	• Global supply (eg through access to international supply market information, improved supplier management and monitoring)
	• Global logistics (eg through computerised transport planning and delivery tracking)
	• General improvements in international business communication (eg through email)

Opposition to globalisation

7.14 The arguments in favour of globalisation are broadly the same as those for international trade in general. However, it should be obvious from TV footage of violent protests outside World Trade Organisation and G8 meetings that there is a contrary viewpoint! Those opposed to globalisation argue as follows.

- It encourages the exploitation of labour in developing nations (poor wages, poor conditions, child labour and so on) for lower-cost production.

- It encourages the exploitation of local markets, using them as dumping grounds for poor-quality or obsolete goods, and leading to increased foreign debt.

- It 'exports' pollution, deforestation, urbanisation and other environmental damage to developing nations.

- It undermines governments in the management of their own domestic economies, particularly through the influence of the World Trade Organisation and the power of global corporations (whose turnover exceeds the total economic output of some nations…)

- It causes unemployment in developed nations, where justified expectations of pay and conditions make labour 'uncompetitive' with cheap-labour competitors.

- It squeezes small, local businesses out of markets, with negative effects on competition, communities and cultures. (There is a well-publicised cultural fight-back by small local retailers against giants like WalMart, for example, and by 'slow food' producers against the McDonald's of the world…)

- It encourages the erosion of local cultures and the loss of local languages.

The impact of international market factors on purchasing

7.15 We will look at international market factors more specifically, in the next few chapters, as they relate to politics (eg international trading blocs and bodies), economics (eg the balance of payments and exchange rates), socio-cultural factors (eg the challenges of cross-cultural management and trading) and so on.

Chapter summary

Key learning points include the following.

- A market is a 'place' where buyers and sellers interact. A market economy is one in which economic choices (what to produce, how, for whom and at what price) are made by the market via the market mechanism: supply and demand.

- Demand (the amount of goods consumers want to buy) usually falls as prices rise, in a downward demand curve. Supply (the amount of goods firms want to produce) usually rises as prices rise, in an upward supply curve. The market eventually stabilises at a price where supply equals demand (equilibrium price).

- Market structure refers to different forms and amounts of competition in a market. There are four basic market structures: perfect competition (many producers with no market power); monopolistic competition (many producers with some market power due to differentiation); oligopoly (a few large producers with high market power); and monopoly (only one producer with absolute market power).

- Each market structure depends on particular market conditions (number of suppliers/buyers, homogeneity or differentiation of goods, barriers to entry and so on). Each has particular characteristics: one market price in perfect competition; differentiation in monopolistic competition; competitive tactics and collusion in oligopoly; and absolute market power in monopoly. Each has advantages and/or disadvantages for a purchaser. You should revise these areas in detail.

- Porter's five forces model suggests that the extent of competition in a given industry environment is determined by: potential market entrants (and barriers to entry); substitute products; buyer power; supplier power; and the intensity of rivalry between competing firms.

- There are strong drivers for international trade (in both product and supply markets) and globalisation (the integration of globally dispersed economic activity). However, both are subject to challenges, risks and barriers which marketers and purchasers will need to take into account at a strategic level.

Self-test questions

Numbers in brackets refer to paragraphs where you can check your answers

1   What are supply markets? (1.2)

2   What factors determine the strength of demand in a given market? (1.4–1.5)

3   List the four market structures in order of *increasing* competition. (1.14)

4   List the conditions for perfect competition. (2.1)

5   What is price discrimination? (3.4)

6   How might products in imperfectly competitive markets be differentiated? (4.2, 5.2)

7   What tactics are typically used by oligopoly suppliers? (5.2)

8   What are the advantages and disadvantages of dealing with (a) an oligopoly supplier and (b) an oligopoly customer? (5.12–5.14)

9   When do (a) buyers and (b) suppliers have more power in an industry? (6.6, 6.7)

10 What are (a) the key drivers *for* and (b) the key arguments *against* globalisation? (7.13, 7.14)

Further reading

From your 'Essential Reading' list, you might look at Worthington & Britton (*The Business Environment:* 5th edition, 2006, FT Prentice Hall), Part 4: MARKETS.

- *Chapter 12: The Market System.* Focus on the introduction and the concluding section 'the importance of the market to business': the detailed mechanics of supply, demand and pricing effects are beyond the scope of the syllabus.

- *Chapter 13: Market Structure:* more detailed coverage of competition, and the nature and effects of perfect competition, oligopoly and monopoly.

- *Chapter 14: International Markets and Globalisation.* Focus on the first sections of the chapter, which explain the international market, and the final section on globalisation. (We cover the economic aspects, such as the balance of payments and exchange rates, in Chapter 6.)

Unless you are interested, you can probably read relatively quickly through most of this material, as much of it lies outside the scope (or beyond the depth) of the syllabus – and we have already covered the essentials. Focus on the mini-case and case study features, which are a good source of illustrative examples for the exam.

CHAPTER 4

Stakeholders

Learning objectives and indicative content

I.4   Identify the different stakeholder groups involved in the public and private sector purchasing functions, and understand the concept of stakeholder co-operation.

- Employees; customers; suppliers; shareholders; local government; local businesses; charities; political parties; pressure groups
- Stakeholder co-operation

Chapter headings

1   Stakeholders in purchasing

2   Why are stakeholders important?

3   Stakeholder analysis and management

4   Stakeholder conflict and co-operation

Introduction

As we saw briefly in Chapter 1, stakeholders are a key part of the purchasing environment because, by definition, they have a legitimate stake in purchasing activity.

Attention in recent decades has broadened from the rights and interests of the primary stakeholders of private sector firms – that is, their members, owners and contracted partners – to include the rights and interests of their secondary stakeholders: groups in the wider external environment who have no direct contractual relationship with the firm.

We start by identifying both primary and secondary stakeholder groups, and analyse (a) the nature of their stake or interest and (b) their ability to influence the organisation to protect their interest or get their needs met.

We then go on to suggest some ways of using this information to manage stakeholder groups, minimising the potential for them to resist or disrupt the organisation's plans. Finally, we explore ways in which the needs of different stakeholder groups may diverge or conflict – and how stakeholder co-operation can be gained, to satisfy those divergent needs.

1   Stakeholders in purchasing

Stakeholders in an organisation

1.1   'Stakeholders' are individuals or groups who have a legitimate interest or stake in an organisation, project or activity (such as purchasing), by virtue of ownership, investment or participation – or because their own goals and interests are affected by it. The nature of the groups' interests will vary, as will their power to influence the organisation to protect those interests.

1.2 As we saw in Figure 1.2, stakeholders are a feature of both the internal and external environments of the organisation. They are often classified as internal, connected and external groups.

1.3 **Internal stakeholders** are the members of the organisation: its directors, managers and employees. They have a key stake in its survival and growth (for continued employment and prosperity); the fulfilment of task goals (as a measure of their competence and success); and the fulfilment of their personal goals (for income, security, career, status and so on).

1.4 **Connected stakeholders** are those in the external micro-environment who are in direct contractual relationship with the organisation. Here are some examples.

- Shareholders, who have a key stake, as owners, in the financial performance of the organisation. In the public sector, this place may be taken by the government, on behalf of the State.

- Other financiers, such as banks (or in the case of charities, donors and funding bodies), whose interest will be in such matters as the security of loans, return on their investments, and efficient use of their contributions.

- Customers and clients, who may have a range of interests: satisfaction of their various expectations and motives for purchasing a product/service (quality, service etc); fulfilment of contract terms (particularly in business-to-business dealings); securing reliable supply; ethical business dealings; accurate information; and so on.

- Suppliers (the primary concern of the purchasing function), who have an interest in: retaining profitable business from the organisation; a mutually beneficial long-term relationship; efficient information flow; timely payment of accounts; feedback and support to enhance their service; and so on.

- Distributors (wholesalers, retailers and so on), who have an interest in: securing reliable supply for resale; securing quality/added value products and services; marketing support; earnings through discount margins or commissions; and mutually beneficial long-term relationships.

1.5 **External stakeholders** are sometimes called 'secondary' stakeholders, because they do not have a direct contractual relationship with the organisation. Here are some examples.

- Government (local and central) and regulatory bodies, which have an interest in: economic activity, supporting national prosperity; direct and indirect taxation revenue; compliance with legislation and government policy; reports and returns used for regulatory and statistical purposes; and corporate social responsibility, to minimise the social impacts and costs of business. (In the public sector, as we mentioned above, government would be a connected stakeholder.)

- Pressure groups, which have an interest in fulfilling their awareness-raising and influencing objectives in regard to a particular cause or issue (eg environmental protection) or the rights of a particular group (eg disabled workers).

- Professional bodies, trade unions and other representative groups, which have an interest in promoting and protecting the rights and interests of their members, promoting professional standards and ethics, and so on.

- The local community and community organisations, which have an interest in employment opportunities; the provision of goods and services; corporate social responsibility and involvement (eg in regard to the local environment or support for local businesses); and financial support (eg for local schools, charities or political parties).

1.6 Traditionally, the interests of secondary stakeholders have been peripheral to business organisations, whose primary responsibility is to their shareholders. However, the emerging concept of **corporate social responsibility** has emphasised that secondary stakeholders have a legitimate interest which should be protected as far as possible.

1.7 Business activity can have a *negative effect* on local communities, for example, through environmental damage, traffic congestion, the squeezing out of small businesses, unemployment as a result of redundancies and so on. These impacts also impose *financial costs* on society, which the business itself does not account or pay for (and which are therefore sometimes called **externalities**).

1.8 It has therefore been argued that business has a responsibility to minimise these impacts, and to 'give something back' to the communities that support them – and provide them with resources, staff and customers. (We will discuss corporate social responsibility or CSR further in Chapter 7.)

Stakeholders of the purchasing function

1.9 In addition to 'organisational stakeholders' in general, each function, unit and project of an organisation may be said to have stakeholders, whose needs and influence must be taken into account. You should be able to identify the key stakeholders in purchasing, from each of the categories listed. The most obvious ones are as follows.

- The organisation's directors and shareholders, who have an interest in purchasing's contribution to corporate strategy and bottom line profit (eg through cost savings, materials quality, supply efficiency and collaborative supply relationships)
- Purchasing managers and staff, who have an interest in fulfilling the function's objectives and perhaps reinforcing its role and status in the organisation
- Line managers in other functions, on whose behalf purchases are made or to whom purchasing advice/policy is directed. These are often thought of as the 'internal customers' of the purchasing function.
- Suppliers, whose own activities and performance are directly affected by their dealings with buyers, and the buyer-supplier relationship. A buying organisation has contractual responsibilities in regard to suppliers (eg to pay for goods supplied) and also ethical responsibilities (eg to allow adequate profits for survival, to pay on time and to manage tenders fairly) – especially if the balance of power is in the buyer's favour, or if the supplier is highly dependent on the buyer for its survival.
- Regulatory bodies, which have a legitimate right to information and compliance in areas such as public sector purchasing, employee health and safety, and the quality and safety of goods (consumer protection).

Public and private sector stakeholders

1.10 It is worth noting, as we mentioned in Chapter 2, that in the private sector, priority is given to a relatively small and well defined group of stakeholders: internal and connected stakeholders – particularly, shareholders. Public sector organisations generally have a wider and more complex range of stakeholders, because in theory they are managed on behalf of society as a whole.

1.11 While private sector businesses often have profit maximisation as their primary objective, public sector and not-for-profit organisations have a range of non-economic and social goals, many of which reflect the interests of wider stakeholders: participants, supporters, donors, beneficiaries, interest groups, communities, the public interest and so on. In practice, this means that public sector and non-profit organisations are more likely to take a range of stakeholder views into account when making major decisions, often consulting with stakeholder groups, taking their feedback into account and carefully communicating decisions and outcomes to them.

1.12 However, it should also be noted that public sector stakeholders often have less direct influence (in the form of market power) to protect their interests. In the private sector, dissatisfied shareholders can threaten to withdraw their finance, employees their labour and customers their business, in order to make their voices heard. In the public sector, taxpayers and ratepayers have no equivalent market sanctions or resource power to influence a state enterprise or agency: they rely heavily on the government, audit authorities and other regulators to represent their interests.

2 *Why are stakeholders important?*

Stakeholder power and influence

2.1 Stakeholders form an important part of the purchasing environment for the following reasons.

- They may seek to influence the organisation, if they perceive that their interests are threatened. Staff and/or suppliers may negotiate for better terms, for example, or activists may threaten a boycott if the organisation uses environmentally-unsound or labour-exploiting suppliers.

- There is strong public and regulatory pressure for business organisations to be 'socially responsible': taking into account the wider social and environmental impacts of their activities on a range of stakeholders.

- Organisations themselves increasingly follow (and publicise) ethical frameworks, acknowledging their responsibility not to trample on stakeholders' interests – whether or not they have an influential 'voice' in the matter.

2.2 Stakeholder groups can apply pressure to influence organisations in different ways and to different degrees.

- Directors and managers exercise direct influence (formal authority or power) over planning, organisation and control. They may also exercise informal power through leadership/charisma, influencing skills (eg in negotiation), or the exercise of discretion when implementing corporate strategy.

- Shareholders may exercise direct influence, as owners, through voting at shareholder meetings. With other financiers, they also exercise power by controlling the organisation's funding and reputation in the financial markets.

- Employees may have power to influence managerial policy and task performance by controlling the labour resource or specialist knowledge or skills, especially if these are scarce and/or valued by the organisation. They might threaten to withdraw their labour (in a go-slow or strike), or negotiate better terms in return for greater productivity or flexibility, say.

- Customers are (in a marketing oriented business) the priority of all organisational planning and activity: they have the power to give or withdraw their custom, as well as the legal rights given to them by sales/service contracts, consumer protection law and so on.

- Suppliers have the ability to influence supply reliability, quality, costs and pricing decisions, the efficient flow-to-market of goods, potential for innovation – and therefore the buying organisation's competitive advantage. They may also have power through the control of strategic resources (supplies which are critical to the buying organisation), needed expertise (eg in the case of subcontractors and consultants) – and perhaps interpersonal influence with managers (eg if trust has been built up between buyer and supplier contacts).

- Government and regulatory bodies have the power to constrain organisational activity by legislation, regulation, tax incentives and disincentives and so on.

- Interest/pressure groups and the community as a whole can lobby for government action and/or mobilise public opinion and consumer action – either in support of organisations (eg Ethical Brand awards, endorsements or 'ticks of approval' from pressure groups) or to influence them to change. Examples include campaigns and consumer boycotts against firms such as Nike (over allegations of worker exploitation), Shell (environmental damage) and McDonald's (consumer health risk), forcing them to change their practices – and issue strong corporate social responsibility statements!

2.3 All these influences may impact on the structure, systems, policies and values of the organisation – and individual functions such as purchasing and supply. The more influence a stakeholder has, the more likely it is that managers will have to take that stakeholder's needs and wants into account.

2.4 It is worth noting that some stakeholders with a strong interest in the organisation's activities may be either powerless (unable to influence the organisation) or voiceless (unable to make their needs and concerns known) – or both. The term **silent stakeholders** is given to those who have no voice in a matter in which they have an interest. Think about the animals used to test products, for example; or the infants who are the ultimate consumers of baby products; or future generations who arguably have a stake in nature conservation or the siting of toxic/radioactive storage facilities…

2.5 The concept of corporate ethics (as well as government policy and interest group advocacy) suggests that organisations should take the interests of powerless and silent stakeholders into consideration.

3 Stakeholder analysis and management

The power/interest matrix

3.1 Mendelow's power/interest matrix is a useful tool for mapping and analysing stakeholder groups. The various stakeholders are placed in four quadrants, defined by: (a) the extent of their *power* to influence organisational activity and (b) the likelihood of their *wanting* to influence it (ie the strength of their interest): Figure 4.1.

Figure 4.1: *Mendelow's power/interest matrix*

Strength of interest

		Low	High
Power to influence	Low	**A**	**B**
	High	**C**	**D**

3.2 Working through each of the segments:

- Stakeholders who have neither strong interest nor much influence in organisational activity (A) are a low-priority group: resources will not be wasted taking their goals into account, and they are likely simply to accept outcomes and directives without resistance. *Minimal effort* will be spent on this group.

- Stakeholders in segment B are important because of their high interest: they may have low direct influence, but unless they are kept in the loop and understand the need for a strategy, they may seek additional power by lobbying or banding together against it. (Community and employee groups may be in this category.) The recommended strategy is to *keep them informed* of strategies and outcomes, through stakeholder marketing, communication and education.

- Stakeholders in segment C are important because of their high influence: they currently have low interest, but if dissatisfied or concerned, their interest may be aroused. (A large institutional shareholder may be in this category.) The recommended strategy is to *keep them satisfied*: their needs should be taken into account when making decisions that will affect them.

- Stakeholders in segment D are known as '*key players*': they have a lot of influence and are highly motivated to use it in their own interests. (Major customers and key suppliers may be in this category.) These stakeholders can be helpful as drivers of change and organisational supporters – but they can also be strong opponents. The recommended strategy is one of early involvement and *participation*, so that the stakeholders' goals can be integrated with organisational goals as far as possible.

Stakeholder management

3.3 Stakeholder management recognises the need to take stakeholders into account when formulating strategies and plans. This may sound like an unhelpful constraint on management decision-making, or a waste of time, but it may be positively helpful in several ways. It enables a manager to gain expert input from stakeholders at the planning stage of a project, to improve the quality of his or her decisions. Moreover, stakeholders are more likely to 'own' and support plans to which they have had input: this will make ongoing collaboration easier. Gaining the support of powerful stakeholders may, in turn, mobilise power and resources within the organisation in support of the manager's plans. And at the very least, sources of resistance to plans (from stakeholders whose goals are different or incompatible with them) can be anticipated and planned for.

3.4 Once key stakeholders have been identified, it is possible to plan a management strategy for each. You might use a standard process, such as the following.

- Goal analysis. What motivates these stakeholders? What are their goals or desired outcomes from your plans? What fears or issues might your plans raise for them? Where might they support you – and where might they oppose you?

- Desired outcomes. What do you want or need from these stakeholders? What levels of support do you want from them? What role(s) would you want them to play in your project or plans?

- Stakeholder marketing. What messages will you need to convey to these stakeholders? How can you 'sell' them the benefits of what you are proposing or doing? How can you confront and overcome any resistance?

- Relationship management. How will you manage communication to, and input from, each of these stakeholders? How will you keep your key supporters motivated? How will you win over or neutralise resistance? How will you engage the interest of potential supporters?

- Issues management. How will you raise potential issues and problems, where stakeholders' goals may differ from yours? How will you gain stakeholders' early involvement, and collaborate with them in minimising or managing the impacts?

3.5   A systematic approach to managing stakeholders is therefore as follows: Figure 4.2.

Figure 4.2 *Managing stakeholders*

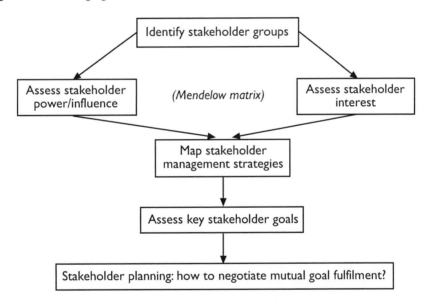

4   *Stakeholder conflict and co-operation*

Conflicting stakeholder goals

4.1   With so many different stakeholder groups, it is inevitable that their interests do not always coincide. Strategy gurus Johnson & Scholes *(Exploring Corporate Strategy)* note that: 'Since the expectations of stakeholder groups will differ, it is quite normal for conflict to exist regarding the importance or desirability of many aspects of strategy.'

4.2   For example, shareholders and investors will want the organisation to maximise profits. In order to do this, however, it may need to downsize its staff or limit pay increases – which would conflict with the interests of employees! It may decide instead to pressure suppliers to lower their prices, or pay them late in order to improve cashflow (conflicting with supplier interests); use low-cost suppliers, perhaps lowering quality standards (conflicting with customer interests); or reduce charitable contributions (conflicting with community and pressure group interests).

4.3   Buyers want to reduce materials costs, but suppliers want to secure higher prices and profitability. The government wants to maximise its tax revenue, but shareholders want to maximise their dividends, employees their take-home pay, and customers their price savings and service quality. Industry needs to build, and dig, and generate waste products – but society wants to protect the natural environment. Once you start thinking about it, there are many, many examples of such competing or conflicting goals and 'win-lose' situations.

4.4   In other words, one stakeholder's gain may well be another stakeholder's loss – and you can't please all of the people all of the time! As Johnson & Scholes note: 'In most situations, a compromise will need to be reached between expectations that cannot all be achieved simultaneously.'

Achieving stakeholder co-operation

4.5   So how does an organisation resolve conflicts of interest between stakeholders? First of all, it will need to undertake stakeholder analysis in order to (a) prioritise stakeholder groups and (b) identify what key stakeholders' needs are. The strategies suggested by the power/interest matrix recognise that not all stakeholders' needs are equal, or need to be met. With a knowledge of key parties' bargaining strength (power) and likely bargaining position (needs and interests), the organisation can begin to negotiate or plan for compromise – or even 'win-win' – solutions.

4.6   In some win-lose situations, a *compromise* may need to be negotiated, so that stakeholders make concessions on some of their aims, in return for achieving others. This is the standard approach to negotiating supply contracts and wage agreements, for example. The two sides (buyer/supplier, employer/trade union) start with widely divergent positions on terms and conditions, but trade concessions and moderate their positions until they reach an agreement they can both live with. The buyer may accept higher prices in return for extra services, say. Employees may accept lower pay rises in return for increased holidays or flexible working arrangements. And so on.

4.7   In some situations, stakeholder interests may overlap, creating situations in which stakeholder groups may seek (or be willing) to support and collaborate with each other, to achieve *mutual gains*. (This is sometimes called a 'win-win' situation: by working together, both parties achieve something they want.)

4.8   One approach is to encourage *co-operation* between stakeholders to 'enlarge the pie' – so that everybody's 'slice' is bigger (rather than each party competing to get a larger share at the expense of the others). Here are some examples.

- Management may be able to convince shareholders that by satisfying the needs of customers (and other stakeholders), it is securing long-term profitability and goodwill: what is good for the customer is good for the firm and its shareholders.

- Purchasing may be able to convince suppliers to invest in improved efficiency or quality, or to help reduce materials costs, because this will help to grow the business – which will ultimately be of benefit to both parties.

- Government already recognises that by supporting business activity and profitability, it is more likely to reap sustainable tax revenue.

4.9 Another approach is to encourage members of one stakeholder group to *join another stakeholder group* (or emphasise where this is already the case), so that they benefit in one group from any sacrifices they make in another. Here are some examples.

- Employees and customers may be encouraged to buy shares in the organisation, so that they will benefit as shareholders from any sacrifices they make in their roles as employees/customers to boost profitability.

- Employees and shareholders may similarly be encouraged to become customers of the product, sharing their interest in quality and value.

- Influential stakeholder representatives may be invited to join the organisation as non-executive directors or consultants, so that they will identify with the organisation's viewpoint.

4.10 A dovetailing of interests may even create positive **synergy**: an effect whereby parties working together are able to achieve *more* than if they worked alone (2 + 2 = 5). For example, a business may support a charity or interest group (eg with cause-related promotions or financial donations), even if the group has previously been hostile to organisational policy. The support would benefit the group – *and* gain the business goodwill, a reputation for social responsibility, the preference of customers who are also supporters of the cause, and so on.

4.11 While bargaining and compromise works, it is not the best possible solution: each party gets what it can live with, but not what it wanted, and this can leave dissatisfaction and conflict simmering below the surface. Managers should seek to dovetail the interests of key stakeholders where possible (to create win-win situations), and should also continually emphasise those shared interests (to gain support and/or minimise opposition) when communicating with stakeholders.

Chapter summary

Key learning points include the following.

- Stakeholders are individuals or groups who have a legitimate interest or stake in an organisation and its activities. The nature of the groups' interests will vary, as will their power to influence the organisation to protect their interests.

- Stakeholder groups include: internal stakeholders (directors, managers and employees); connected stakeholders (shareholders, financiers, customers, suppliers); and external or secondary stakeholders (government, pressure/interest groups, and local community and businesses).

- The emerging concept of corporate social responsibility emphasises that secondary (even silent) stakeholders have a legitimate claim to have their interests protected as far as possible.

- Mendelow's power/interest matrix is a tool for analysing and prioritising stakeholders, suggesting strategies to minimise risk for the organisation.

- Stakeholders often have divergent or conflicting interests and goals. Methods of resolving these include: stakeholder analysis; negotiation of compromise solutions; encouraging of co-operation for mutual gains; and emphasis on shared interests and cross-over membership.

Self-test questions

Numbers in brackets refer to paragraphs where you can check your answers

1   What is the difference between connected and external stakeholders? (1.3–1.4)

2   List two examples of internal, connected and external stakeholders of *purchasing*. (1.9)

3   How does the stakeholder environment vary between the public and private sectors? (1.10–1.12)

4   Why are stakeholders an important part of the environment? (2.1)

5   How do (a) employees and (b) suppliers exert influence on an organisation? (2.2)

6   What are silent stakeholders? Give three examples. (2.4)

7   Draw a power/interest matrix, putting the appropriate strategy in each segment. (3.1, 3.2)

8   Give three examples of conflicting stakeholder goals or interests. (4.2–4.3)

9   Give two examples of stakeholder compromise. (4.6)

10 Suggest two ways in which stakeholder co-operation may be achieved for mutual gain. (4.8–4.9)

Further reading

•   From your 'Essential Reading' list, you might look at Worthington & Britton (*The Business Environment:* 5th edition, 2006, FT Prentice Hall): *Chapter 8: Legal Structures,* which contains a two-page section on stakeholders. We have already covered the same ground, however.

CHAPTER 5

Political Factors

Learning objectives and indicative content

2.1   Explain the impact of political factors affecting purchasing locally, nationally and internationally.

- Political initiatives and drivers; changes in public and private sectors
- Private finance initiatives (PFI), Public private partnerships (PPP) and Design/build/finance/operate (DBFO)
- Government policy and funding
- Political drivers
- International politics and policies
- Trade sanctions
- Political directives

Chapter headings

1   The political environment

2   Local politics

3   National politics

4   Government policy and funding

5   International politics and policies

Introduction

In this chapter, we begin our more detailed survey of the PESTLE factors which make up the wider macro environment of organisations (as introduced in Chapter 1). This chapter covers political factors, and Chapter 6 covers economic factors.

We suggested in Chapter 1 that the PESTLE factors should not be too strictly compartmentalised, because they are all interrelated: as we will see in this chapter and the next, for example, economic factors are the subject of manipulation and management by political forces and bodies. Similarly, political forces are shaped by social and cultural values – and are often applied via legislative or legal measures. Nevertheless, it is worth distinguishing each of the PESTLE factors for the purposes of analysis, especially since exam questions may ask you to focus on one area of the purchasing environment – and the assessors will expect you to know what issues and elements 'belong' to a discussion of each area.

In this chapter, we start by giving an overview of the political environment and how it affects business. We then explore local and national (UK) political structures and processes in more detail: obviously, if you are studying in a country outside the UK, you will be able to use your knowledge of your own political system – but it may be worth getting to grips with the UK system, since this is most likely to be the setting of a case study question.

Finally, we turn our attention to the 'supra-national' level of politics, looking at the purpose and impact of international political bodies on business.

1   *The political environment*

What is politics?

1.1   *Politics* is, broadly, a term for the processes through which power and influence are applied to handle conflicts of interest between stakeholders. (This is the sense in which we talk about 'office politics', for example, or 'gender politics'.) More commonly, it refers to these processes at the level of the State: the ways in which stakeholder interests are harmonised – for example, through competing political parties offering alternative policies and ideologies, the activity of pressure groups, democratic elections, the role of government in making decisions on society's behalf, and the way in which laws and regulations are formulated and enacted.

Overview of how political factors affect business

1.2   Political factors affect businesses in a variety of ways.

- Local government authorities formulate policies and bye-laws which affect local infrastructure, land/building use and service delivery.

- At a national level, the political process includes *legislation* (which directly affects business activity) and the *economic policy* of governments (which influences prices, labour availability, consumer spending, borrowing costs and other important factors of business).

- The government controls much of the economy, as the nation's largest supplier, employer, customer and investor: policy shifts can transform markets. (Think about the defence and aerospace industries, say.)

- As businesses increasingly trade in international markets, the politics of other nations (such as government policy or political instability in an overseas supplier's or subcontractor's country) also create opportunities and risks.

- Political influences cross national boundaries: eg through international institutions such as the European Union (whose directives affect all member countries) and the World Trade Organisation.

- Businesses are influenced *by* political factors – but they also exert some influence *over* them (or seek to do so): by lobbying government decision makers, making financial donations to political parties, influencing public opinion and so on.

1.3   The impact of political factors on a given business will vary according to the type of organisation involved: whether its market is local, national or multi-national; whether it operates in the public or private sector, or in a highly-regulated or de-regulated industry; and so on. We will, inevitably, make some generalisations in this chapter, but you will need to think carefully about which factors apply, and how, in the case of your own organisation, or in regard to an organisation described in the exam.

1.4   In general, however, the likelihood of political change (particularly in democratic systems) complicates management's task of predicting future environmental influences and planning to meet them. Some political changes cannot easily be planned for!

2   Local politics

Local or 'sub-national' government

2.1   Local government authorities (eg County Councils, District Councils and Metropolitan District Councils in England, and Unitary Councils in Wales and Scotland) represent democratic self-government by and for the people of a locality. Authorities have a wide range of responsibilities.

   •   Determining policy and rules (bye-laws), and applying national laws within their areas. This will affect business in various ways: planning regulations might influence business growth, or the siting of warehouse facilities; environmental health policy may affect logistics and storage (eg of foodstuffs or dangerous goods).

   •   Raising funds (via council tax and business rates, and any revenue raised by municipal enterprises) and allocating funds provided by central government and regional bodies in the form of grants. Business will be directly affected by business rates, as a cost – and by business grants and tax relief, as a source of finance.

   •   Administering local authority services, such as housing, social services, education, environmental health, refuse collection, libraries and (on a discretionary basis) sport and leisure services. Some of these services may be contracted out to – or operated in competition with – private sector businesses. Each will have its own procurement needs, and may be a significant player in the local supply market.

Drivers and initiatives in local politics

2.2   A number of *initiatives* (proposals for change) and *drivers* (pressures for change) have recently affected the sub-national political environment, some of which have significant implications for purchasing. The following are just some relevant examples: you may wish to gather your own examples from the website, mailings and activities of your own local council.

2.3   Political power is increasingly devolved to the regions: Scotland and Wales now have their own elected regional assembles (the Scottish Parliament and Welsh Assembly). Businesses operating in those regions will have to adjust their relationships with government. Meanwhile, UK local government is facing pressures to reform its decision-making processes, which again will affect how businesses deal with local bodies.

2.4   Sustainability (including sustainable procurement) has become a policy priority, driven by central government guidelines, academic research and public pressure. The London Borough of Camden recently appointed a sustainable procurement manager, for example, and changed its policies in areas such as the following.

   •   Environmental sustainability: increasing the use of environmental products and saving energy (eg recycled paper, recycled aggregate for highway maintenance)

   •   Social sustainability: ensuring that the workforce reflects the diversity of the area; using local and small business suppliers; supporting the use of local labour and the long-term unemployed; re-contracting school meal provision for more healthy nutrition; and so on.

2.5 Procurement efficiency has also become a policy priority, driven by central government efficiency guidelines (arising from the Gershon Review) and financial imperatives (the need to cut costs in order to improve stakeholder value). Many councils are pooling their procurement on a regional or category basis, for example, in order to gain economies of scale through consolidated buying. Others are developing or joining shared electronic procurement systems (such as e-Procurement Scotland).

3   *National politics*

Branches of national government

3.1 National government consists of three branches.

- The *legislature,* which represents the people between elections, and makes the country's laws. In the UK, this function is carried out by Parliament: a non-elected House of Lords and an elected House of Commons (made up of MPs from a range of political parties). Proposed legislation ('bills') are passed through both houses, before they receive the assent of the reigning monarch and become 'Acts' of Parliament.

- The *executive,* which implements law and policy in practice. In the UK, this function is carried out by the Cabinet and non-Cabinet ministers (assisted by the Civil Service), committees, government departments, local authorities and quangos.

- An independent *judiciary* (judges and the courts), which enforces the laws enacted by Parliament and interprets European Union law. (We will cover this, as part of the legal environment, in Chapter 10.)

Drivers and initiatives in national politics

3.2 Democratic systems are inevitably dynamic, because of the potential for the nation to change governments (with regular elections), and for government to change policies (with pressure group influence and new information). Some of the key changes at the national level, with relevance for purchasing, include the following.

- A broad political consensus on the value of market-based policies (previously identified only with right-wing politics), as a way of achieving employment, tax revenue and 'trickle down' prosperity to benefit all social stakeholders. This has contributed, for example, to new possibilities for partnership between private and public sector firms – as discussed above.

- Increasing internationalisation of social and environmental policy: eg commitments to enact EU directives into UK law, or commitment to Kyoto Agreement targets.

- Proposals to reform the political system (eg the House of Lords, the civil service, new voting systems and new policy-making and delivery systems) – which will alter the relationship between business and government bodies.

- Changing government policy, reflected in legislation, public sector guidelines and funding priorities. The news throws up new examples every day, but you might be able to think of some from recent years such as new legislation on age discrimination in employment, government initiatives on education and skilling (eg Ufl, the University for Industry), or increased funding for the health sector. Specifically in the field of purchasing, there have been initiatives on sustainable procurement, procurement efficiency, and the new Public Contracts Regulations.

- Government responses to emerging national and international challenges. (Think of the impact of the Iraq War on defence spending and procurement, say, or the impact of the Asian tsunami on foreign aid logistics.)

- Increased use of technology in government-to-citizen and government-to-business communication – including public sector take-up of e-procurement systems.

3.3   Again, it will be beneficial for you to scan the quality press and government websites to gather your own relevant and up-to-date examples of government initiatives and policy drivers, as they change with national and international events. A classic example – which may be highly topical in the months when your exams are written – is the pressure caused by the threat of global economic recession, emerging towards the end of 2008: panic in the share markets; the threatened collapse and bailing out of major financial service providers; public demand to secure investments (coupled with outrage at a taxpayer funded 'bail-out' of a perceivably greedy financial sector); and so on. How – and how effectively – has the national government (both parliament and Cabinet) responded to these pressures? What party-political or ideological factors have influenced the response from different political stakeholders?

Political parties

3.4   Political parties are major players in UK politics, because it is from them – in a democratic system – that a government is selected (by virtue of having the most members of parliament). A political party is likely to have a position on a variety of public policy areas, as a platform on which to stand for election – and these positions, and the ideologies underlying them, are a strong influence on the decisions of the party in power. In addition, the minority parties in parliament (the Opposition) provide checks and balances on government power, through public debate and voting on proposed legislation.

3.5   *The media* is another key influencer, with its potential to exert pressure on government (and also business) by arousing or reflecting public opinion.

Pressure groups and interest groups

3.6   *Interest groups* (representing a particular group of stakeholders) and *pressure groups* (promoting a particular issue or cause) also seek to influence government and public opinion in the areas of their interests. Some of these groups may employ professional *lobbyists* to seek to influence government decision-makers.

3.7   Causal pressure groups seek to promote a cause or issue: to raise awareness, mobilise opinion and lobby for changes in government policy or regulation. Examples include: political and human rights groups (such as the Campaign for Nuclear Disarmament or Amnesty International); environmental groups (such as Greenpeace or Friends of the Earth); and social welfare groups (such as Fair Trade, Oxfam, or the Royal Society for the Blind).

3.8   Such groups may seek to influence both government (via lobbying and mobilising public opinion) and businesses whose policies or practices they disagree with (via mobilising consumers to choose alternative products/services). You might therefore add them to the list of potential stakeholders of an organisation. As part of the political process, government and firms may seek to co-opt influential pressure groups to provide advice on their areas of expertise – or to support and collaborate on initiatives (eg a firm getting Fair Trade certification for its brands, or getting the public endorsement of Greenpeace for its environmental policy).

3.9   Sectional pressure groups (or interest groups) seek to promote or defend the interest of particular stakeholders in society.

3.10 Many workers in the UK are represented by **trade unions** relevant to their industry or occupation (such as the National Union of Teachers) under an umbrella group called the Trade Unions Congress (TUC). Trade unions mainly seek to protect their members' rights and interests at work, through their collective power in negotiation with employers. They typically focus on fair pay, benefits and conditions; fair treatment (eg in relation to dismissal from a job); access to information and consultation on issues affecting their work or livelihoods (eg notice of redundancies); access to training and development opportunities; and the right to pursue individual and collective disputes with an employer. However, they also provide funding for political parties, and have traditionally been a strong influence on the policy of the Labour Party, in particular. (Successive Conservative governments sought to reduce their political power by restricting strike action, ending compulsory union membership and other measures.)

3.11 Business firms are represented in the political process by **employer associations** and **trade associations**, under an umbrella group called the Confederation of British Industry (CBI), which promotes the economic interests of commercial organisations, and is often given a key role in industry policy formation and implementation.

3.12 Pressure groups, as part of the broader political scene, may influence organisations in a number of ways. They may influence corporate strategy (eg introducing Fair Trade brands or environmental policies); create pressure or opportunities to develop new products (eg recyclable products, animal-friendly cosmetics) or modify business processes (eg product recycling or supplier ethical monitoring). Firms may also seek to ally or associate themselves with pressure groups which reflect their values, or those of their customers, in order to gain their support and endorsement.

4   *Government policy and funding*

Government influence on business

4.1   As we saw in Chapter 2, some state intervention in economic activity is justified by the need to distribute resources fairly, to regulate the private sector in the public interest, and to correct market failures, ensuring that the factors of production are used in the interests of all citizens.

4.2   The government may influence business activity through a number of mechanisms.

- Economic policy (eg on taxation, inflation and interest rates), which affects investment and market demand – as we will see later in this chapter
- Industry policy (eg protection of domestic producers from imported competition; grants, incentives and sponsorships; and industry regulation) which affects costs and methods of doing business
- Environment and infrastructure policy (eg investment in roads and telecommunications, and environmental protection regulations) which supports – or constrains – business processes
- Social policy (eg education and skills training, workplace regulation and employment law) which affects the availability, quality, cost and management of human resources

- Foreign policy (eg trade promotion, support for exports, EU and World Trade Organisation obligations)

- Public spending on goods and services (the State in its role as buyer) and provision of goods and services (the State in its role as supplier), which generate significant economic activity in themselves.

4.3 Government policy is itself influenced by a variety of factors: party ideology, existing commitments, available and projected future resources, promises made to voters, and the political influence of the kinds of groups discussed earlier. Political influence is particularly important, as it provides a system of 'checks and balances' to curb government influence and protect stakeholder interests.

National government funding

4.4 Grants for *private* sector businesses are available from a huge variety of sources, many of them connected with government institutions. Tracking availability of grants is so complicated that specialist consultancies exist to advise businesses whether they qualify for any kind of grant assistance. They might do so, for instance, if they operate in geographical regions where the government is attempting to stimulate employment. Or they might be engaged in research and development work into scientific areas which the government wishes to encourage.

4.5 Of course, the government also provides primary funding for *public* sector services: schools, hospitals, the police force and so on. Both local and central government raise funds to finance the projects and services for which they are responsible. By far the largest element of public finance is raised from taxation. The central government raises tax revenue from both direct taxes (income tax, national insurance contributions, corporation tax, capital gains tax and so on) and indirect taxes (such as VAT and excise duties).

Public-private partnerships

4.6 An alternative to government funding of public services, explored in recent years, is financing by a mixture of private and public enterprise, often involving some kind of partnership between a public sector organisation and a commercial private sector firm.

4.7 Strategic partnerships are becoming common, particularly for large infrastructure projects. They have been – and are being – used to create national infrastructure such as the Channel Tunnel, the QEII bridge across the Thames at Dartford, and the North Birmingham Relief Road, as well as smaller projects such as hospitals, schools and barracks.

4.8 *Public-private partnerships or PPP (*the Labour government's name for what its predecessor called the *Private Finance Initiative or PFI) are* schemes in which private sector firms and public authorities share capital and expertise, in various structured ways. A private developer may be asked to obtain capital, and/or to design and build a facility – and/or to operate the facility or to charge a fee for its use, for a period designed to recoup the firm's investment plus a reasonable return. (*Full involvement of this kind is known as a Design, Build, Finance and Operate or DBFO project.)*

4.9   PPP projects may take various forms.

- A *Design-Build* contract means that the private partner designs and builds a facility (eg a motorway), which the government will operate once it is completed.

- A *Build-Operate* contract means that the private partner builds the facility (eg a toll road) and operates it for a period, in order to recoup its investment, then transfers ownership to the public sector body.

- A *Turnkey Operation* is where the public sector provides funding and retains ownership of the facility, but the private partner designs and builds it, and also operates it for a period.

- An *Operation and Maintenance* contract means that a private partner is simply contracted, on a tender basis, to operate and maintain a public facility (eg a prison or a waste disposal facility).

4.10   One advantage of such schemes is that the public sector can tap into the expertise of a private partner. This can provide excellent value for money, especially if the private partner has already invested in the required technology. It can also enable a public sector body to complete projects much faster than would otherwise be possible, and without having to cover capital costs from tax revenue.

4.11   On the other hand, critics of PPP argue that the public sector may be surrendering control of the project, with the risk of lower levels of service and public accountability. From the private sector partner's point of view, the arrangement will only be successful to the extent that it gains a reasonable return on its investment (and perhaps also enhanced political influence).

5   *International politics and policies*

The European Union (EU)

5.1   Decisions, law and policy affecting business activity are increasingly being made at a supra-national ('above national') level, through political and trading 'blocs' and agreements. We will examine some of the main international bodies briefly: other issues, such as economic integration and trade sanctions, are more relevant to the economic environment, and will be discussed in the following chapter.

5.2   In Europe, a Common Market was set up in 1957 by the Treaty of Rome, to support free mobility of goods, services, labour and capital across national boundaries: this was seen as being of paramount importance for the overall economic prosperity of the region. The Single European Market was formed in 1992 – and these advances developed further into much closer integration, signalled by the current title of European Union.

5.3   The political institutions of the EU include the following.

- The *European Commission* comprises one Commissioner from each member state (nominated by their governments), supported by a permanent civil service. Its role is: to propose policies and legislation; to implement EU policies and supervise their day-to-day running; and to ensure that EU Treaties are respected.

- The *Council of the European Union (Council of Ministers)* comprises one Minister from each of the member states (varying according to the issue under discussion eg Agriculture, Employment and Social Affairs, Economics and Finance). The council makes the major policy decisions and responds to legislative proposals put forward by the European Commission.

- The *European Parliament* is an assembly of directly elected members, representing each of the member states (in a proportion roughly equal to their populations). The parliament debates and approves legislation, prior to its formal adoption by the Council of Ministers; acts as the community's budgetary authority; supervises the European Commission; and initiates debate on issues requiring policy change.

- The *European Court of Justice* is designed to decide interpretations of EU law, and to quash any measures which conflict with EU Treaties.

5.4 EU policy has an important impact on business, and on purchasing in particular. The concept of economic union, for example, ensures that goods and capital can flow from one member state to another without barriers or trade restrictions (in the form of import quotas, tariffs or customs formalities): this facilitates cross-border supply and logistics. The adoption of a common currency (the euro) facilitates price comparisons and payments, while a common product protection regime (with a single patent office) minimises intellectual property risk.

5.5 Meanwhile, EU directives have influenced UK law on a range of business and employment issues such as working hours, health and safety, equal opportunity, competition and environmental protection.

5.6 The EU procurement directives (enacted in UK law as the Public Contracts and Public Utilities Regulations) provide that decisions on public procurement in the EU for contracts above a certain value must be based on value for money, obtained via competitive tender. The directives focus on areas such as non-discrimination in specifications, and the use of objective decision criteria.

Other regional blocs

5.7 Other regional blocs for the purposes of economic integration, in other parts of the world, include ASEAN (The Association of Southeast Asian Nations) and NAFTA (the North American Free Trade Agreement).

The World Trade Organisation (WTO)

5.8 The WTO (formerly the General Agreement on Tariffs and Trade, or GATT) is an organisation dedicated to promoting free trade between nations. Its main aim is to reduce or remove barriers to trade from tariffs (import taxes and duties) and non-tariff factors (eg quotas, customs red-tape, different regulatory regimes, foreign currency controls, and government subsidies to domestic producers). The usual reason for such barriers is to protect domestic (or trading bloc) industry from the effects of outside competition – a policy called *protectionism*. It is argued, however, that protectionism inhibits economic growth and leads to political ill will and retaliation between nations, stifling international trade.

5.9 The WTO contains high-level policy making councils and a number of subsidiary bodies, such as: the Disputes Settlement Body (which helps to settle trade disputes and breach of rules) and the Trade Policy Review Body (which, among other activities, publishes regular country reports on trade policies).

5.10 While critics argue that the WTO favours the interests of developed countries over developing ones, it has significant influence on purchasing in areas such as opening up markets, facilitating international sourcing and protecting intellectual property rights (designs, patents, copyright and so on).

The Organisation for Economic Co-operation and Development (OECD)

5.11 The OECD has its roots in co-operation to rebuild Western European economies after the Second World War. It comprises 30 members drawn from the richest and most advanced industrial countries in the world, and represents the main forum for their governments to get together to discuss economic matters. The focus is on supporting sustainable growth, free trade and economic development in less affluent non-member countries. The OECD has no direct authority to set policy, but exerts political influence through discussion, persuasion, and the publishing of economic data on member countries.

The Group of Eight (G8)

5.12 Representatives of the eight leading industrial economies (the USA, Japan, Germany, France, Italy, Canada, Britain and Russia) meet annually to discuss issues of mutual interest: human rights, economic management, the environment and so on. These Group of Eight (or G8) summits attract significant media attention – as well as opposition from anti-globalisation protestors!

The influence of supra-national bodies on UK business

5.13 The influence of all these various supra- or trans-national bodies is otherwise either *legislative* (eg the obligation for EU directives to be enacted into the law of member states) or *economic* (eg the imposing or removing of barriers to international trade). They will be discussed further, where relevant, in the chapters on economic and legislative factors.

Chapter summary

Key learning points include the following.

- Political factors include local government processes; national legislation and government policy; overseas government and trade policies; transnational political and economic structures (such as the EU, WTO, OECD and G8); and the interplay of influence between government, business and pressure/interest groups.

- There are a number of drivers (influences for change) and initiatives (proposals for change) in the political environment, and you should try to keep up to date with the changing scene.

- One form of political intervention is government funding, for both the private and public sector. Private-public-partnerships are a relatively new model, private sector involvement in the design, building, finance and/or operation of public works.

- Businesses are increasingly affected by supra-national bodies, such as the European Union, the World Trade Organisation, and the Organisation for Economic Co-operation and Development.

Self-test questions

Numbers in brackets refer to paragraphs where you can check your answers

1   Define 'politics' (1.1)

2   Give an example of local, national and international political factors impacting on business (1.2)

3   What is the role of local government authorities? (2.1)

4   Explain the roles of the three components of UK government. (3.1)

5   What is the role of political parties in the political environment? (3.4)

6   What are 'interest groups' and 'pressure groups', and how do they wield influence on the political scene? (3.6–3.12)

7   Give three examples of government policy that may impact on business. (4.2)

8   Explain two different forms a public-private partnership might take. (4.9)

9   What are the main impacts on business of EU policy? (5.4)

10   What are the main impacts on business of the activities of the WTO? (5.8–5.10)

Further reading

From your 'Essential Reading' list, you might look at Worthington & Britton (*The Business Environment:* 5th edition, 2006, FT Prentice Hall), Part 3: FIRMS.

- *Chapter 3: The Political Environment*

It is worth reading through this material, since it covers a core part of the syllabus, and offers further detail and different examples to our coverage. Again, the mini-case and case study features offer useful illustrations which may be used in the exam.

CHAPTER 6

Economic Factors

Learning objectives and indicative content

2.2   Identify economic factors affecting purchasing locally, nationally and internationally, including:

- Interest rates
- Exchange rates
- Investment programmes
- The business cycle – boom and bust
- International economics

Chapter headings

1   The economic environment

2   The national economy

3   The business cycle

4   International economics

5   Exchange rates

6   The economics of international sourcing

Introduction

In this chapter, we continue our detailed survey of the PESTLE factors which make up the wider macro environment of organisations. This chapter covers economic factors.

The term 'macro-economics' refers to the study of a whole economy – while 'micro-economics' refers to the study of economics as it applies to individual markets, products and firms (such as market supply and demand and market structures, which we discussed in Chapter 3). In this chapter, we look at some of the key macro-economic factors in the purchasing environment.

We start by giving you an overview of how national economies are managed, and how macro-economic factors impact on purchasing.

We go on to look at key concepts and factors in the national economy, including economic activity and growth, and the effects of unemployment, inflation and interest rates. We then show how many of these factors come together in the business cycle of 'booms and busts' (which may be familiar to you from 2009 headlines about 'downturn' and 'recession').

In the final three sections of the chapter, we turn our attention to international economics, examining concepts such as the balance of payments, the impact of exchange rates on firms dealing in international markets, and the economic arguments for and against international sourcing.

1   *The economic environment*

National economic policy

1.1   It is the role of government to manage or control a national economy, in order to provide a stable economic framework from which, ideally, sustainable growth can be achieved.

1.2   The objective of a government's economic policies may be: to achieve sustainable growth in the economy; to control inflation; to achieve low unemployment levels; or to achieve a balance between exports and imports. (It is worth noting that the emphasis on these objectives changes in line with political, social and economic events.)

1.3   In order to achieve these objectives, a government will use a number of different policy tools. For example, *monetary policy* is the government's decisions and actions regarding the level of interest rates and the supply of money in the economy; while *fiscal policy* is the government's decisions and actions regarding the balance between taxation revenue and public expenditure.

Impact on purchasing

1.4   Macro-economic factors affect purchasing in a number of ways.

- The amount of economic activity determines the wealth of a nation, which influences the amount of disposable income its citizens have to spend – which in turn influences the demand for goods and services of various kinds, and the prices at which they can be sold (as we saw in Chapter 3). Lower demand and prices will affect the volume of procurement, and the budget available: on the other hand, it may enhance the role of purchasing, by focusing on the need for cost savings.

- Economic variables determine the strength of an economy and the extent of business confidence in it, which in turn influences the amount people are willing to invest. Changes in the level of investment spending (by both the private and public sectors) are major causes of the upswings and downswings in economic activity which we call business cycles – which again affect demand and prices.

- Employment and unemployment levels may affect the availability of labour and labour costs, as well as disposable incomes and demand.

- Rates of inflation affect prices, and therefore supply costs. They may also make imports relatively expensive or inexpensive, altering a firm's sourcing strategy.

- The overall rate of taxation affects the level of demand in an economy (eg less tax means more disposable income for consumers to spend), and the taxation of specific products (such as alcohol and tobacco) may impact on specialised businesses. At the same time, tax incentives and penalties may influence firms' operational policies (eg 'polluter pays' taxes).

- Exchange rate fluctuations create risk in international sourcing, potentially making foreign currency purchases (imports) more expensive.

- Interest rate fluctuations create risk for corporate finance, potentially making loans more expensive: this will have an impact on companies borrowing to purchase large capital items, for example.

1.5   Basically, any factor that increases *demand* for an organisation's product will also increase its need for *inputs*. Any factor that decreases demand will reduce the need for inputs – but will place more importance on the potential for the purchasing function to control or reduce the costs of those inputs.

1.6   We will now look more closely at some of the key concepts.

2   The national economy

Economic activity

2.1   An economy is a system, which – like the organisation system we looked at in Figure 1.3 – takes in inputs and converts them into outputs. Economic activity can be portrayed as a 'flow' of economic resources into organisations which produce outputs for consumers, which then generates a return flow of income through consumer expenditure.

2.2   One way of portraying this flow of resources and income between firms and domestic households, is as follows: Figure 6.1.

Figure 6.1: *The flow of economic resources*

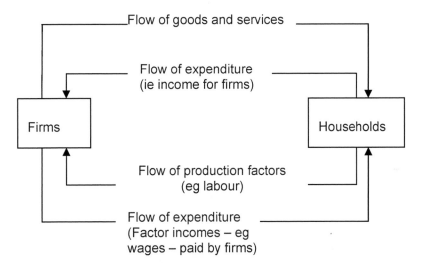

2.3   Total spending in a given economy, however, consists not just of consumer (domestic household) spending, but also of government spending (on providing public services), investment spending (by other firms, on capital items such as plant and machinery) and export spending (foreign purchasers buying our goods). In addition, some household resources are taken out of the flow in the form of tax, savings and import spending (buying foreign goods). The picture is therefore more as follows: Figure 6.2

Figure 6.2: *The circular flow of national income*

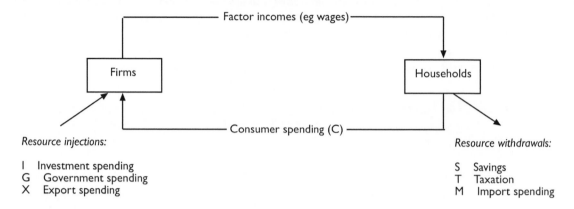

Resource injections:

I   Investment spending
G   Government spending
X   Export spending

Resource withdrawals:

S   Savings
T   Taxation
M   Import spending

2.4   Total spending – or 'aggregate demand' – in an economy can thus be expressed as:

$C + I + G - S - T + (X - M)$.

So if a government wants to increase the country's overall domestic economic income, it can do so by:

*   Trying to increase consumer spending (C)
*   Trying to increase private investment (I)
*   Increasing government spending (G)
*   Reducing taxation (T)
*   Trying to improve the balance of payments on overseas trade (X – M)

Economic growth

2.5   Economic growth may be measured by an annual percentage increase in the gross national product (GNP) per head of the population. In the long run, this depends on:

*   Demand factors: the total amount spent on domestic goods and services in the economy (aggregate demand) and
*   Supply factors: the total potential output of the economy. A growth in capacity may be possible if more or better resources become available (eg more skilled workers, or the discovery of mineral deposits), or if ways are found of using resources more productively (eg through technological development, flexible labour practices or investment in infrastructure).

2.6   The main advantage of economic growth should be a better standard of living for the population as a whole. Greater output capacity should also mean a need for more inputs, increasing purchasing activity. However, there are also disadvantages to growth, including the faster usage of scarce natural resources (pushing up energy costs, for example) and more pollution and waste products: both of these effects may need to be managed by purchasing functions.

Interest rates

2.7 Interest is the amount of money charged by a lender to a borrower for the use of a loan. The 'base rate' (set by the Bank of England in the UK) establishes the key interest rate in the economy.

2.8 The key point about interest rates is that as interest rates *rise,* the costs of *borrowing* increase (because borrowers are charged interest) – but so do the rewards for *saving* (because savings accounts earn interest). Either way, looking at our equation for total spending in an economy, as interest rates rise, economic activity is reduced; as they fall, it is increased. Governments therefore seek to manipulate interest rates to stimulate or slow down demand. This is a key aspect of **monetary policy**: the government's decisions and actions regarding the level of interest rates and the money supply.

2.9 The impact of an interest rate rise for purchasing will be, indirectly, a slow-down in demand for goods – and therefore a reduced need for inputs. In addition, if purchasing activities depend on borrowed funds (as they might do in the case of a major capital purchase, say), there would be a direct impact on costs. A reduction in the base rate would have the opposite effect.

Inflation

2.10 Inflation is a general, sustained increase in prices over time. This may be the result of:

- Demand for goods exceeding supply, pushing prices up (demand-pull inflation)
- Increases in the costs of production, particularly wages, without increased demand, so that producers have to raise their prices to maintain profitability (cost-push inflation)
- Overexpansion of the monetary supply, which boosts excessive demand by making more money available to spend (monetary inflation).

2.11 Once rates of inflation begin to increase, people may fear further price rises and seek higher wages and prices to cover them – creating 'expectational' inflation and a vicious circle called a 'wage-price spiral'. Inflation thus becomes persistent – even if the conditions which caused it are no longer present – because people *expect* it to occur and react accordingly.

2.12 A high rate of inflation is undesirable for a number of reasons. It disadvantages those on lower (and particularly, fixed) incomes, since their spending power is reduced. It causes uncertainty about the future value of money, which makes it harder for businesses to evaluate future expenditure, or the real value of large-scale capital items over their lifetime, or the likely return on investments: this may act as a disincentive to investment and long-term decision-making. In international trade, if the rate of inflation is higher in the UK than in other economies, exports become relatively expensive and imports relatively cheap: the balance of trade, and local employment, will suffer.

2.13 The control of inflation has therefore been a major policy objective in most developed nations since the 1970s. Strategies vary according to the contributory factors (and different economic theories).

2.14 Demand-pull inflation can be reduced by 'slowing down' the economy with measures such as the following.

- Reduced government spending
- Higher taxation to cut consumer spending (fiscal policy)
- Raising interest rates, increasing the costs of borrowing for both consumer and business spending (monetary policy).

2.15 Cost-push inflation can be managed by government intervention to reduce production costs and limit price rises. This can be done by:

- Applying controls over wage and price rises (prices and incomes policy)
- Encouraging increased productivity in industry (eg by funding technology development)

2.16 Monetary inflation can be controlled by limiting the money supply (monetary policy) in various ways:

- Trying to control or reduce bank lending
- Maintaining interest rates at a level that might encourage people to take their money out of the supply by increasing their savings
- Trying to achieve a balance of trade surplus (more exports than imports)

2.17 However, this still leaves substantial problems if the underlying cause of inflation is an increase in the cost of significant imported raw materials, such as oil, say.

Employment

2.18 The creation and maintenance of employment is a key focus of government economic policy, because – as we saw in Figure 6.1 – the flow of economic resources depends on wage income flowing into households (and out again in consumer spending).

2.19 High unemployment is undesirable for a number of reasons. Unemployed workers do not produce anything, making the total national income less than it could be. They may also lose their skills over time, through lack of use, creating a loss of productive capacity, and incurring costs of retraining. Rising unemployment is costly for governments because it means less tax (on income and spending) coming in – and more financial assistance benefits going out. And, of course, unemployment has personal and social costs: personal hardship and distress, and possibly knock-on effects such as increased crime and family breakdown.

2.20 Various types of unemployment have been identified.

- **Frictional unemployment** occurs where there is a shortage of a particular type of worker in one region, but a surplus in another. Surplus workers are therefore temporarily unemployed, for the time it takes for them to find a new job.
- **Seasonal unemployment** occurs in some industries, such as construction, farming and tourism, because the demand for workers fluctuates in seasonal cycles.
- **Structural unemployment** occurs where an industry undergoes long-term changes which result in lower demand for workers: the automation of mining and construction are two clear examples.

- **Cyclical unemployment** occurs when (as we will see below), industries or economies periodically go through times of decline and recession: the demand for output falls, and so does the demand for workers.

2.21 Governments can try to create jobs and/or to reduce unemployment in various ways. They may themselves create jobs and recruit more people into the public sector, or may encourage growth in the private sector of the economy. They may support education and training in vocational skills (or retraining, to combat structural unemployment), and job search/outplacement services (to reduce frictional unemployment).

3 The business cycle

'Boom and bust'

3.1 The business cycle (or trade cycle) is the periodic fluctuation in levels of economic activity, output and employment: from 'boom' to 'bust' (and back again). The understanding of business cycles can be crucial for purchasing, especially investment in capital goods like plant and machinery: this represents a hefty up-front expense in the anticipation of future returns (extra production capacity and sales revenue) – which may be at risk if the sector is hit by a downturn in demand due to the business cycle.

3.2 There are four main phases in a typical business cycle: Table 6.1

Table 6.1: *Phases in the business cycle*

Depression	There is low consumer demand; production capacity is unused; prices are stable or falling; business profits are low; there is high unemployment; and business confidence is low.
Recovery	Consumer spending rises; investment picks up; prices are stable or rising; profits and employment start to rise; and confidence grows.
Boom	Consumer spending is rising fast. Production capacity is reached, and there are labour shortages, so output can only be increased by new investment in labour-saving technology: investment spending is high. Increased demand stimulates price rises, and business profits are high.
Recession	Consumption starts to fall off; production falls; unemployment starts to rise; profits fall and some businesses fail; many investments suddenly become unprofitable and new investment falls.

3.3 Wide fluctuations in economic activity may damage the overall economic wellbeing of society – through the inflation and risk-taking of the booms, as well as the high unemployment of the busts. Governments generally seek to stabilise the economic system, trying to avoid extremes.

3.4 Purchasers may, however, need to anticipate and adapt resourcing decisions to suit each stage of the cycle. Here are some examples.

- Investment, purchasing and stock control decisions should be tailored to the anticipated level of demand (lower in a downturn and recession, and higher again in recovery).

- Costs may need to be reduced to cope with recessionary phases, particularly if the firm has to reduce the price of products/services in order to stimulate demand and maintain sales.

- Recruitment may need to be suspended in advance of recession, to allow the workforce to be reduced by natural wastage rather than redundancies. In highly cyclical industries, companies might be more proactive in developing a numerically flexible workforce (eg by subcontracting and outsourcing) – to which purchasing may contribute.

3.5 It is worth noting that forecasting the pattern and timing of the business cycle is very difficult in practice! The cycle is affected by complex factors such as oil prices, international political stability and the performance of other economies. The effects of the US mortgage lending ('sub prime') crisis, for example, precipitated a global financial crisis and warnings of recession towards the end of 2008.

The Budget

3.6 We are all familiar with the headlines associated with each year's Budget presentation by the Chancellor of the Exchequer – income tax going up or down, extra duty on petrol, tobacco and alcohol – but there is more to it than this. The Budget is the overall report on the government's finances for a given year: its expenditure (public spending) and receipts (mainly from taxation) – and its estimate of the gap between them. This shortfall is called the **Public Sector Borrowing Requirement** (PSBR): the combined deficits of central government, local authorities and public corporations.

3.7 In times of recession, when unemployment is high, the government's tax take is low, as incomes and expenditures fall. Furthermore, government expenditure is high, as more people claim financial assistance from the state. So there will probably be a budget deficit, and the government will have to borrow funds to cover its obligations. The **national debt** is simply the accumulated government debt that has been run up (and not repaid) by year after year of PSBRs. During periods of economic boom, rising incomes and expenditure increase the tax take, benefit payouts fall, and the government may be able to pay back some of the national debt.

3.8 **Fiscal policy** is the term for policies aimed at managing the relationship between taxation and public spending.

- A government may seek to operate with a budget deficit (spending more than it receives in tax revenue), in order to stimulate total spending in the economy. Higher public sector spending should also have positive 'spin-off' effects, such as improved infrastructure (roads and so on). However, a high PSBR (large government borrowings) may force up interest rates and act as a disincentive to private sector investment in the economy, by making it too expensive for firms to borrow and invest profitably.

- Alternatively, a government may seek to operate with a budget surplus (spending less than it receives in tax revenue), in order to slow down total spending in the economy and bring inflation under control.

3.9 It is worth noting that this either/or view (held by Keynesian economists) is hotly contested by monetarist economists, who argue that government's role is to run a 'balanced budget': no deficit or surplus.

4   International economics

4.1   The main features of the international economic environment that will affect purchasing are as follows.

- The need to balance the flows of exports from and imports to the national economy (for reasons which will be discussed below). Measures intended to do this will affect the attractiveness of purchasing imported supplies.

- The policies of international trading blocs and partners in regard to protecting domestic producers (protectionism) or liberalising trade.

- The need to manage risks arising from exchange rates: that is, the price of one currency expressed in terms of another currency.

The balance of payments

4.2   The balance of payments is the statistical accounting record of all a country's external trade dealings in a given period (usually a year). It records the flows of value/money, rather than goods: imports are recorded as negative amounts (debits), as money is leaving the country to pay for the goods, while exports are recorded as positive amounts (credits), as money is coming into the country to pay for the goods.

4.3   These flows include:

- *Current transactions*, or payments for goods and services. The current account is subdivided into 'visible trade' (import and export of goods) and 'invisible trade' (import and export of services, interest, profits, dividends and money transfers). The balance of in-coming and out-going flows in visible trade is called the 'balance of trade' and the balance in current transactions overall is called the 'current balance'.

- *Capital transactions,* or flows of funds for investment purposes: long-term transactions such as the purchase of shares or real estate, or inter-government loans; and short-term transactions such as trade credit and foreign currency borrowing and lending.

Balance of payments surplus and deficit

4.4   A 'balance of payments surplus' usually refers to a balance on the current account where the value of exports is greater than the value of imports. A 'balance of payments deficit' refers to a balance on the current account where the value of imports is greater than the value of exports.

- A persistent *surplus* sounds good, but can cause problems. It may create excessive demand – greater than total domestic supply – putting upward pressure on prices. Moreover, one country's surplus is another's deficit, and the exporter may find its trade subject to tariffs or other import controls.

- A persistent *deficit* creates more severe problems. Since it represents a leakage of income from the national economy, it may erode growth. It is also likely to force exchange rates down, which will make the price of imports higher in domestic terms: this will have a clear implication for purchasers importing goods, as well as creating price inflation.

4.5   Governments can use a number of measures to reduce a balance of payments deficit (which is the bigger problem). The aims will be straightforward.

- To *increase exports* eg by giving support, information or financial subsidies to exporters, and/or

- To *reduce imports* eg through trade restrictions or protectionism: import quotas, controls or tariffs (taxes on imports, which give a cost/price advantage to domestic producers of the same goods). This may not be possible, however, under EU rules or WTO treaty obligations.

4.6   Another approach will be to devalue the currency, lowering the exchange rate, and making exports cheaper and imports more expensive in domestic terms – as we will explain in the next section of the chapter.

Trading blocs

4.7   A trading bloc is an economic arrangement created among a group of countries. There are more than 30 trading organisations and blocs around the world, including: ASEAN (The Association of Southeast Asian Nations); EFTA (The European Free Trade Agreement); and NAFTA (the North American Free Trade Agreement). Trade *within* each of these three major trading blocs is expanding on a vast scale – while trading *between* blocs, or indeed with non-members, tends to decline.

4.8   Unlike the European Union, which has moved towards political integration, most trading blocs are solely about **economic integration**. This type of integration can take various forms.

- A **free-trade area** (such as EFTA and NAFTA) represents the least restrictive economic integration between nations. Essentially, in a free-trade area all barriers to trade among members are removed, and no discriminatory taxes, tariffs or quotas are imposed.

- A **common market** (such as the Andean Common Market – Ancom – comprising Venezuela, Columbia, Ecuador, Peru and Bolivia) is the closest form of integration: a trading group with tariff-free trade among members *and* a common external tariff on imports from non-members, *and* collective regulation on quotas and other non-tariff barriers. Commercial law is also drafted centrally, and overrides the domestic laws of member states.

Tariff and non-tariff barriers to trade

4.9   Outside trading blocs, international trade may be subject to barriers in the form of taxes and duties (tariffs) and non-tariff measures. Here are some examples.

- Quotas: limits on the quantities of specified products that are allowed to be imported

- Complex customs procedures and paperwork, for goods to cross borders

- The need to comply with different quality, health and safety, environmental protection and other regulations in different countries

- Government subsidies to domestic producers (which make it more difficult for overseas firms to compete on price)

- Exchange controls: limits on the ability of a domestic importer to obtain the foreign currency needed to pay his overseas suppliers.

4.10 However the trend – supported by bodies such as the World Trade Organisation – is to remove such barriers and to encourage free trade and competition.

5 Exchange rates

What are exchange rates?

5.1 As we noted earlier, the exchange rate is the price of a currency (say, pounds sterling or euros) expressed in terms of another currency (say, US dollars).

5.2 The exchange rate between two currencies is determined by the relative supply and demand for each currency.

- Demand for pound sterling may rise, for example, when foreign buyers need to pay for UK exports; or foreign investors want to invest in the UK (perhaps because interest rates are attractively high); or speculators want to buy sterling on the foreign exchange market, in the anticipation that its value is rising.

- Conversely, supply of sterling will rise when people sell their pounds in exchange for foreign currencies: UK residents wishing to buy imports or invest abroad, say, or speculators selling sterling in anticipation of the value falling.

5.3 If demand for a currency, relative to supply, is rising (eg if there is a balance of payments surplus: more exports than imports), the foreign exchange markets will tend to quote the currency at a higher exchange rate. If supply is rising, relative to demand (eg if there is a balance of payments deficit: more imports than exports), the exchange rate will tend to be lower.

5.4 Exchange rates which are left to be determined by supply and demand on the foreign exchange (forex) markets, without government intervention, are called 'freely floating' exchange rates. Exchange rates which are subject to occasional government intervention to prevent unwanted fluctuations or changes are called 'managed floating' exchange rates.

The impact of exchange rates

5.5 Exchange rates are important for firms in international product or supply markets.

5.6 *Importers* want the value of their currency to be as *high* as possible. If the value of sterling is strong or rising against a foreign currency, UK purchasers can acquire more of that currency to pay their foreign suppliers: imports will be cheaper in domestic terms. If sterling weakens, purchasers' ability to acquire overseas currency is reduced, and imports are more expensive in domestic terms. This is the major consideration for purchasers.

5.7 For *exporters*, the position is reversed. They want the value of their currency to be as *low* as possible. If the value of sterling is low against a foreign currency, overseas purchasers will be able to buy more pounds to pay for UK goods: UK exports will be more affordable to overseas purchasers. If the value of sterling is high, UK goods will be more expensive to foreign buyers, and UK suppliers will find it harder to compete with other international suppliers (with weaker currencies). They may be forced to reduce their selling price, with an adverse effect on profits.

5.8   Firms producing goods for the domestic market *in competition with foreign imports* similarly want the value of sterling to be *low*, as this makes imports more expensive in domestic terms, favouring domestic suppliers. If sterling rises, imports will be more competitive.

5.9   *Fluctuations in foreign exchange rates* therefore represent a source of financial *risk* for purchasing organisations. An overseas supplier will normally quote a price in its own currency, and the buyer will need to purchase currency in order to make payment. If sterling weakens between the time when the price is agreed and the purchase of the currency, the buyer will end up paying more. The risk is even greater if staged payments are to be made.

Managing exchange rate risk

5.10   There are a number of ways of managing exchange rate risk.

- The purchaser might be able to transfer the risk to the suppliers, by getting them to quote prices in sterling. (This might be a tough negotiation, unless the purchaser has strong power in the relationship, or can offer concessions in exchange.)

- If fluctuations are not extreme, it may be possible to estimate the rate that will apply at the time of payment, and negotiate prices accordingly (perhaps with a contract proviso that prices will be *re*-negotiated if the exchange rate fluctuates by a stated percentage or reaches a stated rate).

- It may be possible to agree to pay for the goods at the time of contract (ie at a known exchange rate), without waiting for delivery – although this creates another kind of risk.

- Another approach would be to use one of the available tools of currency management, such as a **forward exchange contract**. Under this arrangement, the organisation contracts now to purchase the overseas currency at a stated future date, at a rate of exchange agreed now. There is a cost to doing this, but the uncertainty is removed.

- If exchange rate risks are severe, a purchaser may consider sourcing from the domestic market, from a single currency market such as the EU, or from other markets with less volatile currencies. (We will examine the economics of international sourcing briefly below.)

The single currency

5.11   One of the long-standing objectives of the EU has been 'monetary union' or a single currency area. The euro became general currency within the EU in 2002, although some member states (including the UK) opted to keep their own currencies. In other members, euro notes and coins replaced the old national notes and coins, such as the Deutschmark in Germany and the franc in France. The establishment of the euro irrevocably fixed exchange rates between participants' currencies.

5.12   The argument still rages as to whether the UK should join the single currency and adopt the euro. The arguments for and against can be summarised as follows: Table 6.2.

Table 6.2: *Arguments for and against the UK adopting the euro*

Arguments for a single currency	Arguments against a single currency
Greater stability of economic policy	Loss of control over economic policy
Facilitating trade and investment, without the risks/costs of currency transactions	The need to 'bail out' weaker economies in order to hold the system together
Currency stability, enabling lower interest rates for borrowing	Cost and confusion in moving to a new currency and coinage
Preserving the City of London's position as a premier financial market	Lower confidence arising from loss of national pride
Transparency of transactions, wage and price comparisons	

6 *The economics of international sourcing*

6.1 It may be worth drawing together some of the key economic factors impacting on a purchaser's decision on whether to source from international suppliers.

6.2 Overseas economies may have lower costs of production (labour costs, environmental compliance costs), which can be passed on to purchasers as lower prices. This is the overwhelming reason why companies now source internationally, or outsource production to low-labour-cost countries. However, there is increasing pressure for buyers not to *exploit* overseas workers, with an emphasis on Fair Trading (fair prices paid to suppliers) and ethical monitoring of suppliers (to ensure that their workers have fair terms and conditions).

6.3 International sourcing will incur additional costs of: procurement staff training and systems preparation; larger order and stock quantities (because of longer lead times for delivery); transport and logistics; compliance (with different laws and regulatory regimes); transport and exchange rate risk (and risk management: insurances, forward contracts and so on); contracting and payment (given the complexity and distance); supplier selection and monitoring; quality assurance; and so on. Low prices are only one part of the total purchasing cost!

6.4 International trade is often subject to trade restrictions or protectionist measures, in the form of taxes and duties (tariffs) and non-tariff measures, including quotas, customs red tape, legal requirements, government subsidies for domestic producers and exchange controls. However, these are being reduced with increasing trade liberalisation, particularly within trading blocs such as EU or ASEAN.

6.5 Additional risk is posed by the fact that economic factors are constantly changing, and international factors may be harder to predict. As an example, consider the troubles facing organisations that source from (or outsource to) China at the moment.

- Economists forecast that the over-supply of cheap Chinese labour will not last much beyond 2010: annual wage increases of 15% will soon erode its cost advantage.
- The introduction of new labour laws at the beginning of 2008 may also increase costs in China.

- Changes in Chinese tax regulations may affect Chinese suppliers' ability to reclaim VAT on some commodities (including chemicals, clothes, metals and machinery) – and the costs may be passed up the supply chain to international buyers.

6.6 This would make a great exam case study question: should a given firm look to source its supplies from an overseas market – and what risks might it incur by doing so?

Chapter summary

Key learning points include the following.

- Macro-economic factors affect buyers in a number of ways: by influencing the amount of disposable income; by influencing the level of business confidence; by influencing employment levels, rates of inflation, rates of taxation, exchange rates and interest rates.

- Economic activity can be shown as a flow of resources between firms and households. Refinements to the basic model take account of injections to the system (investment spending, government spending) and withdrawals from the system (savings, taxation), as well as the level of net imports/exports.

- The national micro-economic environment includes factors such as: economic activity and growth; employment; inflation; taxation; interest rates; business cycles; and government intervention via monetary and fiscal policy. Each of these areas may have an impact on purchasing by affecting demand, costs and risk.

- The business cycle (or trade cycle) is the periodic fluctuation in levels of economic activity, output and employment: from 'boom' to 'bust' and back again. Buyers may need to adapt resourcing decisions to suit each stage of the cycle.

- The main features of the international economic environment are: the balance of payments (and government action to increase exports and/or decrease imports); and exchange rates (which affect the price of imports and demand for exports). International sourcing has both economic benefits and costs/risks.

- Buyers must increasingly consider whether to source from abroad. Overseas economies may have lower costs of production. However, there are additional costs to be considered as well: training staff, systems preparation etc. In addition, there are risks associated with international purchasing that do not apply to domestic sourcing (eg unpredictable political and economic fluctuations).

Self-test questions

Numbers in brackets refer to paragraphs where you can check your answers

1   Distinguish between macro- and micro-economics (Introduction)

2   Distinguish between monetary policy and fiscal policy. (1.3)

3   Explain the circular flow of national income. (2.3–2.4)

4   List three causes of inflation and how they can be controlled. (2.10, 2.11, 2.14–2.16)

5   How might a rise in interest rates affect a business? (2.9)

6   Describe the four phases in the business cycle. (3.2)

7   Explain the effect on UK importers of a balance of payments deficit. (4.4)

8   Explain the effect on UK importers of a rise in the value of sterling against the currency of the supplier's country. (5.6)

9   List three ways of managing exchange rate risk. (5.10)

10   What are the economic arguments for and against international sourcing? (6.2ff)

Further reading

From your 'Essential Reading' list, you might look at Worthington & Britton (*The Business Environment:* 5th edition, 2006, FT Prentice Hall), Part 3: FIRMS.

•   *Chapter 4: The Macro-Economic Environment*

It is worth reading through this material, since it covers a core part of the syllabus, and offers further detail and different examples to our coverage. Again, the mini-case and case study features offer useful illustrations which may be used in the exam.

CHAPTER 7

Social Factors

Learning objectives and indicative content

2.3   Explain how social factors can affect purchasing locally, nationally and internationally

- •   Culture

- •   Demographics

- •   Local practices

- •   Language

- •   Behaviour

- •   Communications

- •   Ethics

- •   Local working practices and working hours

Chapter headings

1   The socio-cultural environment

2   Cultural factors

3   Demographic and socio-economic factors

4   Corporate social responsibility (CSR) and ethics

5   Socio-cultural factors in international supply chains

Introduction

In this chapter, we explore another group of PESTLE factors: socio-cultural factors. These are broadly 'people' factors, and, more specifically, factors arising from the values and behaviours of people in *groups*: societies, organisations, ethnic groups and so on.

We start the chapter with our usual overview of the impact of socio-cultural factors on purchasing.

We go on to examine what we might call 'local' aspects of culture (that is, the factors within a particular national or organisational culture which influence its members' behaviour) – as opposed to 'international' aspects of culture (the ways in which *differences* in culture can impact on businesses dealing with international stakeholders).

We look at how culture manifests itself in a society or organisation, and at some of the key statistical factors in a population (known as 'demographics') which impact on purchasing. We then go on to include the 'extra E' of the STEEPLE model – ethical factors – as one of the ways in which organisations respond to the social environment.

Finally, we look at the particular socio-cultural challenges of international and cross-cultural business dealings.

1 *The socio-cultural environment*

1.1 Organisations operate within society, are made up of members of society – and do business (as buyers and sellers) with other organisations and markets of which the same can be said. Society cannot fail to influence business activity!

1.2 Factors in the socio-cultural environment include a wide range of 'people' factors.

- **Demographics**: population size, structure (eg breakdown by age or ethnic group), distribution, movements and characteristics (eg education and employment)

- **Socio-economics**: measures of social class, status, income and wealth, and their impact on consumer spending

- **Social infrastructure**: structural support for education, communications, travel and other activities

- **Culture**: 'the collective programming of the mind which distinguishes the members of one category of people from another' (Hofstede). Culture is the shared assumptions, beliefs, values, behavioural norms, symbols, rituals, stories and artefacts that make our society (or ethnic group, or organisation) distinctively 'us' – or as one writer put it, 'How we do things round here'.

- **Ethics**: the moral values which a society (or organisation) adopts as a guide to defining right and wrong conduct

- **Consumer trends and fashions**: eg patterns of consumer preference, 'hot' products and 'hot' issues which have become or will become important for a society

- **Human resource management** (HRM): attitudes and policies about how people should be employed and managed in organisations.

1.3 These kinds of factors may impact on purchasing in a number of ways.

- A wide range of factors will influence the attitudes and purchasing behaviour of consumers, determining – and potentially changing – the level of demand (and hence supply volume) or the type of goods and services demanded (and hence supply requirements). You might like to run through the list of factors given above and think how each might affect demand for an organisation's goods and services.

- Demographic factors may affect the availability of skilled labour resources, both in purchasing and in the organisation as a whole (so that purchasing may have to contribute to solutions such as outsourcing or subcontracting).

- Cultural factors will influence the attitudes and behaviour of suppliers, affecting the way purchasers are able to negotiate, establish rapport and generally do business with them.

- Cultural, HRM and ethical factors will influence the attitudes and behaviour of purchasing staff, affecting how they can be motivated and managed – and of other members of the organisation, affecting how they perceive and work with the purchasing function.

- *Changes* in socio-cultural factors may require a purchasing response. (A new generation of ICT users, for example, may create pressure to adopt electronic purchasing. The trend towards outsourcing may give purchasing a new role in subcontractor management.)

- *Differences* in socio-cultural factors pose particular challenges for purchasers working with suppliers or colleagues in other countries, or from different backgrounds. This may be a significant barrier to international sourcing (eg different languages, business customs, negotiating styles and regulations). It may also hamper effective communication and collaboration within a multi-cultural purchasing team.

1.4 We will look at some of the key social factors in a little more detail.

2 Cultural factors

Elements of culture

2.1 Culture is the shared ways of behaving and understanding that are distinctive to a particular group of people. This group may be a nation or ethnic group, a social class, a profession or occupation, a gender, or an organisation: each may have its distinctive way of thinking and doing things. These are sometimes called 'spheres' of culture.

2.2 An influential writer on culture, Fons Trompenaars, suggested that culture operates on three levels: Figure 7.1. You might like to picture our pyramid as an 'iceberg', of which only the top third appears above the surface.

Figure 7.1: *Elements of culture*

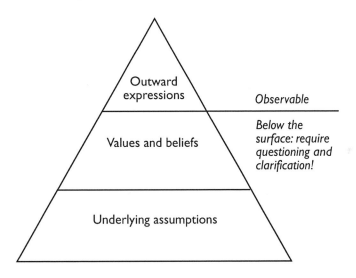

2.3 The most easily recognisable elements of culture, because they are directly observable, are its outward expressions: the part of the iceberg above the water. These elements include behaviour, artefacts and rituals.

- **Behaviour** includes accepted norms of personal and interpersonal conduct (eg negotiation and communication styles); customs and rules defining the right/wrong behaviour in a given situation; fashions and fads; and so on.

- **Artefacts** are products of the culture such as its arts and technology, its myths and heroes, its language and symbols.

- **Rituals**: patterns of behaviour which have symbolic or traditional value, such as social formalities, ceremonies and rites of passage.

2.4   Beneath these outward expressions are the **values and beliefs** which give them their special meaning and significance within the culture. They may be explicit in sayings or mottos, but are often not directly expressed so much as reflected in behaviour, artefacts and rituals. So, for example, a society that believes that age deserves respect will develop behaviours honouring older people, rewarding seniority in organisations, adopting wise elders as role models and so on.

2.5   Beneath values and beliefs lie assumptions: ideas which shape the culture's ways of thinking and behaving – but which have become so ingrained that they are no longer consciously recognised or questioned. The rights of the individual, or the legitimacy of authority, may come into this category, for example.

2.6   The 'underlying' elements of culture – like the part of the iceberg that lies under the water – are the ones that often cause problems. They are difficult to manage, whether in societies or organisations, because of the potential for misunderstanding (and, from there, conflict). An important skill of cross-cultural management and purchasing, as we will see, is being aware that, when dealing with other cultures, we don't always know what it is that we don't know!

2.7   Different countries and cultural sub-groups (different social classes, ethnic backgrounds, religious groups, age groups and so on) may have significantly different norms, values and assumptions, which influence how they do business and manage people, and how consumers develop product/service preferences and buying patterns. An organisation will have to adapt its products, services and processes to the needs of the culture in which it operates.

Organisation culture

2.8   Organisation culture has been defined as 'a pattern of beliefs and expectations shared by an organisation's members, which produce norms that powerfully shape the behaviour of individuals and groups in the organisation' (Schwartz & Davies). It has been summed up as 'the way we do things around here'.

2.9   You should be able to think of examples of each of Trompenaars' elements or manifestations of culture, as they might apply within a work organisation (perhaps using your own organisation as an example).

- Behaviours, for example, might include whether people are familiar or formal with colleagues; the rules of behaviour formulated as part of the disciplinary or ethical code; standard procedures and channels of communication; the 'short-cuts' developed over time in departments; and so on.

- Artefacts may include dress codes, office décor, symbols (such as corporate logos), corporate marketing literature – and indeed all work outputs. Things such as office size may take on a symbolic value, reflecting status or power.

- Rituals may include business formalities, ceremonies (such as performance awards), 'pizza Fridays' and so on.

- Beliefs and values will be both expressed (in corporate mottos and marketing) and underlying (eg in attitude to risk or quality, employee relations, and the importance given to empowerment, teamwork and so on).

2.10   The corporate culture may embrace positive values such as quality/excellence, innovation and social responsibility – or may tolerate negative behaviours such as absenteeism, cutting corners and office politics. One of the key tasks of management is to shape (and if necessary, change) the culture in directions that will help the organisation to function and compete in its market. However, it is important to note that an organisation's culture is also partly shaped by its environment, as it will adopt elements of the other cultural spheres (nation, region and industry sector) in which it operates.

The impact of cultural factors on purchasing

2.11 Cultural factors may influence purchasing (and other organisational processes) in a number of ways.

2.12 Organisations will have to adapt their products and services to the culture of their market (or different market segments), and this will impact on the materials and other inputs required. These cultural factors may change over time. Think how the materials specifications of clothing manufacturers have changed, say, with value-driven changes in demand for animal fur or organically grown cotton. Or how food specifications have changed with growing awareness of obesity and food intolerance issues, or growing ethnic/religious groups with special dietary preferences.

2.13 Organisations may need to adapt their marketing and supply chain management to culture-driven changes, trends and fashions. You should be able to identify a range of such 'hot' cultural topics in your country or region. Here are some obvious examples.

- Growing public concern about environmental and ethical issues. So, for example, purchasers will need to select 'green'/responsible suppliers, utilise 'green' materials, implement recycling policies; monitor supplier performance in relation to ethical labour practices; or broaden the supply base in order to comply with diversity policies. The organisation as a whole may seek to develop eco-friendly and Fair Trade products to satisfy a growing market demand, and may seek to position itself as a socially responsible producer and employer.

- Growing concern for fitness and health. Food producers may have to modify their products (and purchasers their inputs), in order to make them low-fat-low-salt or otherwise healthier. There is an increasing market for sports- and health-related goods and services. Employers may have to formulate work-life balance or corporate health programmes in order to retain quality employees.

- Growing use of personal electronic devices (such as mobile phones, MP3 players, digital cameras, palm-top computers – or all four rolled into one!) This has opened new markets for some producers (eg Apple moving into mobile telecom with the i-Phone) and all but destroyed the market for others (eg photographic processing and portable compact disc players). It has also altered the way organisations promote their products (eg with entertainment 'content' or SMS text messaging).

2.14 The organisation will reflect its national culture *and* will have its own organisation culture: even the purchasing function itself may have a distinctive culture (differing from the sales and marketing function, say). Some organisations may expect a flexible 'can do' attitude to price, customisation and delivery from purchasers and their suppliers, for example, while others may be more bureaucratic, bound by rules and procedures. Changes in purchasing policy and practice will be hard to sustain, if they do not 'fit' – and are therefore not supported or reinforced by – the corporate culture.

2.15 Purchasers may need to be particularly aware of cultural differences for cross-cultural or international teamworking and supplier management. 'Business gifts' which are considered essential in one culture, for example, may be interpreted as 'bribes' in another. (This will be discussed later in this chapter.) Similarly, marketers will need to be aware of the different values, tastes and preferences of overseas customers, and adapt products and messages accordingly.

3 Demographic and socio-economic factors

Demographics

3.1 Demography is the study of population and population trends. Demographic data is useful for purchasing (and business in general) because the population represents the source of demand for goods and services (and hence input requirements). The structure of the population has implications for demand in particular markets or market segments. Think of the effect that an increasingly *ageing* population would have on the business – and purchasing spend – of a childcare provider, or an aged care provider, a toy manufacturer, or the NHS. Think of the effect of an increasing *ethnically diverse* population on a food retailer or restaurateur; or the effect of increasing numbers of *single-person households* on the way goods are portioned and packaged...

3.2 The population also represents a source of skilled labour, which may affect purchasing recruitment – and also supply prices (as a cost of production for suppliers). Think of the effect on a rural employer in an area where employment-age people are increasingly moving to the city, say; or of the effect on purchasing recruitment and training of increasing numbers of women entering the workforce.

3.3 So what are the key demographic trends in the UK environment at the moment, from a purchasing point of view?

Population size

3.4 Population size is important for a number of reasons. If the population is too small, it may have insufficient labour and skills to exploit its resources and provide necessary services. If a population is too large, it may make excessive demands on the country's physical environment and resources, or may create a demand for public services that the public or private sector may not be able to supply. More importantly, perhaps, is the rate of change in the size of a population, with the potential to create either of the above problems.

3.5 Changes in the rate of population growth are caused by factors such as changes in the birth rate (or fertility rate), changes in the death rate (or mortality rate) and changes in the rate of emigration (people leaving the country) and/or immigration (people coming into the country).

3.6 The long-term growth in the world's total population has been due mainly to the reduction in the mortality rate: improved medicine and hygiene have reduced early loss of life through disease and childbirth. However, less developed countries also have a high birth rate, while developed countries have a declining birth date (in some countries, below the 'replenishment' rate of two children per couple). Developed countries are therefore facing a situation in which they need to import labour, in order to maintain productivity: a key driver for immigration.

3.7 In the UK, the overall population is increasing, mainly due to immigration. The number of people who are economically active has also been increasing, mainly through women entering the paid workforce. Both these factors tend to boost demand for goods and services.

Age structure

3.8   However, in the long term, the UK working-age population is expected to *shrink*. Birth-rates have been falling and life expectancy has been rising, creating an increasingly *aged* population and workforce. A larger proportion of the population will be retirees, and dependent on the (relatively smaller) younger working population for national income – and pensions.

3.9   An ageing population will change patterns of demand: shrinking the youth market and growing the 'grey'/mature-age market. So, for example, durability may replace fashionability as the key attribute of product design and the purchasing of materials and components. Distribution systems may increasingly favour home delivery, at the expense of inner city or out-of-town retail outlets. Renewed emphasis may be placed on value-for-money products, with a pressure on purchasing to reduce costs.

3.10   An ageing population may also impact on labour supply: forcing firms to pay more for young workers, or to retrain and retain older workers – or to outsource activities to economies with younger and lower-cost labour pools (in which purchasing may play a part). Age discrimination in recruitment was outlawed in the UK for the first time in October 2006, partly in recognition of the need for greater acceptance of mature-age workers.

Regional distribution

3.11   There have been significant changes, over time, in where people choose to live and work. The UK has seen a shift from urban areas to non-metropolitan regions, but this trend may reverse as the government pushes local authorities to create or expand towns. In other countries, such as Australia, there is a problem with young people moving from the country into cities, eroding rural economies and threatening agricultural production. These sorts of trends affect public service provision and infrastructure, as well as patterns of regional demands for goods: some small geographically isolated communities may not be profitable for banks or retail chains, for example.

Gender

3.12   The UK working population has become increasingly diverse in terms of gender, as legislation and changing social values have supported women's right to work. This has highlighted employment issues such as equal opportunity and equal pay. It has also shifted gender roles in household buying, with women enjoying independent spending power. Nevertheless, markets may still usefully be segmented and targeted by sex, since women and men have distinct purchasing preferences and patterns.

Ethnicity

3.13   UK society as a whole has become increasingly diverse in terms of race and ethnic background. Few societies are now homogeneous in terms of culture or ethnic background, although there may be regional pockets where immigration and settlement have been more intense. Ethnic diversity has brought a wide variety of cultural factors and differences to bear on organisations.

- Creating markets for the foods and clothing styles of other cultures

- Creating cross-cultural and multi-cultural management situations within firms and supply chains

- Highlighting the need to reflect social diversity in the workforce and supply base.

Social units

3.14 More and more people in the UK live outside the traditional family unit. Over 30% of all households are now one-person households and around 10% are lone-parent families (mostly women). Grown-up children tend to stay at home longer, for economic reasons. Many families are 'blended' through divorce and remarriage. These kinds of changes will be reflected in the demand for products (eg single-serve packaged foods, and convenience items for 'time-poor' households) and in working arrangements (eg family friendly policies and part-time working to allow lone parents to participate in the workforce).

Socio-economic class

3.15 Definitions of *social class* are commonly derived from demographic factors including wealth or income, educational attainment and occupational status. Some classifications you may have heard of include: lower/working-class (producers of goods and services), middle class (managers and organisers) and upper class (titled landowners and the very wealthy); or A, B, C1 (upper, middle and lower middle class), C2 and D (skilled and unskilled working class) and E (casual workers and welfare dependents).

3.16 The class structure of society will determine the level of demand for goods and services (and hence inputs), because of different classes' spending power, and what they spend their money on.

4 *Corporate social responsibility (CSR) and ethics*

Business ethics

4.1 'Ethics' are simply a set of moral principles or values about what constitutes 'right' and 'wrong' behaviour. For individuals and groups, these often reflect the assumptions and beliefs of the families, national cultures and educational environments in which their ideas developed. Ethics are also shaped more deliberately by public and professional bodies, in the form of agreed principles and guidelines which are designed to protect society's best interests.

4.2 An exam question may pose a scenario in which ethical issues arise – in which case you may wish to use the extended version of the PESTLE model (STEEPLE). The ethical environment includes factors such as: the core ethical values of the organisation and wider society; particular issues which raise ethical concern (eg supplier/worker exploitation, animal testing or the potential for fraud in purchasing); relevant ethical frameworks (eg Fair Trading certification, a corporate Code of Conduct or the CIPS Code of Ethics); and other pressures towards ethical behaviour (eg pressure groups, consumer support for ethical brands, or consumer boycott of allegedly unethical brands).

4.3 Ethical issues may affect purchasing at three levels. At the *macro* level, there are the issues of the role of business and capitalism in society: the debate about globalisation, the exploitation of workers, the impacts of industrialisation on the environment and so on. This is the sphere addressed by the Ethical Trading Initiative, for example: an alliance of companies, non-governmental organisations and trade unions committed to working together to promote internationally-agreed principles of ethical trade and employment.

4.4 At the *corporate* level, there are the issues which face individual organisations as they interact with their stakeholders. Some of these matters will be covered by legislative and regulatory requirements, and an organisation may have a 'compliance based' approach to ethics which strives merely to uphold these minimal requirements. The sphere generally referred to as **corporate social responsibility** covers policies which the organisation adopts for the good and wellbeing of stakeholders, taking a more proactive 'integrity based' approach: voluntarily seeking to 'do the right thing' in a given situation. This includes issues such as environmental protection and sustainability, fair trading, impact minimisation and community investment.

4.5 At the *individual* level, there are the issues which face purchasers within the organisation and supply chain: refusing to be party to fraud, say; not discriminating in the award of tenders; or deciding whether to accept gifts or hospitality from suppliers which might be perceived as an attempt to influence the placing of a contract. This is the sphere which is often covered in Codes of Ethics, such as that published by CIPS for its members. You should read through the CIPS code, if you haven't already done so: check the CIPS website at http://www.cips.org.

Corporate social responsibility (CSR)

4.6 The term 'corporate social responsibility' is used to describe a wide range of obligations that an organisation may feel it has towards its secondary stakeholders, or the society in which it operates. It is sometimes expressed in terms of minimising **externalities**: the costs of business activities which are not reflected in the costing of a product/service and paid for by consumers, but which are borne by the wider community – such as the costs of pollution (and associated ill health), traffic congestion or environmental degradation.

4.7 One CIPS examiner has written that: 'CSR means the commitment to systematic consideration of the environmental, social and cultural aspects of an organisation's operations. This includes the key issues of sustainability, human rights, labour and community relations, and supplier and customer relations beyond legal obligations. The objective [is] to create long-term business value *and* contribute to improving the social conditions of the people affected by our operations.'

4.8 Any or all of the following considerations may be relevant in assessing a purchasing organisation's CSR obligations.

- *Sustainability* issues: conserving the world's limited natural resources (eg by minimising the use of non-renewable resources, minimising fuel use in transporting goods, or using recycled materials); and supporting small and local suppliers

- *Environmental* issues: 'green' materials, pollution control, waste management, the avoidance of environmental disfigurement, promoting recycling and so on – and ensuring that suppliers do the same

- *Ethical trading and business relationships*: ensuring product safety/quality for consumers; improving working and social conditions for employees and suppliers, particularly in developing nations; avoiding the abuse of buyer power to squeeze supplier prices (fair trading); upholding ethical employment practices (such as equal opportunities and employment protection); adherence to ethical codes and so on.

4.9   There are many ways in which a purchasing function can contribute to CSR objectives. For example, it can draw up and enforce codes of ethical practice in sourcing or adhere to the rules laid down in the CIPS ethical code, Ethical Trading Initiative or Fair Trade framework. It can encourage (or even insist on) ethical employment and/or environmental practices in its suppliers. It can adhere to health and safety, equal opportunities and other ethical practices in its own workplace and so on. (We will consider 'green' purchasing separately in Chapter 9.)

Why should an organisation set ethical standards and CSR objectives?

4.10   Milton Friedman took the view that 'the social responsibility of business is profit maximisation': providing a return on shareholders' investment. Spending funds on objectives *not* related to shareholder expectations is irresponsible, and the public interest is arguably already served by profit maximisation, through corporate taxes.

4.11   'Consequently,' argued Friedman, 'the only justification for social responsibility is *enlightened self interest*' (or ethical egoism) on the part of a business organisation. So how does CSR serve the interest of the firm?

- Law, regulation and Codes of Practice impose certain social responsibilities on organisations, and there are financial and operational penalties for failure to comply (eg 'polluter pays' taxes).

- Voluntary measures may enhance corporate image and build a positive brand. A commonly quoted example is the environmental and sustainability strategy adopted by The Body Shop. You might like to check out the website of the Medinge Group, which publishes profiles of each year's top *Brands with a Conscience*: http://www.medinge.org.

- Above-statutory provisions for employees and suppliers may be necessary to attract, retain and motivate them to provide quality service and commitment – particularly in competition with other employers/purchasers.

- Increasing consumer awareness of social responsibility issues creates a market demand for CSR (and the threat of boycott for irresponsible firms).

- Social responsibility helps to create a climate in which business can prosper in the long term. In the same way, ethical sourcing helps to create a climate in which mutually-beneficial long-term relationships with suppliers can be preserved.

5   Socio-cultural factors in international supply chains

Cultural differences

5.1   We noted earlier that *differences* in socio-cultural factors have a particular impact on purchasing in international or cross-cultural markets. In this section, we will briefly explore the sources of those differences, and what purchasing can do to overcome potential risks and problems arising from them.

5.2   Different countries (or world regions) have different cultural norms, values and assumptions which influence how they do business and manage people.

5.3   Culture researcher Geert Hofstede *(Cultures and Organisations)* formulated one of the most influential models of work-related cultural differences, identifying five key dimensions of difference between national cultures.

- *Power-distance:* the extent to which unequal distribution of power and status is accepted or involvement/participation expected

- *Uncertainty-avoidance:* the extent to which security, order, control and predictability are preferred to ambiguity, uncertainty, risk and change

- *Individualism:* the extent to which people prefer to live and work in individualist ('I') or collectivist ('we') ways

- *Masculinity:* the extent to which gender roles are distinct, and whether masculine values (assertiveness, competition) or feminine values (consensus, relationship) prevail.

- *Long-term orientation:* the extent to which thrift and perseverance are valued (long-term orientation) over respect for tradition, fulfilling solid obligations and protecting one's 'face' (short-term orientation).

5.4   You should be able to recognise the challenges faced by a purchaser in a country at one end of the spectrum, in dealing with a supplier at the other end of the spectrum, on each dimension. For example, a purchaser in a low uncertainty-avoidance culture such as the UK will be flexible about procedure and forthright about disagreements: a supplier from a high uncertainty-avoidance culture such as Japan may be uncomfortable working without written rules and procedures, and may be offended or stressed by disagreement.

5.5   You may also be able to think of more specific examples of cultural differences, to do with aspects such as the following.

- Attitudes to the participation of women in business. (Equal opportunity is less of a value in some Middle Eastern and Latin cultures, for example.)

- Negotiating and conflict styles. Many Asian cultures, for example, have a strong reluctance to lose 'face' or respect, or to cause others to do so, and are therefore reluctant to criticise or challenge in public

- Decision-making styles. Many Asian cultures seek consensus or group agreement in decision-making, rather than leader-imposed or majority-rule decisions.

- The perceived propriety of business gifts and hospitality. These may be considered an important sign of mutual respect in some cultures – where in the West they are regarded as unprofessional and unethical attempts to influence decisions, and are often covered in corporate Ethical Codes. This may be a particular issue for purchasers.

- Business customs and formalities. Each culture has its business rituals: eg the importance of business cards in Japan, the importance of social conversation prior to getting down to business in Middle Eastern cultures, or the comparative informality of interpersonal dealings in North America.

Other differences impacting on international sourcing

5.6   There may be a number of other potential differences to take into account.

- Differences in working practices, which can be a source of misunderstanding or frustration for overseas purchasers and managers. Examples might include long lunch breaks in some European countries, and greater (or less) emphasis on worker involvement in decision-making.

- Different standard working hours, wage rates and conditions of employment. This can pose ethical issues and reputational risks for purchasers. Oxfam faced severe embarrassment, for example, when it was found that its overseas suppliers of 'Make Poverty History' armbands were exploiting their workers, by Western standards.

- Different legal and regulatory regimes (eg on quality standards, worker terms and conditions, health and safety, intellectual property protection and so on). The rules in a different country may be more stringent than at home (creating compliance difficulties) – but are often *less* stringent (creating quality, ethical and reputational risks for the purchaser). US toy makers, for example, have recently fallen foul of the less stringent regulation of their Chinese subcontractors: many toys had to be recalled owing to the use of toxic lead paint (banned in the US and EU).

- Language differences, which may create a barrier to effective communication in materials specification, negotiation and contracting, relationship management and so on

- Differences in communication infrastructure and tools (eg lack of internet, fax or even phone access for doing business) – an effect made more acute by possible differences in time zone (requiring communication tools for 24/7 dealings, such as email)

- Different education and skill levels and emphases, and different professional qualification standards: this may affect the selection and management of outsource providers, for example

- Different standard business terms (eg credit periods, standard contract clauses, payment methods) and so on.

Managing diversity and socio-cultural differences

5.7 Schneider & Barsoux *(Managing Across Cultures)* argue that 'rather than knowing what to do in Country X, or whether national or functional cultures are more important in multi-cultural teams, what is necessary is to know *how to assess the potential impact* of culture, national or otherwise, on performance.'

5.8 At the organisational and departmental level, there should be a plan to evaluate this potential impact and to implement programmes to encourage: awareness of areas of difference and sensitivity; behavioural flexibility (being able to adapt in different situations and relationships); and constructive communication, conflict resolution and problem-solving, where differences emerge.

Chapter summary

Key learning points include the following.

- Factors in the socio-cultural environment include: demographics, socio-economics, social infrastructure, culture, ethics, consumer trends and human resource management. All these factors can influence the demand for goods and trading and employment relationships. Particular challenges are posed by changes and differences.

- Culture comprises the shared ways of behaving and understanding that are distinctive to a particular group of people. Trompenaars suggests that culture operates on three levels: outward expressions, values and beliefs, underlying assumptions. Only the first of these is outwardly observable.

- Organisational culture is 'a pattern of beliefs and expectations shared by an organisation's members, which produce norms that powerfully shape the behaviour of individuals and groups in the organisation'. More simply, it is 'the way we do things around here'.

- A number of demographic factors influence purchasers: population size; age structure; regional distribution of the population; gender; ethnicity; social units; and socio-economic class.

- Ethics are moral principles or values about right and wrong. They apply to purchasing at a macro, corporate and individual level. Corporate social responsibility (CSR) describes the range of obligations that an organisation might have towards its secondary stakeholders.

- International trade poses challenges from differences in culture, language, local working practices and business customs, different legal regimes and communications.

Self-test questions

Numbers in brackets refer to paragraphs where you can check your answers

1   Define 'culture' and identify its different manifestations, according to Trompenaars. (2.1, 2.2)

2   What is organisation culture? (2.8)

3   List three current demographic trends and explain their impact on purchasing. (Section 3)

4   How do definitions of socio-economic class impact on purchasing? (3.16)

5   Give two examples of (a) macro and (b) individual ethical issues. (4.3, 4.5)

6   What are 'externalities'? (4.6)

7   Cite three arguments in support of CSR. (4.11)

8   Explain the Hofstede model of cultural differences. (5.3)

9   List four socio-cultural differences which pose a challenge for international purchasing. (5.4, 5.5)

10   How might 'communication' be a point of difference with an impact on international purchasing? (5.6)

Further reading

From your 'Essential Reading' list, you might look at Worthington & Britton (*The Business Environment:* 5th edition, 2006, FT Prentice Hall), Part 3: FIRMS.

•   *Chapter 5: The Demographic, Social and Cultural Context of Business*

It is worth reading through this material, since it covers a core part of the syllabus, and offers further detail and different examples to our coverage. Again, the mini-case and case study features offer useful illustrations which may be used in the exam.

CHAPTER 8

Technological Factors

Learning objectives and indicative content

2.4   Identify and explain how technological factors can affect purchasing at local levels, nationally and internationally

- Technology as a way of opening up new markets
- New communication technologies
- Government initiatives with technology
- Evolving nature and scope of e-procurement
- Different paces of technology development nationally and internationally, in developed and developing economies
- E-sourcing

Chapter headings

1   The technological environment

2   Technological development

3   Developments in ICT

4   E-sourcing and e-procurement

Introduction

In this chapter, we look at another group of PESTLE factors: technological factors, which have to do not just with machines, but with the choices organisations have to make around automation, computerisation, innovation, knowledge and change in business processes.

We start, as in previous chapters, by giving an overview of the impact of different technology applications on products, markets and business processes.

We then go on to discuss how new technologies develop, how nations differ in the extent of their technological development or sophistication, how development can be encouraged – and how new technology may be seen as a drawback as well as a benefit!

In the final sections, we explore some of the key developments in technologies relevant to purchasing, and how they are being applied, finishing with a brief survey of purchasing technology: e-sourcing and e-procurement systems.

1   The technological environment

What is technology?

1.1   Technology refers not just to 'machinery', but to means and methods of production, including: the apparatus (tools and equipment), techniques (ways of using tools, work methods) and organisation (how tasks are structured and resources deployed). When we talk about the technological environment, therefore, we are usually talking about:

- Developments in mechanised, automated or computerised ways of doing things (apparatus and techniques): for example, email, the internet, computer-aided design and manufacture (CAD/CAM) or radio frequency identification (RFID); *and*

- The changes to business structures and processes that those developments make possible (organisation): for example, electronic communication, e-procurement, integrated materials planning, just in time supply, stock/delivery tracking, virtual teamworking and so on.

An overview of technology's impact on purchasing

1.2 Technological developments have a range of impacts on business and purchasing activity.

1.3 Automation and computerisation raise productivity by allowing faster, more accurate, more consistent work than human beings can achieve alone. A supplier with access to advanced design, manufacturing, goods handling and transport technology should be able to fulfil orders faster, more cheaply and with more consistent (though not necessarily higher) quality.

1.4 Technology opens up new *product* markets through the potential for product innovation: think of the relatively new markets for digital cameras, MP3 players, music/book downloads, plasma TVs and so on. These new markets impact on purchasing by creating new sourcing requirements.

1.5 Technology also opens up new *supply* markets, eg by giving purchasers access to information on international suppliers via the internet, and facilitating communication and transaction processing. Technology may also be a differentiating or cost-saving factor, lowering barriers to entry and allowing small new producers or service providers access to established markets.

1.6 Technology changes business processes. It may be used to perform operational functions more safely (eg automated production and materials handling) or easily (eg recording and tracking stock movements using barcoding or RFID). In recent decades, it has changed both production processes and supply and distribution processes.

- Production processes, with an emphasis on labour-saving equipment and machinery – impacting purchasing through the need for investment appraisal and capital purchases. Examples include the increasing use of automated (or robotic) production, computer-aided design and manufacture, computerised quality/process monitoring and so on.

- Supply and distribution processes. Examples include: access to new global supply and product markets through e-commerce and faster transport; electronic sourcing and procurement systems (for e-auctions, order cycle processing, delivery tracking and so on); and new methods of service delivery (such as ATM machines, online entertainment ticketing and online banking).

1.7 Technology changes the amount of labour and types of skills required by businesses (eg through the use of labour-saving automation) and how they can be organised and managed (eg the use of information and communication technology to facilitate off-site and mobile working, and 'virtual' teamworking). This may in turn support the use of outsourcing and subcontracting, which may be driven and managed by the purchasing function. It may also create a changing skill profile for purchasers (eg use of e-procurement tools).

1.8 Technology influences the competition in an industry. It impacts on the competitive forces discussed in Chapter 3: for example, by raising entry barriers (eg if high investment in technology is required to enter the market); lowering entry barriers (eg by giving new players a differentiating advantage); or altering the balance of power between buyers and suppliers (eg by making it easier for buyers to switch, because they have more information – or harder, because they are 'locked in' to a shared computer network, say).

The impact of information and communication technology (ICT)

1.9 Information and communication technology (computers + telecommunications) has had a particular impact on purchasing.

- Dramatically increasing the speed of communication and information processing. Real-time answers to enquiries, updating of information and processing of transactions can be conducted via a computer network or the internet.

- Offering wider access to environmental and supply market information (especially from global sources). The internet offers constant access to formal information resources (in the form of websites, databases, libraries, expert agencies and so on) and informal resources in the form of network contacts. This has had the effect of opening up new supply markets, by giving purchasers access to information about suppliers and supply markets worldwide.

- Facilitating 24-hour, 7-day, global business. The internet and e-mail allow companies to offer service and maintain communication across office hours, international time zones and geographical distances.

- Supporting paperless communications (eg electronic mail messages), business transactions (eg online ordering and payment) and service delivery (eg online ticket reservations, information and education services, and so on). Information storage and retrieval is less wasteful of physical space and resources – and of administrative time.

- Offering opportunities for cost savings, through a wider supply base, streamlined processes and lower prices (eg via e-auctions)

- Freeing up buyers' time – previously taken up by routine and repetitive clerical tasks – for creative, strategic and relational aspects of their roles

- Enhancing management information (eg via databases and systems which record, store and analyse a wide range of transaction, business and environmental data).

- Creating 'virtual' supplier relationships, teams and organisations, by making location irrelevant to the process of collaboration.

2 Technological development

New technology development

2.1 Technological development may mean new technological innovations or improvements in various directions, such as added speed or power, increased miniaturisation, increased performance/quality/reliability, lower prices/costs and so on. (Think about how personal computing and mobile phones have changed in the last few years, for example.) Obviously this is a vast topic, and we can only a highlight a few points of interest: your own experience, and attention to media stories, will suggest many more examples.

2.2   The Austrian economist **Joseph Schumpeter** distinguished three stages in the process by which new technologies develop and become adopted by an industry or market.

- *Invention:* scientifically or technically new ideas are devised for a product or process.
- *Innovation:* the ideas are developed into marketable products and processes, which are introduced to the market. Innovation or product development includes prototyping, feasibility studies, technical and market testing and so on.
- *Diffusion* (or dissemination): the innovation proves successful and gradually comes to be widely available for use, through increasing adoption by individuals and organisations – which makes them increasingly cost-effective over time.

All three stages are required for what we call 'technological change', resulting in the cumulative economic and environmental impacts of new technology.

2.3   Schumpeter's distinctions helpfully highlight the fact that innovation is more than just 'new ideas': application and market success are necessary to create genuine technology development. In other words, the real impact of new technology on an economy occurs at the diffusion stage, where technologies are introduced and used.

2.4   It is worth noting, however, that this model suggests a linear process from invention to diffusion. In fact, it is a cyclical process: once an innovation is introduced into a market and deployed in practice, there will be a flow of feedback information which will usually stimulate further technical development and adaptation. This suggests that, in order to stimulate technological development, investment is required not just in invention, research and development – but in getting technology to market.

2.5   Schumpeter went on to analyse the effect of technological change on the performance of an economy. In the 1920s, Nikolai Kondratieff had identified peaks and troughs in economic prosperity in major Western economies (which you might equate to the business cycles discussed in Chapter 6). Schumpeter observed that the upswings (or 'upwaves') in economic activity coincide with major technological innovations, and the 'downwaves' coincide with lack of further innovation (once previous innovations have become an accepted part of the economy and no longer yield dynamic improvements). There was a major upswing towards the end of the 20th century, for example, resulting from developments in information and communication technology.

Technological development and product lifecycles

2.6   The product lifecycle (PLC) is a model which compares the 'shelf life' of a product to the life of a living organism, which goes through various stages. The basic principle of the PLC is that products have a finite life. A standard lifecycle curve may be illustrated as follows: Figure 8.1.

Figure 8.1: *A standard product lifecycle*

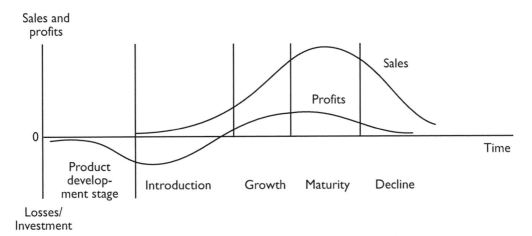

2.7 Once a product reaches the stage of maturity, and is faced with the prospect of decline, organisations need to protect their profits and competitive position by either of the following measures.

- Introducing new products, so that as one product declines, another reaches peak profitability in its place *or*

- 'Refreshing' the mature product: re-inventing or modifying it, so that it can be re-introduced to the market as 'new and improved', renewing the lifecycle.

2.8 Schumpeter argued that innovative organisations refresh existing products before they reach decline, hastening the obsolescence of the old product – and therefore shortening the product lifecycle. (You might think of new versions of computer operating software, for example, or new 'generations' of i-Pods: no-one wants the old versions once the new ones come out, so the old version quickly declines.)

2.9 Dynamic and innovative technological environments support faster and more frequent product development and updating: new features, greater miniaturisation, better recyclability and so on. The availability of new and updated products sends existing products into decline more quickly, so product lifecycles in these environments are generally getting shorter. Bradley *(The Purchasing Environment)* claims that the product lifecycle of a car in Europe is 5–7 years (because new models and features are constantly coming onto the market), while in developing countries it is often more than 30 years (because the pace of innovation is slower).

2.10 Frequent product innovation and modification requires flexible purchasing strategies – among other challenges.

The pace of technological development in different economies

2.11 The pace of technological development varies from economy to economy, according to factors such as the following.

- The availability of infrastructure (eg telecommunications cabling or band width)
- The extent of government investment in innovation and infrastructure development
- Government support and incentives for private sector investment (eg innovation forums or tax incentives)

- Education and research support from the academic community – which also requires investment in universities and labs, eg in the form of research and innovation grants

- The availability of markets in which to deploy and test new technologies (which, as we have seen, is how innovation really impacts on an economy)

- The extent and pace of cultural adaptation (eg the willingness of a society to accept new technologies, and its ability to afford technology products). Some cultures may adopt new technology products early; some may prefer to wait and see, or wait until the prices come down; some may prize tradition so highly that new technologies are actively resisted.

2.12 Developing economies often lack the resources to invest in systematic technology innovation and adoption. This hampers their economic development still further, since (as we saw in Chapter 6), technological advancement is one of the defining factors in economic development. Even within rapidly developing economies, such as China, there may be regional variations in infrastructure and access, due to geographic isolation or lack of resources.

Technology transfer

2.13 If an organisation or developed nation wishes to trade with a less advanced country, it may need to boost its technological capability. The process whereby more advanced nations share their technology with less developed economies is called **technology transfer**.

2.14 Technology transfer may take place in a variety of ways. Individual trading partners may supply their subsidiaries, suppliers or joint venture partners in developing nations with any of the following.

- Technological knowledge, management expertise, consultancy and training

- Investment or co-investment funding for new technology or research and development.

- Access to design patents for new technology products and processes (so that they do not have to be developed from scratch)

- Finished technology products, machinery and tools – such as computers, mobile phones, production equipment, vehicles and so on.

2.15 International agencies, or national governments, may similarly provide: consultancy; education and training; business networking opportunities (to encourage the sharing of technological know-how and innovation ideas); and/or investment or co-investment funding in the form of grants or loans (often for research and infrastructure projects).

Government support for technology development

2.16 National governments frequently aim both to invest in technology research and infrastructure, and to encourage the private sector to do so, in order to boost national competitiveness. In the UK, for example, HM Treasury offers tax incentives for investment in research and development activity, and for small business investment in ICT.

2.17 The UK government's pioneering Global Watch Service was designed to help UK businesses to identify and access innovative technologies and practices from overseas, but it was replaced in April 2007 by a simpler and more streamlined scheme called Knowledge Transfer Networks (KTNs). KTNs were set up by government, industry and academia to facilitate the transfer of knowledge between the industrial and scientific sectors. (You may like to check out the website: http://www.ktnetworks.co.uk.)

2.18 The Department for Innovation, Universities and Skills (DIUS) is responsible for supporting science, research and innovation through education and skills training. It is also responsible for allocating the science budget into research. (You may like to check out the website: http://www.berr.gov.uk/dius.)

2.19 In addition to direct investment in technology development, governments can create *demand* for technology products and innovation – for example, by public spending on defence or e-procurement – which will stimulate private sector research and development.

2.20 For more (and continually updated) information on government initiatives in this area, you might like to browse through the website of the Department for Business Enterprise and Regulatory Reform (BERR), which has links to the DIUS and other relevant sites.

- BERR: http://www.berr.gov.uk
- The Innovation Page: http://www.berr.gov.uk/dius/innovation

2.21 Private sector firms also stimulate invention and innovation in various ways: by providing experts to innovation think tanks, by inviting contributions from independent inventors, and by making innovative products and processes available in the market.

Caution about technological development

2.22 Organisations can get very enthusiastic about the possibilities of new technology. However, they must recognise that a given technology may not be the most effective, or cost-effective, solution to every business challenge. Here are some drawbacks of technology.

- High capital investment and set-up costs (design and development, hardware and software costs) – which may put more sophisticated applications (such as electronic data interchange or EDI) beyond the reach of small firms.

- High initial learning curve costs: training of users, cost of initial errors while users learn the system, potential confusion of running the system in parallel with old methods during the initial period

- Reliability issues, especially at an early stage of development, with the risk of 'bugs' in the software and initial teething troubles. Reliability may continue to be a problem, however, with the risks of network breakdown, power failure or viruses contaminating the system – and this can often cause chaos if the firm has become dependent on the technology (eg to communicate with suppliers or access information), with no backup systems in place.

- Compatibility issues, if the system is required to work together with the different systems of suppliers, say – or if key suppliers do not have access to the technology.

2.23 In addition, as we noted earlier, the pace of technological development varies from economy to economy: there may be large variations in infrastructure sophistication, compatibility and technology access/adoption in international markets.

2.24   There may also be ethical issues in the adoption of technology by a business.

- Smaller suppliers may not be able to afford to invest in collaborative technologies (such as an EDI network for transaction processing), and it may be unethical – and damaging to long-term relationships – to force them to do so.

- Automation of processes previously carried out by people has implications for staffing, and these will need to be handled responsibly: redundancies should be minimised (eg by retraining and redeploying staff, or freezing recruitment in advance to let normal resignations and retirements reduce staff numbers) and carefully managed to minimise hardship and conflict.

- Any significant change can be a source of insecurity, resistance and temporary loss of performance (as people learn new ways of doing things). Technological changes require stakeholder education, consultation and management.

3   *Developments in ICT*

3.1   Computerisation has been applied to a wide range of areas – some of which you will be using in everyday life. The following is just a brief survey of some of the tools which have emerged, with particular relevance to purchasing.

Operational systems

3.2   Operational systems are very diverse, including: materials and production planning systems, stock control systems, computer-aided design and manufacture (including robotics), and warehouse systems (including automated materials handling and stock/delivery tracking).

Point of sale and tracking systems

3.3   *Point of sale devices* involve the use of barcoding and radio frequency identification (RFID) tagging to record sales at point-of-sale terminals, which are linked to IT systems. Electronic point of sale (EPOS) systems can be used to track product sales, stock availability and location. They can also be connected to inventory management systems (for automatic stock replenishment), payment systems (via electronic funds transfer) and management information systems (for sales analysis, demand forecasting and inventory).

3.4   *RFID* is perhaps the 'hottest' technology in this area. EPOS and inventory control systems have for some years used barcoding as the main technology for automatic data capture. However, the use of RFID tags (transponders) offers significant advantages, compared to conventional optical scanning of barcodes.

- The tag doesn't have to be scanned or 'seen' by the reader: it can be used for updating inventory of moving and 'hidden' items in complex storage and transport environments.

- Data can be flexibly interrogated and updated for stock control, re-order triggering and so on.

- A *CIPS Practice Guide* argues that RFID can offer improved product availability; improved utilisation of resources; lower total operating costs; and enhanced safety, security and quality control.

Marks & Spencer is among the major organisations trialling and rolling out RFID systems in the UK.

Communications and relationship management systems

3.5 You should be able to draw on your own personal experience of 'newish' (and constantly developing) communications tools and systems, including: email; electronic banking and funds transfers (used in business for direct payments to supplier or employee bank accounts); mobile telecommunications and mobile computing (eg using mobile phones and palmtop computers to connect to the internet).

3.6 More specialised business-use communications systems include **electronic data interchange** or **EDI** (direct computer-to-computer communication within a network). This has been one of the most important developments in IT for purchasing. Instead of exchanging paper-based documents, inter-organisational enquiries and transactions are sent via cable or telecommunications links, directly from one computer system to another. EDI can be used for the following purposes.

- Query handling: sending marketing, transaction and technical information (product and price details, technical product or process specifications, terms and conditions of trade)

- Transaction handling: generating quotes, purchase orders, delivery instructions, receipt acknowledgements, invoices and so on

- Funds transfer (electronic payments to supplier or employee accounts, using direct transfer or credit card).

3.7 Communications developments (particularly the internet, email, web-casting and video-conferencing) have also facilitated 'virtual' teamworking and organisation. **Virtual teams** are interconnected groups of people who may not be present in the same office and may even be in different areas of the world, but who use ICT links to: share information and tasks (eg technical support provided by a supplier); make joint decisions (eg on quality assurance or staff training); and fulfil the collaborative functions of a team.

3.8 Partners in the supply chain, for example, can use ICT links to access and share up-to-date product, customer, stock and delivery information (eg using web-based databases and tracking systems). Electronic meeting management systems allow virtual meeting participants to talk and listen to each other on teleconference lines, while sharing data and using electronic 'whiteboards' on their PCs or laptops. This supports enhanced supplier relationships and the management of outsourcing, particularly international outsourcing (or 'offshoring'): you don't need to be within reach of people to monitor their performance, stay in touch – or even have meetings!

Management information

3.9 Management information is data collected, processed and formatted in such a way as to be useful to managers to aid them in planning, control and decision-making. Management information tools include the following.

- Databases and database management: capturing and storing data (eg on customers, products/inventory, suppliers or transactions in progress) in a structured way, so that they can be shared by different users, and interrogated flexibly for a variety of applications.

- Decision support systems: eg spreadsheets and computer models, used to examine the effect of different inputs and scenarios on the outcomes of a plan or decision.

- Management information systems: integrated systems for recording, storing and analysing a wide range of sales, purchase, point-of-sale, inventory, maintenance,

HR, financial and business intelligence data, to support management decision-making.

3.10 Database systems now have widespread application in business. Databases can be interrogated and the data analysed (using a process called 'datamining') for applications such as: identifying the best suppliers (for purchase decisions) or customers (for targeted marketing effort); developing the supplier or customer base (by identifying potentially valuable contacts and relationships to pursue); and enhancing supplier and customer relationships, by using information to personalise, target and streamline communications.

3.11 Perhaps most importantly, databases ensure continuity of knowledge, service and relationships. People move on, and have limited memory capacity at best: databases allow historical and current data about supplier performance, customer preferences and inventory levels to be stored and retrieved as needed.

The internet and e-commerce

3.12 The internet is a worldwide computer network allowing computers to communicate via telecommunications links. The network can also be accessed from laptop computers, personal digital assistants (such as Palm Pilots) and 3G mobile phones. The internet has exploded in the last decade as a business tool, for:

- Marketing: supporting advertising, direct marketing, customer communication, public relations and market research (eg using online surveys and browsing/transaction histories).

- Direct distribution: of products (through online product ordering, or the downloading of electronic products such as music, video or educational content) and services (eg information, ticketing, consultancy and e-learning).

- Customer service and technical support: through email enquiries, FAQs (frequently asked questions), access to database information etc.

- Partnership development: through better information-sharing and communication with suppliers and business networks.

3.13 The term 'e-commerce' (short for electronic commerce) refers to business transactions carried out online via ICT – usually the internet. E-commerce has facilitated direct marketing, linking customers direct with suppliers. It is a means of automating business transactions and workflows, and usually a means of streamlining and improving them. (However, it must be remembered that at some point, goods may have to be physically transported from the producer to the purchaser – and at this point, the speed of transaction-processing may not be matched by the speed of delivery!)

3.14 For the purchasing function, the internet has provided particular benefits.

- Wider choice of suppliers, including global and small suppliers. (Purchasing professionals still have to make strategic and tactical choices: ICT merely provides better-quality information for doing this.)

- Savings in procurement costs, through electronic communication, greater accuracy and electronic transaction processing. In a research project in 1997, management consultants McKinsey noted that the biggest effect of the internet for business overall is the huge saving in transaction and interaction costs – the costs of 'the searching, coordinating and monitoring that people and companies do when they exchange goods, services or ideas'.

- Support for low inventory and efficient stock turnover (eg just in time supply).

- Improved supply chain relationships and coordination, arising from better data-sharing.

Intranets and extranets

3.15 An *intranet* is a set of networked and/or internet-linked computers, which is accessible only to authorised users within the same organisation or work group.

3.16 Intranets are used in employee communication: only employees are able to access relevant web pages and internal email facilities. Intranets may provide employees with access to a wide range of internal information: performance databases and reporting systems; employment and training information; noticeboards; internal email facilities; mailings of employee newsletters and work updates; internal training software and so on.

3.17 An *extranet* is an intranet that has been extended to give selected outside users authorised access to particular areas or levels of the organisation's website or information network. Examples include the registered-user-only pages of corporate websites and the member-only pages of professional bodies' websites (such as CIPS).

3.18 Extranets are particularly useful tools for customer and supplier relationship management. They may be used to publish news updates and technical briefings which may be of use to clients or supply chain partners; to exchange transaction data and messages; or to share training resources (as part of collaborative quality management, say).

4 *E-sourcing and e-procurement*

E-sourcing

4.1 CIPS defines e-sourcing as 'using the internet to make decisions and form strategies regarding how and where services or products are obtained'. In other words, it concerns the first part of the purchasing cycle from need recognition to contract: purchasing research, definition of requirements, tendering, supplier selection and contract award. This technology is mainly used by specialist buyers.

4.2 E-sourcing may take a number of forms, depending on the purchasing methods used.

- *Electronic catalogues.* Suppliers exhibit their products in electronic catalogues, and buyers work with those details (product specifications, prices etc) to purchase materials and services.

- *E-tendering*, using electronic RFQ (request for quotation) procedures. RFQs and specifications are posted online or sent to different suppliers, and competing bids for the contract are received and evaluated electronically.

- *E-auctions*, where a seller offers goods for sale and potential buyers bid competitively: all bids are 'open', so buyers may raise their offers during the auction; the highest bid at the time limit wins. (You may be familiar with this system from e-Bay, for example.)

- *Reverse auctions*, where a *buyer* specifies its needs/demands, and suppliers submit quotes competitively: again, all bids are open, so suppliers may lower their prices during the auction, and the lowest bid at the time limit wins.

- *Market exchanges*: electronic marketplaces where multiple buyers and sellers meet and exchange goods.

Advantages of e-sourcing

4.3 The website of the Office of Government Commerce claims a number of benefits for e-sourcing: Table 8.1.

Table 8.1: *Advantages of e-sourcing (in the public sector)*

Benefit	Explanation
Process efficiencies	Reducing time and effort spent on tendering and contract management; reduced paperwork; fewer human errors
Compliance	Eg with the provisions of the Efficiency Review and the National Procurement Strategy for Local Government
Cost savings	Reducing the direct costs of tendering (for both buyer and suppliers); more efficient comparison, supporting savings through competition
Collaboration	Making it easier for purchasers to work together on common sourcing projects across different departments and regions: creating 'virtual buying organisations' to increase bargaining power
Strategic focus	Allowing purchasing professionals to focus on value-added and strategic procurement activity (such as supplier screening, supply base development and relationship management), rather than administration

E-procurement

4.4 CIPS defines e-procurement as 'using the internet to operate the transactional aspects of requisitioning, authorising, ordering, receipting and payment processes for the required services or products'. In other words, it involves the 'purchase to pay' part of the purchasing cycle: from purchase approval to the receipt of the product, followed by payment. This technology makes it possible for users who are *not* purchasing specialists to manage the buying process according to systematic purchasing disciplines – so it is often used to devolve buying to user departments.

4.5 E-procurement tools include the following.

- *Desk-top procurement systems*: allowing users to place electronic orders with approved suppliers, within the framework of a supply contract already set up by the purchasing function

- *Electronic data interchange*: the exchange of transaction documents in a standardised electronic form, directly from a computer application in one organisation to an application in another

- *Online track and trace*: the ability to trace the location and progress of deliveries, using barcodes or RFID tagging and/or global positioning systems (GPS)

- *Electronic payment*: automated generation of invoices for orders (self-billing); matching of invoices with orders and goods received; payment by electronic funds transfer; or the use of credit-card style purchasing cards

- *Electronic point of sale (EPOS) systems*: getting sales and inventory updates from point of sale terminals, which may also trigger automatic re-ordering if stocks are low

- *Contract management systems*: electronic contracts; reporting of any performance discrepancies; contract updating and so on

- *Database information:* centrally stored and managed data concerning supply markets, customers, supplier performance or other areas, which can be updated and interrogated in real time.

4.6 The consequences of computerising purchasing systems can be dramatic. The DTI's booklet *Supplying the Challenge*, for example, described the process at confectionery company Mars. 'Buyers have replaced paper and files with electronic information and links to company operational data: now the company is reaping the rewards through more co-ordinated – increasingly pan-European – buying, better scheduled deliveries, and more information available more quickly to [internal] customers throughout the organisation. Everyone creating a requisition does so on a computer screen. Buying authorisations are registered on-screen and buyers create priced orders from the information brought together by the system. This alone saves huge amounts of time and money. Perhaps more important, the system helps Mars plan further ahead and control its purchasing better.'

4.7 An article in *Supply Management* cited the example of supermarket giant Sainsbury's which in the last decade has completely re-engineered its supply chain. Among other changes (involving the structure of the distribution system), Sainsbury's has fully automated two of its warehouses, in order to minimise human error and implement zero defect order fulfilment. It has also introduced real-time information and collaborative commerce across the extended supply chain. This includes:

- Computerised inventory management, to enhance control over the supplier-to-store replenishment network

- Data-mining applications, gathering information at point of sale, measuring on-shelf availability on an hour-by-hour basis, and facilitating real-time re-ordering.

4.8 You should gather your own examples of e-purchasing systems in action, from your own experience and from your reading in *Supply Management.*

Chapter summary

Key learning points include the following.

- Technology embraces apparatus, techniques and organisation. Technological change has had major impacts on purchasing and operations – and you should review these in detail.

- New technology develops in three stages: invention, innovation and diffusion. This happens at different rates in different economies, depending on infrastructure, support, investment and adoption. Developed nations can support developing nations via technology transfer.

- Despite the immense advantages of new technology, there are also (potentially) operational, financial and ethical drawbacks that must be considered.

- A number of key technological developments in relation to purchasing were discussed in Section 3 of this chapter: point of sale and tracking systems; communications and relationship management systems; management information systems; the internet, intranets and extranets.

- E-sourcing is the application of the internet to the pre-contract stages of the purchasing cycle, while e-procurement covers the purchase-to-pay stages of the cycle. Both offer benefits of a wider supply base, cost savings (through efficiency) and lower prices (eg through e-auctions).

Self-test questions

Numbers in brackets refer to paragraphs where you can check your answers

1   Explain the impact of technology developments in opening up new markets. (1.4, 1.5)

2   Explain the impact of technology developments on business processes. (1.6)

3   Explain the impact of technology developments on competition. (1.8)

4   Explain the three stages of new technology development and innovation. (2.2)

5   Explain the impact of technology developments on product lifecycles. (2.9)

6   Identify three mechanisms of technology transfer. (2.14)

7   What are the potential drawbacks of technological change? (2.22)

8   What are (a) RFID and (b) intranets? (3.4, 3.15)

9   Give three examples of computerised applications supporting purchasing and operations management. (Section 3)

10   Give three examples of (a) e-sourcing and (b) e-procurement tools. (4.2, 4.5)

Further reading

From your 'Essential Reading' list, you might look at Worthington & Britton (*The Business Environment:* 5th edition, 2006, FT Prentice Hall), Part 3: FIRMS.

- *Chapter 6: The Resource Context.* Focus on the short section titled 'Technology'.

- *Chapter 16: The Technological Environment: E-Business.*

It is worth reading through this material, since it covers a core part of the syllabus, and offers further detail and different examples to our coverage. Again, the mini-case and case study features offer useful illustrations which may be used in the exam.

CHAPTER 9

Environmental Factors

Learning objectives and indicative content

2.5 Identify environmental factors affecting purchasing at local levels, nationally and internationally, and explain their potential impact

- Environmental policy
- Pollution, removal of rain forests, ie issues relating to environmentally friendly practices
- Reducing and disposing of waste in the purchasing function
- Legislation on emissions
- Kyoto agreement and its impact upon commercial operations

Chapter headings

1 The natural environment

2 Current environmental concerns

3 Pressure for environmental responsibility

4 Environmental policy

5 The contribution of purchasing to 'green' business

Introduction

In this chapter, we cover the final E in the PESTLE model: factors relating to the natural environment.

Note that when you read or use the phrase 'environmental factors', you need to be clear whether it refers specifically to the last E in PESTLE – that is, what we have called the natural environment or 'green' factors (in the sense in which people are concerned about 'the environment') – or whether it is referring to the business or purchasing environment as a whole.

This is a highly fashionable topic at the moment, and a high governmental and organisational priority – for reasons both of sustainability (a stewardship duty to maintain a viable environment for future generations) and of marketing (given increasing stakeholder pressure for nations and organisations to demonstrate responsibility).

We start this chapter with a brief overview of the natural environment, before exploring in more depth some of the key issues and trends which are currently of concern: pollution control, for example, and global warming.

We go on to outline the legislation, regulation and international agreements aimed at securing environmental protection, including the Kyoto agreement.

Finally, we explore the processes whereby a business may develop and pursue an environmental policy – and some of the issues that may arise as it does so.

1 *The natural environment*

Factors in the natural environment

1.1 This aspect of the purchasing environment may be called the 'ecological' environment (ecology being the study of organisms in their natural environment); the 'natural' environment (ie relating to nature); or the 'natural resource' environment (since the organisation draws resources from nature). Unfortunately, within the PESTLE framework, it tends to be called 'environmental factors': if you see this phrase, you will need to think carefully whether, from the context, it refers to factors in the natural environment or to factors in the purchasing environment as a whole. 'The environment' has become a kind of popular shorthand for nature and 'green issues' – but an examiner may not see it that way!

1.2 Here are some factors in the natural environment which are relevant to purchasing.

- The weather – and more generally, climate factors. These may affect commodity prices, supply and logistics: for example, drought and flood affecting agricultural production, or the risk of hurricanes disrupting shipping and road transport. Weather effects, in particular, cannot be reliably forecast, and represent a significant supply risk.

- Natural resources, such as oil, coal and other minerals, and farmed/gathered materials and ingredients used in products, such as cotton, wool and foodstuffs. The availability, quality and price of such supplies will be of key interest to buyers.

- The impact of business on the natural environment, in terms of land use, pollution and so on.

- Specific issues of environmental concern, such as deforestation (particularly the loss of rainforests), the reduction of world fish stocks through overfishing, the loss of biodiversity, or climate change ('global warming'). We will discuss a number of the 'hot' eco-issues further on in the chapter.

- Governmental, pressure group and public concern, and pressure applied on organisations, in any or all of the above areas. Some are the subject of international agreements and targets (eg Kyoto). Others are the subject of legislation (eg on electronic and electrical waste, and lead emissions by cars). Some are the subject of incentives (eg 'polluter pays' taxes and consumer 'green brand' awards), while others are subject only to public awareness and consumer pressure for social responsibility.

Local, national and global issues

1.3 Some issues may be local in their scope and effects: for example, a factory discharging effluent into a local river; the risk of local flooding; or local traffic congestion and pollution (noise, dirt, vibration and air pollution) caused by transportation.

1.4 Some issues are national in their impact (for example, in the UK, national resource issues such as water or energy consumption, deforestation and the loss of arable land to urbanisation) and in their management (for example, UK legislation such as the Clean Air Act, and public sector sustainability targets). Other countries will have a different set of problems: drought, water management and salination (increasing salt concentration in water and soil) in Australia, say, or deforestation in Asia and South America, because of logging and/or demand for land to be cleared for agriculture. You should identify the key environmental issues affecting your own country.

1.5 Some issues are international in their scope and management. Increasingly, the world faces genuinely 'global' problems, such as climate change, resource depletion or damage to the ozone layer. Although it has been slow happening, there are now also concerted international responses to environmental issues: for example, EU directives, the Kyoto Agreement on climate change, and OECD recommendations.

1.6 To get a flavour of these different levels of concern, you might like to check out the environmental policy statements of:

- Your local government body
- The UK Environment Agency (http://www.environment-agency.gov.uk)
- The European Environment Agency (http://www.wwa.eu.int/com/environment)

1.7 You might also browse the websites of international environmental pressure groups such as Greenpeace (http://www.greenpeace.org/international) or the David Suzuki Foundation (http://www.davidsuzuki.org) – and any commercial organisations you are interested in.

Impact on purchasing

1.8 The kinds of factors outlined above may influence purchasing activity in various ways.

1.9 Increasing consumer concern will place pressure on organisations to adapt their products and processes to be more environment-friendly, because consumers will prefer 'green' brands (such as The Body Shop) – and may boycott brands with a poor environmental reputation (such as BP or Shell following an oil spill). Purchasing will have a key role in 'greening' products and processes, as we will see later: it will also be affected by a rise or fall in demand due to green consumption.

1.10 Government policy and legislation creates compliance issues. The UK Waste Electrical and Electronic Equipment (WEEE) Regulations 2006, for example, follow an EU Directive which makes manufacturers, sellers of branded products, importers (including purchasers) and exporters of electronic and electrical products responsible for the costs of their collection, treatment, disposal and recycling.

1.11 There may be financial penalties for poor environmental performance (eg fines for non-compliance or 'polluter pays' taxes). On the other hand, there may also be a cost in implementing a corporate environmental policy (eg more expensive materials, recycling processes, tighter controls and general change management) – and in implementing a national policy (eg the Climate Change Levy used to fund the Carbon Trust).

1.12 Costs of obtaining natural resources and commodities may rise as supplies fall, whether because of long-term factors (such as depletion), or short-term supply factors (eg weather affecting agricultural production, or political unrest disrupting gas supplies from Russia, say).

1.13 Cost savings may be achievable by a firm, for example by reducing its energy consumption, reducing its product packaging or using recycled materials.

1.14 Natural events (eg severe weather or earthquake) pose a risk for supply, potentially disrupting production or transport infrastructure. Purchasers may need to secure 'back-up' sources of supply and purchase insurances to cover the risk. They may also choose to support the supply chain: when a 2007 earthquake in Tokyo forced one of

Toyota's key component suppliers to halt production, for example, Toyota provided 200 staff to help the supplier with its recovery.

2 Current environmental concerns

Resource depletion and management

2.1 The factors in the natural environment which are currently known about, and of concern, are many and various, as you may have noted if you browsed any of the websites cited earlier – or if you think about all the various environmental pressure groups you've heard of! Start collecting a dossier of examples of 'green' issues that interest you, and what corporations are (or are not) doing about them: they will give you a stock of useful illustrations for an exam answer. We will just look at some key issues, briefly, here.

2.2 A number of issues are of current concern, in regard to resource depletion and management.

- There is an increasing depletion of non-renewable resources: resources which cannot be replenished once supply is exhausted. Key examples include oil, coal and other minerals, agricultural land and rainforests (given the long time-scale for regeneration of such complex eco-systems). There is increasing pressure on businesses (and society in general) to limit or minimise the use of non-renewable resources, in order to support sustainability.

- There is also a challenge in keeping renewable resources productive. The world is unlikely to 'run out' of resources such as soil, water, fish stocks and clean air – but the quality and productivity of those resources is being reduced by overuse, pollution and other forms of environmental damage. The yield of agricultural land, for example, is significantly reduced by overuse, erosion, salination, irrigation difficulties, pollution and other effects.

- Both the above factors create a challenge of finding new resources: for example, vegetable-based fuels or bio-fuels, and renewable energy sources such as water, wind and solar power. The UK has recently set a target of 10% of its electricity coming from renewable sources, for example, and Virgin Airlines – among other private sector firms – are investing heavily in research on bio-fuels, to offset their impact on the environment through the use of non-renewable (and pollutant) fuels.

2.3 A related area of concern is the increasing rate of species extinction and the loss of **biodiversity** through the destruction of natural habitats which support varied ecosystems and plant and animal species. This may represent a depletion of resources (eg plants with medicinal properties as yet unresearched), but also represents issues of social cost and legacy: the desire not to leave future generations with an impoverished biosphere and environmental problems.

2.4 CIPS defines biodiversity as 'the total variety of life on Earth'. Its *Corporate Social Responsibility* guidelines argue that: 'In principle, most people support the idea of preserving diversity of habitats, genetic profiles and species. It is a responsibility of organisations to minimise any adverse impact on these areas'.

Environmental damage

2.5   It has been recognised, ever since the early days of the Industrial Revolution, that industrialisation has an impact on the natural environment. Again, this may take many forms, depending on the location and nature of industrial activity.

2.6   There is an increasing loss of arable land available for food production, due to industrial and urban development, putting pressure on food supply chains and prices.

2.7   There has also been destruction of rainforest land on a massive scale, both for forestry (for wood and paper industry products) and to clear more arable land to support the development of rainforest communities. This damages the environment on several levels.

   •   Rainforests are complex eco-systems which house a high proportion of the world's plants, insects and other unique species: the destruction of habitats causes a drastic loss of biodiversity

   •   Rainforests are some of the few remaining large-scale forested areas. Trees and other plants are a key mechanism in maintenance and 'cleaning' of the earth's atmosphere, taking in carbon dioxide and generating oxygen. The destruction of forests therefore contributes to a build up of carbon dioxide in the atmosphere, making it both less breathable and more prone to global warming (as discussed below).

   •   Rainforests contain unique plant species, which have been used for their medicinal properties by indigenous communities. Their destruction represents a loss of potential – as yet unresearched – resources.

   •   Rainforests are also the habitat of small indigenous groups, whose culture and way of life is threatened by the encroachment of industrialised society.

2.8   Another range of issues surrounds various forms of industrial pollution and their effects. Examples include air pollution, through vehicle and factory emissions, dust and chemical sprays; soil pollution, through the seepage or burial of industrial waste, or the use of chemical fertilisers; the contamination of wetlands, rivers and oceans, through the seepage or discharge of effluent (liquid waste), or accidental oil and chemical spillages; and noise pollution, through machine and vehicle noise.

2.9   The discharge and disposal of waste products, particularly in terms of non-biodegradable, toxic and radioactive materials, is the subject of legislation in many countries, with regulations on safe handling, transport and disposal. This has created pressure for the development of recyclable products and materials, and for producers to take responsibility for the collection and disposal of potentially damaging waste products (such as obsolete electrical and electronic goods).

2.10   The syllabus highlights pollution and removal of rainforests as examples of issues relating to environmentally friendly practices – but as you can see, the list of potential environmental damage is much longer than that. You might think of further examples from the news media or your own experience: the scarring of areas of natural beauty for mining; the loss of bird and animal species as natural habitats are taken over for housing or transport infrastructure; and so on.

2.11   Local authorities and firms increasingly have policies about waste reduction, recycling, land reclamation or re-beautification, safe waste disposal, pollution and emissions control, the preservation of 'green corridors' and habitats, and so on. In addition, businesses are implementing policies such as the following.

- Reducing product packaging, or using sustainable raw materials in packaging (eg recycled paper)
- Seeking to use sustainable raw materials (eg not using rainforest wood/paper products, using recycled materials where possible)
- Discouraging plastic carrier bag usage by shoppers (in retail environments)
- Developing recyclable materials and products, and encouraging recycling via reverse logistics provisions
- Setting targets to reduce waste products and/or to reduce the amount of waste sent to landfill (as opposed to re-use or recycling)
- Eliminating the use of chemicals and pesticides (in food production, say)
- Reducing transport emissions through 'green' vehicles and route planning

Climate change

2.12　Climate change or 'global warming' is perhaps the 'hottest' topic in environmental politics (no pun intended!), with a number of major research reports and a major film *(Al Gore's An Inconvenient Truth)* raising the profile of the issue for governments and pressure groups worldwide.

2.13　The science of climate change is still under debate, with some scientists claiming that the causes of atmospheric temperature fluctuations are not clear, or that such fluctuations occurred naturally long before human (let alone industrial) intervention in the environment. However, there is fairly widespread political consensus on the prevailing theory.

2.14　Essentially, 'greenhouse gases' in the atmosphere, including carbon dioxide, fulfil an essential function in keeping the earth warm. Excess levels of these gases, however, can raise the temperature too far, causing the melting of polar ice-caps, the rising of sea levels and changes to global climate patterns. Greenhouse gases are produced by natural as well as industrial processes, but current levels in the atmosphere appear to be higher than in pre-industrialisation eras, and have been attributed to factors such as transportation and energy use.

2.15　Global warming and climate change may have a range of severe consequences, including the flooding of coastal areas and the displacement of communities; the disruption of agriculture and food production; and the increase in severe weather events such as hurricanes and droughts (which – among other ill effects – may disrupt supply!).

2.16　In order to counter the threat, societies and corporations are urged to reduce greenhouse gas emissions, and to reduce their 'carbon footprint': that is, the total impact of their activities on the amount of carbon dioxide (CO_2) in the atmosphere. Emissions-reducing projects include renewable and 'clean' energy (such as wind farms or hydro-electric plants), energy efficiency projects and re-forestation projects.

2.17　Here are some practical measures that can be taken by individual firms.

- Setting policies and targets for reducing carbon emissions (and ideally becoming carbon neutral) and monitoring carbon footprint
- Minimising the use of non-renewable (fossil fuel) energy in all activities, and sourcing or generating 'green' (renewable) electricity
- Reducing business travel and the air freight of goods (and/or labelling air-freighted products to give consumers the choice); planning road haulage to

minimise fuel use and emissions; moving towards the use of bio-diesel in lorry fleets; and using 'green' company car fleets

- Carbon offsetting (ideally, where no other method of reducing CO2 emissions is available). Individuals, companies or governments can purchase financial instruments called 'carbon offsets' (representing the fruits of emissions-reducing projects) to compensate for their own greenhouse gas emissions. (The Kyoto Protocol sanctioned offsets as a way for governments and private companies to earn 'carbon credits' which can be traded in a compliance market.)

- Carbon labelling: supporting the work of the Carbon Trust to develop the labelling of consumer products and services with their carbon impact

- Developing and selling products with a lower carbon impact (eg low-energy use household appliances, non-HFC-gas refrigerators and air-conditioning systems, clothes which can be washed at lower temperatures)

- Mobilising and supporting key suppliers and logistics providers in reducing their carbon emissions, and making this a criterion for supplier selection and evaluation.

- Mobilising and supporting customers in reducing their carbon emissions. Marks & Spencer, for example, are now educating their customers on carbon footprint reduction (in a joint campaign with the World Wildlife Fund, WWF), supporting the carbon labelling of their products, and siting retail outlets to encourage the use of public transport and cycling (to reduce car usage).

2.18 The **Kyoto Protocol** is a proposal of the international Framework Convention on Climate Change, aiming to reduce greenhouse gases – and therefore to prevent human-driven climate change. The protocol came into effect in 2005, and now has over 180 signatories: a significant achievement in securing global co-operation! It requires signatories to commit to targets for reducing national CO2 emissions: the UK has adopted the target of cutting national carbon dioxide emissions by 20% by 2010, for example.

2.19 The protocol also established the 'Clean Development Mechanism' (CDM), which validates and measures emissions-reduction projects (renewable energy production, changes in land use, re-forestation and so on). This allows entities that have difficulty meeting their emissions quotas to offset, by buying CDM-approved Certified Emissions Reductions.

2.20 The USA is the only developed country not to ratify the Kyoto treaty, but debate continues to rage about the usefulness of the protocol and the impact of reducing emissions on national economies and employment.

2.21 You may like to estimate your own carbon footprint: check out http://www.carbonfootprint.com/calculator or http://footprint.wwf.org.uk.

3 *Pressure for environmental responsibility*

Environmental law and regulation

3.1 The impetus for firms to become environmentally responsible may come from a number of sources.

3.2 Some areas may be specifically covered by legislation and regulations. For example, the EU has a set of Emissions Standards for all new road vehicles, trains, barges and 'non-road mobile machinery' (such as tractors). Other EU directives include a wide range of areas such as: the disposal of waste electrical and electronic products; the control of landfill use and waste incineration; the protection of water quality, freshwater fish, and bathing waters; the control of agricultural chemicals; the reduction or elimination of pollution; the protection of habitats; the control of the discharge of dangerous substances; and the safe disposal of batteries!

3.3 The Environment Agency in the UK has the responsibility of regulating business and industry: implementing EU directives nationally, issuing permits, monitoring compliance and carrying out risk assessments. There are five basic approaches to regulation.

- Direct regulation: enforcing legislation, and issuing permits, which typically set limits to control pollution levels, and require operators to carry out management processes.

- Environmental (or 'polluter pays') taxes, such as the Landfill Tax or Climate Change Levy.

- Offset or trading schemes, such as the EU Emissions Trading Scheme (for greenhouse gases) and the Landfill Allowances Trading Scheme. Participants can choose either to operate within their allowance (eg by reducing emissions or resource use), *or* buy extra allowances in the market to offset any excess: they can also sell surplus allowances if they perform better than expected.

- Voluntary or negotiated agreements, jointly agreed by businesses (usually to avoid the threat of legislation or compulsory regulation). The motor industry, for example, has a voluntary agreement with the EU on emission reduction targets, and other agreements are in force in the chemical industry and agricultural sector (on the use of pesticides). The Environment Agency monitors compliance.

- Education and advice: the promotion of regulatory requirements, risk assessment consultancy, and showcasing emerging issues and successful initiatives.

Pressure groups and green consumerism

3.4 In addition, you should be aware of the wide range of pressure groups which promote environmental causes and issues; protest (and encourage consumer action) against poor environmental performers; and/or showcase and reward good environmental performers (eg with 'Green Brand' awards, endorsements and collaborative campaigns). You might like to do your own research into one or two such pressure groups which interest you: the Wetlands Trust, Greenpeace, WWF and so on.

3.5 You might also like to browse websites which help consumers to locate 'green' products and brands. For example:

- The Find Green: http://www.thefindgreen.com

- Guide Me Green http://www.guidemegreen.com

3.6 One of the strongest pressures on corporations to be environmentally responsible has been the rise in green consumerism: the willingness of consumers to choose products, brands and providers on the basis of environmental responsibility. Consumers are increasingly well informed about the environmental performance of firms, and the environmental impact of products (including their energy use, recyclability and carbon footprint), through the internet and the activity of green consumer groups.

3.7   Organisations have faced major consumer boycotts as a result of poor environmental performance. Shell Oil, for example, has been called to account for alleged pollution of waterways in Nigeria; McDonald's for its excess packaging; and cosmetic and pharmaceutical companies for animal testing of products.

3.8   Conversely, organisations such as The Body Shop – and, more recently, Marks & Spencer – have created a strong brand identity and customer loyalty through environmental leadership.

4   *Environmental policy*

Establishing an environmental policy

4.1   Pressures such as those discussed above have led many organisations to take direct action on environmental responsibility.

4.2   The first step for a firm wishing to establish an environmental policy will be to determine its objectives. This may not be easy: it is not always clear whether Product X is more or less friendly to the environment than Product Y – particularly since the science (eg in the case of climate change) is still being debated. A systematic effort must be made to assemble information from the widest possible range of sources – although, again, it must be remembered that pressure groups may not be the best source of *unbiased* information and views... Research data is now being widely disseminated via Environment Agencies, and some helpful tools have been developed.

4.3   The support of senior management will be essential if any environmental policy is to succeed. If there is no overall corporate policy on environmental issues, the purchasing function may find it difficult to gain stakeholder 'buy in' to the proposal. On the other hand, senior managers may be glad to have change champions in this area, leading the way – and making them look good!

4.4   The next step will be to lay down guidelines on measures that can be instituted within the organisation, usually by negotiation with other functions. For example, purchasing may see the need to minimise packaging, but this may conflict with the ideas of marketing staff.

4.5   Once an organisation takes an environmental stand, it is likely that such attitudes will begin to spread along its supply chain. A 'green' buyer will demand similar commitments from its suppliers, who in turn will pass on the philosophy to second-tier suppliers. A momentum towards better environmental standards is then underway. Of course, this reasoning does not begin – or end – in the purchasing department. On the contrary, it is often an overall corporate policy that leads to change and development. Even so, purchasing staff have an important role to play in giving effect to environmental objectives.

4.6   Ideally, an organisation's environmental policy may also spread along the supply chain in the downstream direction as well – towards consumers – so that they are educated to require green products.

Example: M & S's Plan A

4.7   Here is an example of such a policy in action. In 2007, Marks & Spencer launched a new CSR programme called 'Plan A' (so called because 'There is no Plan B'), built on five 'pillars', three of which are environmental.

- *Climate change:* 'We'll aim to make all our UK & Irish operations carbon neutral by 2012. We'll maximise our use of renewable energy and only use offsetting as a last resort. And we'll be helping our customers and suppliers to cut their carbon emissions too.'

- *Waste:* 'We'll significantly reduce the amount of packaging and carrier bags that we use, and find new ways to recycle materials. By 2012, we aim to ensure that none of our clothing or packaging needs to end up as landfill.'

- *Sustainable raw materials:* 'From fish to forests, our goal is to make sure our key raw materials come from the most sustainable sources available to us, protecting the environment and the world's natural resources for future generations.'

4.8   Each of these objectives is broken down into practical action steps (100 in all), involving M & S's own practices; mobilising and supporting suppliers to adopt green practices; and educating and supporting customers to do the same (eg with 'pledges' of participation).

4.9   This is regarded as a cutting edge example of an eco and ethics plan. If you want to know more, the outline of the plan (and progress reports) makes accessible reading: check out http://plana.marksandspencer.com.

Benefits of having a strong environmental policy

4.10   Why should an organisation go to the trouble and cost of developing and implementing an environmental policy? We discussed the arguments in Chapter 7 as part of our justification for corporate social responsibility in general, but to recap:

- A proactive and voluntary display of environmental responsibility may help to stave off more demanding and intrusive legislative requirements and regulation.

- Strong environmental policy goals give the organisation clarity and unity of direction for controls, performance measurement and improvement in this area.

- Strong environmental policy goals give guidance to supply chain partners and customers, gaining their support and compliance.

- A reputation for environmental responsibility may build an attractive brand which will be supported by green consumers; a point of differentiation from competitors for competitive advantage; and a source of customer loyalty.

- A reputation for environmental responsibility may also enhance the organisation's attractiveness as an employer (employer brand) and/or as a customer (for suppliers who are equally committed to green values) and/or as a promotional partner for influential pressure groups (whose members may support the organisation's products).

- Poor environmental performance, and lack of a policy for improvement, may subject the organisation to pressure group opposition, consumer boycott, penalties for non-compliance with legislation and regulation, or environmental (eg polluter pays) taxes.

- Environmental responsibility may be an issue of sustainability: maintaining the resources and markets the organisation itself will require to keep doing business in the future. Squandering resources and alienating communities is counterproductive: 'shooting oneself in the foot'.

5 The contribution of purchasing to 'green' business

5.1 Areas of environmental concern in which purchasing staff have a role to play are summarised by Saunders (*Strategic Purchasing & Supply Chain Management):* Table 9.1.

Table 9.1: *Environmental concerns relevant to purchasing staff*

• Recycling and reusing of materials and waste products (which may require new reverse logistics processes to recover products from consumers)
• Safe disposal of waste products that cannot be recycled
• Supplier selection policies (and tender criteria) to support firms that conform to environmental standards eg with regard to air, water and noise pollution
• Supplier and product selection policies that reflect concern for conservation and renewal of resources
• Safe and animal-friendly testing of products and materials
• Concern for noise, spray, dirt, vibration and congestion in the planning and operation of transportation

5.2 We might also add the following points.

- Acting as the interface between suppliers and product development/design departments, to encourage knowledge-sharing, research and innovation for 'greener' product specifications and collaborative processes

- Gathering and presenting information to demonstrate long-term cost reduction, risk management and sustainability benefits of green policies, in order to secure stakeholder buy-in

- Monitoring, managing and perhaps supporting the environmental performance of suppliers on an ongoing basis, to ensure their compliance with the buyer's environmental standards (in order to minimise the reputational risk of being associated with an environmental disaster)

- Sourcing materials and services for environmental protection and reclamation (eg re-planting trees or cleaning up polluted areas).

5.3 A commitment to avoid buying materials that are harmful to the environment, if alternative products are available at a similar price and quality, should not be controversial. However, *cost* has been a significant obstacle in the past: 'green' products have typically been more expensive than their 'non-green' equivalents. The last few years have seen radical changes in this situation, and in many cases actual savings are to be made in choosing a green or sustainable alternative. (Energy efficient light-bulbs, for example, may cost more upfront but the savings will come further down the line in reduced energy use.)

5.4 If no cost-effective or value-adding green alternatives are available, the buyer may need to work with suppliers to reduce the damaging environmental impact of a product – or with production colleagues to see if the product can be replaced.

5.5   As you will note from our comments above, co-operation with suppliers is an important feature of green procurement. This fits in neatly with modern ideas on supply chain relationships.

5.6   Finally, a timely reminder: human beings are also part of the natural environment! It is comparatively easy to identify and avoid buying products which are dangerous in themselves. It may be less easy to identify harmless products that are, nevertheless, manufactured using processes which place workers in danger, or dangerous to dispose of, or dangerous if stored or used incorrectly by consumers. Attention will have to be given to the whole lifecycle of the product.

Chapter summary

Key learning points include the following.

- Factors in the natural environment can have an important impact on purchasers: the weather; availability of natural resources; the impact of commercial operations on the natural environment; specific issues of concern, such as deforestation and pollution.

- The natural environment includes factors such as: resource depletion and management; preservation of biodiversity; minimisation of environmental damage (pollution, erosion, waste, deforestation etc); the supply risks posed by weather; climate change – and the influence of legislation, international agreements (such as Kyoto), government policy, pressure groups and public concern on any or all of these issues.

- Increasingly, organisations have faced pressure to exhibit environmental responsibility. This pressure has come from legislation and regulation, the activities of dedicated pressure groups, and the growing concern for environmental issues among consumers.

- The result of this, for many organisations, has been the development of specific environmental policies. There are clear commercial advantages in this process, but such policies are unlikely to succeed unless they are supported by commitment from top management.

- Purchasing can contribute to 'green' operations in a number of areas of materials specification, supplier selection and management, and advocating and justifying change.

Self-test questions

Numbers in brackets refer to paragraphs where you can check your answers

1 List three major factors in the natural environment. (1.2)

2 Give one example each of a local, national and international environmental issue. (1.3–1.5)

3 What can purchasing do to minimise supply risk due to weather? (1.14)

4 Explain the importance of (a) 'biodiversity' and (b) rainforests? (2.3, 2.7)

5 List three ways in which industrial activity may damage the environment. (2.6–2.10)

6 Give three examples of measures to reduce a company's carbon footprint. (2.17)

7 Explain the purpose and achievements of the Kyoto Protocol. (2.18–2.20)

8 Identify five approaches to environmental regulation. (3.3)

9 Explain the benefits of having a strong environmental policy. (4.10)

10 List seven ways in which purchasing can contribute to environment-friendly operations. (5.1, 5.2)

Further reading

From your 'Essential Reading' list, you might look at Worthington & Britton (*The Business Environment:* 5th edition, 2006, FT Prentice Hall), Part 3: FIRMS.

- *Chapter 6: The Resource Context.* Focus on the short section titled 'Natural resources'.

- *Chapter 8: Corporate Responsibility and the Environment*

It is worth reading through this material, since it covers a core part of the syllabus, and offers further detail and different examples to our coverage. Again, the mini-case and case study features offer useful illustrations which may be used in the exam.

We have also suggested a number of websites throughout this chapter: do check them out if you have time. Some of them (such as the carbon footprint calculator) are positively *fun* – as well as very educational!

CHAPTER 10

Legal Factors

Learning objectives and indicative content

2.6   Explain and provide examples of the main sources of English law.

- Statute law
- Common law
- European law

Chapter headings

1   The sources of English law

2   Contracts and the sale of goods

3   Employment law

4   Equal opportunity

5   Health and safety at work

6   Other law affecting purchasing

Introduction

In this chapter, we cover the last group of PESTLE factors (although the syllabus orders them as PESTEL): the legal environment.

The syllabus focuses on the three main types or sources of English law: statute law (legislation), common law (general principles established in decided legal cases), and European law. It is difficult to separate these three aspects, in discussing the legal environment, because each impacts on the others, in ways that we will describe.

The syllabus also asks you to 'provide examples' – so it is difficult to know whether particular UK legislation, common law principles or European directives could be examined, and if so, which ones. We have chosen to give you a broad survey of the areas of legislation specified in the earlier (2007) version of the syllabus, just in case these topics still attract the attention of the examiner.

1   The sources of English law

The legal environment

1.1   In any community, some agreed rules are essential in order to be able to control the actions of individual citizens for the common good. 'Law' broadly consists of a body of rules laid down by society to regulate human conduct: if these rules are broken, penalties and other sanctions can be imposed. The broader 'legal environment' consists of legislation, regulations, voluntary codes of practice and other requirements formulated by governments (by enacting legislation or statutes), courts (by setting legal 'precedents' or case law) and regulatory bodies.

1.2 This is a particularly important area for environmental monitoring and purchasing management for the following reasons.

- The organisation's response is not 'optional' or left to managerial discretion: compliance is required and enforced by various sanctions and penalties
- The requirements are constantly changing, as courts and tribunals define them through their decisions, and as legislators and regulatory bodies issue new provisions and amendments
- Purchasing involves a number of activities which are the specific focus of law and regulation, including the development and fulfilment of contracts, the employment of staff, and competitive tendering (in the public sector).

1.3 The English legal system incorporates the law of England and Wales. (Within the UK both Scotland and Northern Ireland have different legal systems.) The law within this system derives from four main sources: common law, equity, statute law and EC law.

Common law

1.4 **Common law** is the body of law which applies throughout England and Wales. It consists of statements and interpretations of fundamental legal principles, declared by judges in the course of deciding legal disputes. Here are some examples.

- The common law principles of the **law of contract**: when contracts are validly formed; how contract terms should be interpreted; when contracts are terminated; and what remedies are available for breach of contract. (These aspects are discussed in Section 2 of this chapter.)
- The common law principles of **tort**: the set of rules that determine when one person must pay compensation to another for harm wrongfully caused, as a result of intentional malice, recklessness or negligence.

1.5 **Equity** is a similar collection of discretionary rules and remedies devised by judges to decide cases on the basis of fairness and good conscience, where the complexity and rigidity of common law might work against fair solutions.

1.6 Common law and equity can be grouped under the heading of **case law** (eg if an exam question specifies 'three sources of English law'). The doctrine of 'judicial precedent' states that when judges determine principles when making their decisions in legal disputes, those principles should be followed in similar later cases, where possible. Case law is the body of legal principles established by judges' decisions in previous cases. Legal cases are usually referred to in the form *Smith v Jones (200X)*: you will come across this formula often if you continue your studies into legal aspects of purchasing!

Statute law

1.7 **Statute law** is the law created by Parliament and its delegated bodies. Statutes (Acts of Parliament and other statutory instruments) are binding on everyone in the jurisdiction and supersede both the common law and equity. Examples include the Sex Discrimination Act 1975, the Freedom of Information Act 2000 and the Sale of Goods Act 1979. We will discuss a number of statutes relevant to purchasing in this chapter, since statute law is designed both:

- to codify and enforce the principles of *common law* on a particular matter; and
- to implement *European law* within the English legal system.

European Community (EC) law

1.8 The Council of the EU and the European Commission exercise law-making powers that have an effect on the English legal system.

- *Regulations* are designed to achieve uniformity of law among the member states, and have direct force of law in all member states without the need for further legislation – even if legislation conflicts with them.

- *Directives* are designed to harmonise the law of member states, in the form of instructions to member states to bring their laws into line with EU law by a certain date. Examples include the Working Time Directive (implemented by the UK Working Time Regulations) and the Public Procurement Directive (implemented by the UK Public Contracts Regulations). There are EU directives on areas such as equal opportunity; privacy and data protection; environmental issues (including the Waste Electrical and Electronic Directive, or WEEE); intellectual property protection; and several other areas.

1.9 Perhaps the most obvious EU directive with an impact on purchasing is the Public Procurement Directive, and we will focus on this in our coverage. EU directives cannot be separated from statute law in many cases, because the EU law has been (or is being) implemented into UK statute: we will indicate where this is the case.

Civil and criminal law

1.10 It may also be helpful to know that there are two basic branches of English law.

- **Civil law** assists 'individuals' (including groups or organisations) to recover property or enforce obligations owed to them: eg in disputes over breach of contract, defamation, unfair dismissal or discrimination.

- **Criminal law** assists the State to suppress crime and to punish (and, theoretically, reform) offenders: eg cases of theft or murder.

1.11 In civil law, one individual, group or organisation (the claimant) sues another (the defendant) to obtain redress for some wrong, usually in the form of financial compensation (called damages). The court hearing, initially held in a county court or high court, is called litigation. Most legal cases relevant to purchasing will be of the civil type (eg disputes over contracts), although some breaches may constitute a criminal offence (eg fraud).

1.12 We will now look at some of the main areas of law affecting purchasing.

2 Contracts and the sale of goods

Common law in regard to contracts

2.1 A contract is an agreement between two or more parties which is intended to be enforceable by law. This is different from a social agreement, such as arranging to borrow a friend's car for the day: if one party does not carry out his part, he will not be taken to court by the other to enforce the agreement. However, if the agreement is between two commercial enterprises, it is *presumed* that there is an intention to 'enter into legal relations': that is, to use the law to enforce the agreement if necessary.

2.2 The law of contract is concerned with four basic questions.

- *Is there a contract in existence?* The answer depends on the presence of five essential elements: agreement (offer and acceptance); consideration (some form of exchange, eg payment of money for goods); intention to create legal relations; legal capacity to enter into contracts (eg being over 18 and of sound mind); and correct form (since *some* types of contract, such as share transfers and hire purchase agreements, must be in writing – although in general, oral agreements are binding if the other elements are present).

- *Is the agreement one which the law should recognise and enforce?* Some contracts will be wholly or partly unenforceable, because of undermining factors such as a mistake or misunderstanding in what a party thought he was agreeing to.

- *When do the obligations of the parties come to an end?* The most common method of terminating a contract is when both parties have performed their contractual obligations (ie the terms of the contract) to mutual satisfaction. However, contracts can also be terminated by the failure of one or both parties to meet an essential term of the contract ('breach of contract').

- *What remedies are available for the injured party if the other party fails to meet his obligations?* Possibilities include monetary compensation for the loss suffered (damages), or a court order for the other party to carry out his obligations.

2.3 In general, parties are at liberty (in common law) to make their own bargains, and the courts will not interfere with the terms they agree upon, as long as both parties clearly understand what those terms are. This is called 'freedom of contract'. (One reason why purchasers need to be careful when drawing up contracts: once you make an agreement, you will generally have to abide by it, unless you are released from your obligations by the other party.) However, there are some exceptions, which illustrate the intervening role of *statute law*.

- If the parties have failed to express all the terms of their agreement, the court may *imply* terms based on their presumed intentions. Sometimes, such terms are automatically implied by statute. For example, the Sale of Goods Act 1979 (discussed below) lays down implied terms which will apply to *all* contracts for the sale of goods – unless specifically excluded in the contract.

- Some types of contract clause may be *disallowed*, because they conflict with statutory principles. For example, clauses limiting the liability of a party (exclusion clauses) may not be allowable under the Unfair Contract Terms Act 1977, so that firms cannot disclaim responsibility for loss or harm suffered by consumers as a result of negligence, say.

The effect of case law

2.4 There is a vast body of case law defining how common law principles and statutory provisions are to be interpreted and enforced in different circumstances – and you will need to get to grips with key cases at later stages of your CIPS studies. To give you a flavour of how it works, however, we will cite a couple of examples.

2.5 We have said that for a valid contract to exist, there must be offer and acceptance. But what happens if an offer is withdrawn? In the case *Routledge v Grant (1828)*, Grant offered to buy Routledge's horse and gave him six weeks to decide whether or not to accept. Before the six weeks had elapsed Grant withdrew his offer. The dispute went to court, and the judge decided that since Routledge had not yet accepted, there was no contract, and Grant was entitled to withdraw the offer, even though he had stated that he would keep it open for a given time. Judges in similar cases will now adopt this precedent as a legal principle.

2.6 The Sale of Goods Act 1979 provides that if a buyer enters into a purchase contract based on a description of the goods, it is *implied* that the goods delivered should correspond to the description. If they don't, the buyer can reject the goods and refuse to pay for them. But how close to the description do the goods have to be? In *Moore v Landauer (1927),* there was a contract for tinned fruit to be delivered packed in cases of 30 tins each. The correct number of tins was delivered – but in cases varying between 24 and 30 tins each. The judge held that the contract was not satisfactorily performed, even though the market value of the goods was the same: the buyer could reject all goods and not pay. Again, judges in similar cases now adopt this precedent as a legal principle, where possible.

The effect of statute: the Sale of Goods Act 1979

2.7 The Sale of Goods Act 1979 draws together the legal principles relating to contracts in which a seller transfers property (ownership or title) in goods to a buyer in exchange for a money consideration (price). Sections 12–15 of the Act set out terms which are *implied* into all contracts of sale of goods, principally to protect the buyer: Table 10.1.

Table 10.1: *The Sale of Goods Act*

S	Implied term	Explanation
12	**Title (ownership)**	The seller is deemed to undertake that he has a right to sell the goods (eg as a true owner of the goods, or without infringing a patent)
13	**Sale by description**	In a sale by description, the offer includes some description (specification and quantity of goods, time of delivery etc), on which the buyer relies in accepting. The seller is deemed to undertake that the goods will correspond with the description.
14	**Satisfactory quality and fitness for purpose**	Where the seller supplies goods in the course of a business, he is deemed to undertake that:
		The goods will be of satisfactory quality: working and in good condition (so far as may be reasonably expected) and free from 'minor defects' (except defects drawn to the buyer's attention or which pre-contract inspection ought to have revealed)
		The goods will be fit for the purpose for which they are commonly used, or for any specific purpose made known by the buyer to the seller
15	**Sale by sample**	Sale by sample occurs when the contract gives the buyer an opportunity to examine a small part of goods to be bought, as typical of the whole (bulk). The seller is deemed to undertake that:
		The bulk will correspond with the sample in quality
		The buyer will have a reasonable opportunity to compare the bulk with the sample
		The goods will be free from defects which would not be apparent from reasonable examination of the sample

2.8   Other sections of the Act deal with the following issues.

- •   When ownership passes from a seller to a buyer (sections 16–20)

- •   The seller's duty to deliver, and the buyer's duty to accept and pay for, goods in various circumstances (sections 27–31)

- •   Remedies for breach of contract by the buyer, eg if the seller isn't paid (sections 41–50)

- •   Remedies for breach of contract by the seller, eg if goods aren't delivered as contracted (sections 51–54).

You shouldn't be required to know the detailed provisions at this stage of your studies: you will encounter them when you progress to Level 4.

2.9   Similar provisions, in the context of the supply of goods and services, are contained in the *Supply of Goods and Services Act 1982.*

2.10   You should be able to come up with examples for each scenario envisaged by the implied terms covered in Table 10.1. For example, a supermarket might purchase products described as 'biodegradable plastic bags' from a supplier, but subsequently find out that the bags are not biodegradable. An office manager might buy wallpaper based on samples, only to find that the batch of paper delivered is of a slightly different colour – and the supplier hadn't warned that this could happen.

2.11   If an important implied term (called a 'condition') is not met, the buyer is entitled to insist that it *is* met or, more usually, to receive *damages*: monetary compensation for any economic loss resulting from the breach of contract. The purpose of damages is to restore the injured party to the same position he would be in if the contract had been performed. If a seller fails to deliver goods, for example, damages should equal the difference between the agreed contract price and the cost of obtaining the goods elsewhere.

Another relevant statute: the Unfair Contract Terms Act 1977

2.12   The express terms of a contract may attempt to exclude or limit terms implied by statute: a supplier stating, for example, that he accepts no responsibility for goods not conforming to description or sample.

2.13   However, this might unfairly limit the rights of buyers, and is therefore subject to certain restrictions. The *Unfair Contract Terms Act 1977* restricts the exclusion or limitation of liability for:

- •   Negligence (s 2): that is, the breach of a contract obligation (express or implied) to take reasonable care *or* the breach of the common law duty to take reasonable care.

- •   Breach of implied terms (s 3). Liability for breach cannot be excluded at all in consumer contracts (to protect consumer interests), and only in other contracts if the exclusion is 'reasonable' and fair, taking into account other factors: whether the buyer was forced by circumstances or inducements to agree to the term, whether the buyer understood (or ought to have understood) the implications of the term and so on.

3   *Employment law*

Introduction

3.1   Employment law deals with the legal relationship between employers and employees, securing both individual employment rights (such as protection from unfair dismissal or the right to equal pay and opportunity) and collective employment rights (such as the right to trade union membership and consultation). Some aspects of the employment relationship are governed by the *common law* on contracts: principles such as duty of care (in relation to health and safety) and so on. However, this is an area that has been increasingly addressed by *statute law*. Key areas of employment legislation are summarised in Table 10.2.

Table 10.2: *Key UK employment legislation*

Field	Purpose	Key statutes
Equal opportunity	Outlawing various forms of discrimination	Race Relations Act 1968 Sex Discrimination Act 1975/86 Disability Discrimination Act 2005
Pay	Providing minimum wages and employee information on pay Providing equal pay for men and women doing 'work of equal value'	Wages Act 1986 National Minimum Wage (Enforcement) Act 2003 Equal Pay Act 1970
Heath and safety at work	Providing healthy and safe working environments and practices	Factories Act 1961 Health & Safety at Work Act 1974
Employment protection	Protecting employees from unfair dismissal and redundancy	Employment Protection Act 1975 Employment Acts (1980s, 2002) Employment Rights Act 1996 Employment Relations Acts 1999/2004
Industrial relations	Regulating the rights and activities of trade unions and employee representatives	Industrial Relations Act 1971 Trade Union and Labour Relations Acts 1974/1976/1992 Trade Union Reform and Employment Rights Act 1993
Flexible working	Giving working parents the right to request flexible working arrangements Protecting the rights of fixed-term (short-contract) employees	Employment Act 2002

3.2   We have included the key statutes mainly to highlight (a) the amount of legislation employers have to take into account and (b) the frequency with which legislation changes!

3.3   You might also note a strong relationship between the political environment and the legal environment. Much of the legislation of the 1980s was passed by Conservative governments seeking to remove constraints on business, reducing individual protections and limiting trade union power. Legislation by the subsequent Labour governments has gone the other way, supporting trade union activity and individual rights (the minimum wage; family friendly working hours; minority rights and so on). Meanwhile, the influence of *EU law* has increased steadily.

Outsourcing and redundancies

3.4   Most employment protection law should be considered beyond the scope of the syllabus, but the provisions relating to the protection of employee rights in the event of outsourcing is arguably more directly relevant to purchasing.

3.5   The *Transfer of Undertakings (Protection of Employment) Regulations 2006* – known as TUPE – are intended to preserve employees' rights when an undertaking, or part of one, is transferred to a new employer *or* when a 'service provision change' takes place (eg where services are outsourced or re-assigned from one contractor to another).

3.6   The criteria for employees to be protected under the Act are as follows.

    •   That there is a transfer of economic activity
    •   That the employees were employed immediately before the transfer
    •   That they were employed in the activity being transferred and
    •   That their contracts would have been terminated by the transfer.

3.7   The act protects such employees in various ways.

    •   Employees employed when the business changes hands automatically become employees of the new employer, with the right to the same terms and conditions as set out in their original contract of employment and any negotiated agreements (unless variations are justified on economic, technical or organisational – ETO – grounds).

    •   Representatives of any employees affected by the transfer (eg their recognised trade unions) have the right to be informed and consulted about the timing, reasons and implementation of the transfer.

    •   If employees are dismissed because of the transfer, and the dismissal is deemed justified on ETO grounds, this is defined as redundancy: employees have other rights (eg to notice, redundancy pay and time off to look for other work) under various Employment Protection and Employment Rights Acts.

3.8   The legislation also protects the new employer, by placing a duty on the old employer to provide information about the transferring workforce: this is called 'employee liability information'.

3.9   From Table 10.2, you can see that this is part of a much broader body of employment rights and protection law. Dismissals, redundancies and trade union consultations are complex matters – and beyond the scope and depth of this syllabus. If in doubt, a purchasing officer would in any case consult the HR or legal department of the organisation before taking any action in regard to staff.

Other workplace legislation

3.10 We will now look in more detail at the legislation specifically mentioned in the 2007 syllabus, while we await confirmation as to what the examiner might consider appropriate 'examples' for you to provide (or for exam questions to focus on). This may seem like a bit of a 'pick and mix' approach, but again, it should serve to alert you to the sheer variety of areas in which requirements may affect purchasing managers; the frequency with which legislation changes; and the impact of long-term cultural and policy shifts on business practice.

4 Equal opportunity

The law on equal opportunity

4.1 'Equal opportunity' in an employment context means that everyone has a fair chance of getting a job, accessing training and benefits and competing for promotion, regardless of individual differences or minority status. It is, effectively, non-discrimination or anti-discrimination.

4.2 UK legislation outlaws discrimination in a number of key areas.

4.3 The **Sex Discrimination Act** 1975 (and subsequent amendments) prohibits certain types of discrimination in employment against women (and men) by reason of sex, marital status (eg if an employer believes that a single man will be able to devote more time to the job), and change of sex or gender reassignment. The Employment Equality (Sexual Orientation) Regulations 2003 also outlaw discrimination on the grounds of sexual orientation. Special provision is made under the **Equal Pay Act** 1970 (and 1984 amendment regulations implementing the European Equal Pay Directive), for women to have the right to claim equal pay and conditions for work of equal value to that of a man in the organisation.

4.4 The **Race Relations Act** 1976 (amended 1996, 2000 and 2003 – which gives you some idea of the need to keep up to date!) covers discrimination on grounds of colour, race, nationality, and ethnic or national origin. The Employment Equality Regulations 2003 also prohibit discrimination on the grounds of religion or belief.

4.5 The **Disability Discrimination Act** (1995, amended 2005) covers discrimination against disabled persons. In addition, the employer has a duty to make reasonable adjustments to working arrangements or to the physical features of premises where these constitute a disadvantage to a particular disabled employee.

4.6 The **Employment Equality (Age) Regulations** 2006 ban discrimination on the basis of age (old or young) in terms of recruitment, promotion, access to training and rights to claim unfair dismissal or receive redundancy payments. It also bans companies from setting compulsory retirement ages below 65 (unless this can be objectively justified), and introduces the right for employees to request working beyond retirement age (which must be considered by employers, although not necessarily granted).

4.7 There are three basic types of unlawful discrimination under the legislation.

- **Direct discrimination** is where one group is treated less favourably than another. Using age as an example, direct discrimination would include not providing medical insurance to employees aged 50 or older.

- **Indirect discrimination** is where an employer applies a provision, criterion or practice to all groups equally, but this has the *effect* of putting one group at a particular disadvantage, without justification. Examples might include: changing shift patterns to include early morning starts, as this would disadvantage women (who are usually responsible for child care).

- **Harassment** is defined as unwanted conduct (verbal or non-verbal) which violates a person's dignity, or creates an intimidating, hostile, degrading, humiliating or offensive environment for a person. Examples include: placing vital objects on a high shelf, where a disabled person cannot reach; derogatory comments about a woman's appearance; or racist jokes.

4.8 Since October 2007, it has been the responsibility of the new Commission for Equality and Human Rights (CEHR) to promote equality and tackle discrimination in the areas of sex, race, disability and age, religion/belief and sexual orientation. (Previously, separate commissions existed in each area.) Discussion is currently under way with a view to harmonising all the various legislation in this area within a single Equality Act. Keep an eye on the CIPS student website for updates as the discussion unfolds…

Equal opportunity in practice

4.9 In order to respond to the legislative provisions, organisations may have to pay particular attention to policies and practices for recruitment, selection and employee development. There is always a risk that a disappointed job applicant (or training applicant or promotion prospect) will attribute his lack of success to discrimination – especially if a given ethnic minority, sex or other group is already poorly represented in the organisation (or in management posts), or if policies on equal opportunity are not clear.

4.10 Here are some common compliance issues.

- Job advertising: employers should not imply or state any intention to discriminate, and should not place advertisements where minority groups will be disadvantaged in accessing them. This may rule out recruiting by word-of-mouth, using the existing workforce, for example, if it is not broadly representative.

- Selection interviewing: employers should not ask non-work-related questions of some groups but not others (eg only asking women about plans to start a family)

- Employers should formulate selection tests which are performance-relevant and do not favour particular groups.

4.11 In addition to compliance, some employers have begun to address the underlying problems of equal opportunities, appointing equal opportunities managers to put issues higher on the corporate agenda, and providing awareness training for managers to encourage a 'managing diversity' orientation.

4.12 Flexible policies on working hours and career shapes facilitate employment for women with family responsibilities. Under the Employment Act 2002, mothers and fathers of children under six years of age (or disabled children under 18) have the right to request a flexible working arrangement. Career-break and return-to-work schemes may also be developed, including training for women returners. The provision of workplace childcare facilities is another possibility.

4.13 The accelerated development of women and minority groups can be achieved by 'fast-tracking' school leavers and graduates, and posting managerial vacancies internally, giving more opportunities for movement up the ladder for groups currently at lower levels of the organisation. Positive action may be taken to train disadvantaged groups, or to encourage them to undertake training in which they have previously been under-represented (the one area in which positive discrimination is permissible). The Metropolitan Police in London, for example, piloted a scheme of pre-training training (in literacy, numeracy, current affairs, physical fitness and interpersonal skills) to prepare applicants from minority groups to compete on an equal basis for training places.

4.14 In the area of disability, similar positive action policies may include the provision of wheelchair access, braille or large-print versions of documentation, text-based telecommunications systems and so on. You might like to think what adjustments might be made to facilitate work (and avoid harassment) for members of religious groups in the workplace.

5 Health and safety at work

Statute law on health and safety at work

5.1 In 1972, the Royal Commission on Safety and Health at Work reported that unnecessarily large numbers of days were being lost each year through industrial accidents, injuries and diseases, because of the 'attitudes, capabilities and performance of people and the efficiency of the organisational systems within which they work'. Since then, major legislation has been brought into effect in the UK, most notably:

- The Health and Safety at Work Act 1974
- Various regulations implementing EU directives on health and safety, including:

  - The Manual Handling Operations Regulations 1992
  - The Workplace (Health, Safety and Welfare) Regulations 1992
  - The Provision and Use of Work Equipment Regulations 1992
  - The Health and Safety (Display Screen Equipment) Regulations 1992
  - The Control of Substances Hazardous to Health Regulations 1994
  - The Fire Precautions (Workplace) Regulations 1997
  - The Management of Health and Safety at Work Regulations 1999

5.2 We will not be able to cover their provisions in detail here. Just be aware that the framework for HR policy in the area of health and safety is extensive, detailed – and constantly changing!

Why focus on health and safety?

5.3 Wider attention has been given to health and safety issues, with consumer demand for social responsibility by organisations (underpinned by the competitive need to attract and retain quality labour) and widespread exposure of abuses through disasters such as the Bhopal chemical plant and Piper Alpha oil rig explosions. So why should organisations plan for health and safety at work?

- To protect people from pain and suffering (obviously, we hope)
- To comply with relevant legal/policy standards

- To minimise the costs of accidents and ill-health (including disruption to work, sickness benefits, repairs, replacement staff, legal claims etc)

- To enhance their ability to attract and retain quality staff

- To avoid negative PR and enhance their employer brand and reputation for corporate social responsibility.

The Health and Safety at Work Act 1974

5.4   Under the Health and Safety at Work Act 1974, every employer has a general duty to ensure the health, safety and welfare at work of all employees, so far as is reasonably practicable. Various aspects of this responsibility, included in the Act and subsequent Regulations, are set out in Table 10.3.

5.5   Other regulations cover particular safety and health risks in the workplace, and in particular industries: guidelines are available from the Health and Safety Executive. You may also encounter particular measures (eg in relation to manual handling and dangerous substances) in your studies for subjects such as *Purchasing Operations*.

Health and safety in practice

5.6   Apart from obviously dangerous equipment in offices and factories, there are many hazards to be found in the modern working environment, and the prevention of accidents is a major aspect of health and safety policy: advising and warning about safe and unsafe procedures, activities and attitudes.

5.7   The Workplace (Health, Safety and Welfare) Regulations 1992 provide for a range of safety measures. Machinery and equipment should be properly maintained, and fenced if dangerous. Floors, passages and stairs must be properly constructed and maintained. Falls and falling objects should be prevented by erecting effective physical safeguards. Windows, doors and gates should be made of safe materials and fitted with any necessary safety devices. Fire precautions should be taken; appropriate firefighting equipment and clearly marked (and unobstructed) escape routes should be provided. Fire alarms should be installed and regularly tested.

5.8   Various high-risk activities may be the subject of policies and procedures.

- The lifting of heavy objects ('manual handling operations')

- The safe handling, storage and disposal of hazardous chemicals and other substances. Hazards may include poisoning, burning and allergies, as a result of exposure – and also serious conditions (such as cancers and lung diseases) linked to substances such as lead, radioactive materials, asbestos and coal dust.

- The use of computer workstations. Attention may be given to the ergonomic design of workstations (to avoid strain), the control of monitor flicker/glare, and user practices (poor posture, insufficient work breaks and so on).

5.9   Many organisations now also have policies relating to personal health and safety: alcohol and drug abuse (affecting work behaviour); non-smoking workplaces; and positive health promotion (eg stress management, health checks, education, fitness programmes and so on).

5.10   Gather some examples from your own organisation's health and safety policies and practices, for use as illustrations in the exam (if required).

Table 10.3 *Employer and employee duties in managing health and safety*

Employee's duties	Employer's duties
HEALTH AND SAFETY AT WORK ACT 1974	
• To take reasonable care of himself and others affected by his acts or omissions at work • To cooperate with the employer in carrying out his duties (including enforcing safety rules) • Not to interfere intentionally or recklessly with any machinery or equipment provided in the interests of health and safety	• To provide safe systems (work practices) • To provide a safe and healthy work environment (well-lit, warm, ventilated, hygienic and so on) • To maintain all plant and equipment to a necessary standard of safety • To support safe working practices with information, instruction, training and supervision • To consult with safety representatives appointed by a recognised trade union • To appoint a safety committee to monitor safety policy if asked to do so • To communicate safety policy and measures to all staff, clearly and in writing
THE MANAGEMENT OF HEALTH AND SAFETY AT WORK REGULATIONS 1992	
• To inform the employer of any situation which may pose a danger	• To carry out risk assessment, generally in writing, of all work hazards, on a continuous basis • To introduce controls to reduce risks • To assess the risks to anyone else affected by their work activities • To share hazard and risk information with other employers, including those on adjoining premises, other site occupiers and all subcontractors entering the premises • To initiate or revise safety policies in the light of the above • To identify employees who are especially at risk (other legislation cites pregnant women, young workers, shift-workers and part-time workers) • To provide fresh and appropriate training in safety matters • To provide information to employees (including temporary workers) about health and safety • To employ competent safety and health advisers.
HEALTH AND SAFETY (CONSULTATION WITH EMPLOYEES) REGULATIONS 1996	
	• To consult all employees on health and safety matters (such as the planning of health and safety training, changes in equipment or procedures which may substantially affect health and safety at work, or the health and safety consequences of introducing new technology)

6 *Other law affecting purchasing*

6.1 The syllabus doesn't specifically mention the following areas, but it is worth being aware of them as potential examples of statutory influences on purchasing activity.

Competition law

6.2 Governments generally want to support free competition (as discussed in Chapter 3), as this is arguably in the best interests of consumers and the economy as a whole.

6.3 The Competition Act 1998 is one measure designed to protect competition in the UK.

- Chapter 1 of the Act prohibits agreements and concerted practices (eg cartels and price fixing agreements) which prevent, restrict or distort competition, or are intended to do so, and which may affect trade within the UK. An agreement is unlikely to be considered as having an appreciable effect on the market unless the combined market share of the parties involved is greater than 25%.

- Chapter 2 prohibits abuse by one or more undertakings of a dominant position in a market, which may affect trade within the UK. A 'dominant position' is largely determined by the extent to which the undertaking(s) can act independently of competitors: this would usually mean a market share of more than 40%. 'Abuse' includes conduct such as imposing unfair purchase or selling prices; limiting production or technical development to the detriment of consumers; or applying different trading conditions in such a way as to place certain parties at a competitive disadvantage.

6.4 The Fair Trading Act 1973 also gives wide powers to the Office of Fair Trading to investigate and regulate monopolies and mergers, while the Enterprise Act 2002 makes it a criminal offence to operate a price cartel.

6.5 Similar measures, in regard to competition within the EU, are provided by the Treaty of Rome Articles 81 (anti-competitive agreements) and 82 (abuse of a monopoly position).

Public sector procurement

6.6 The *Public Contracts Regulations 2006* (as discussed briefly in Chapter 2) apply to public authorities and utilities for purchases above a given financial threshold. The purposes of the regulations, and the **EU public procurement directives** on which they were based, are: to open up the choice of potential suppliers to public sector bodies, reducing costs through competition; to open up new, non-discriminatory and genuinely competitive markets for suppliers; to facilitate the free movement of goods and services within the EU; and to ensure that public sector bodies award contracts efficiently and without discrimination.

6.7 The regulations set out rules for the following areas.

- The open advertising of tenders through the EU

- Contract award procedures and time limits for the issuing and receipt of tenders

- Award criteria. In general, buyers are obliged to award the contract on the basis of the lowest quoted price, or on the basis of the 'economically most advantageous' tender (in which case they must explain by what non-price criteria they mean to assess 'economic advantage'). This is designed to ensure that criteria are clearly defined, non-discriminatory – and not leaving room for manipulative post-tender negotiation.

- Suppliers' right to feedback: unsuccessful bidders have the right to a debrief, at their request, in order to understand why they did not win the contract.

6.8   You will study these requirements in detail later in your CIPS studies.

The key point being…

6.9   Of course, there are many other relevant areas, such as corporate governance, fraud prevention, protection of intellectual property (copyrights and patents), data protection and freedom of information. But we have to stop somewhere! The key point is: purchasing professionals really need to monitor the legal environment…

Chapter summary

Key learning points include the following.

- The legal environment consists of statute law (Acts of Parliament and other statutory instruments); European Community law; and case law, including principles of common law and equity determined as a result of legal precedent.

- Contract law is concerned with legally binding agreements between two or more parties. The Sale of Goods Act 1979 draws together the legal principles relating to contracts, including implied terms as to title, sale by description, satisfactory quality and fitness for purpose, and sale by sample.

- Employment law deals with the legal relationship between employers and employees, both individually and collectively. Legislation in this area covers issues such as employment protection (including TUPE transfers).

- Equal opportunity law is designed to outlaw discrimination in areas such as sex and sexual orientation, race, disabilities, age and religion.

- Legislation on health and safety at work is designed to ensure that employees are protected as far as possible from accidents and ill health arising from the working environment. Duties are imposed on both employers and employees to achieve this.

- Other areas of legislation relevant to purchasers include: competition law; and the particular regulations applying to purchasing in the public sector.

Self-test questions

Numbers in brackets refer to paragraphs where you can check your answers

1   Explain the importance of the legal environment. (1.2)

2   List the sources of English law. (1.3)

3   What are the five essential elements of a contract? (2.2)

4   What implied terms are provided by sections 12–15 of the Sale of Goods Act 1979? (2.7)

5   What remedies are available to a buyer if an important implied term of a sales contract is not met? (2.11)

6   When do the TUPE Regulations 2006 apply, and what are an employer's duties under the Regulations? (3.5–3.7)

7   In what areas is discrimination outlawed under UK equal opportunities legislation? (4.3–4.6)

8   What are an employee's duties under the Health and Safety at Work Act? (Table 10.3)

9   Identify three potential causes of accidents in the workplace, and suggest what might be done to minimise the risk. (5.7, 5.8)

10   What are the purposes of the EU public sector procurement directives? (6.6)

Further reading

From your 'Essential Reading' list, you might look at Worthington & Britton (*The Business Environment:* 5th edition, 2006, FT Prentice Hall), Part 3: FIRMS.

•   *Chapter 7: The Legal Environment*

It is worth reading through this material, since it covers a core part of the syllabus, and offers further detail and different examples to our coverage. Again, the mini-case and case study features offer useful illustrations which may be used in the exam.

CHAPTER 11

Financial Concepts

Learning objectives and indicative content

3.1   Identify the legal obligations relating to financial reporting of public, private and not-for-profit organisations

   •   UK legal requirement to put accounts into the public domain

Chapter headings

1   Why should purchasers understand finance?

2   The regulatory framework

3   Sources of finance

4   Costs and cost analysis

Introduction

In this chapter and the next we look at the financial tools available for analysing the external purchasing environment.

We begin by examining why a purchasing professional should be interested in financial analysis. We also introduce the concepts of financial accounting and management accounting.

From there, we consider the regulatory framework – the rules and regulations governing the preparation of accounting statements.

Next we look at the sources of finance for public and private sector organisations.

Finally we look at different methods of analysing costs.

1   Why should purchasers understand finance?

Why prepare accounts?

1.1   Business accounting is the process of recording financial transactions carried out by an organisation, and summarising them so as to present a financial picture. This process is undertaken by all manner of organisations: commercial businesses (from the very small 'sole trader' to large companies), charities, government authorities and so on.

1.2   Recording each transaction carried out by a large business is a costly and time-consuming task. For example, imagine the number of sales transactions carried out in a single day – never mind a month or year – in a large department store. Or the number of purchase invoices received from the suppliers of a large business such as British Telecom.

1.3 In order to prepare accounts, all of these transactions must be captured and recorded. Moreover, they must be totalled and summarised at regular intervals (perhaps monthly or annually) so as to display an overall picture. This is an activity of some complexity, and is usually handled by people with professional qualifications in accounting.

1.4 It is clear that a great deal of effort, time and money is required in order to carry out the accounting function. However, there are many reasons why all this effort is justified. One reason why organisations prepare accounts is that they are obliged to do so by external regulations. For example, in the case of limited companies there is a legal requirement to prepare accounts annually and to file a copy of those accounts with an official called the Registrar of Companies. The content of the accounts, and the nature of the accounting records supporting the annual figures, is very closely regulated by the Companies Acts. Failure to satisfy the regulations may give rise to fines and in some cases to more serious punishments.

1.5 Another reason for preparing accounts is to satisfy the tax authorities. The tax payable by an organisation depends on how much profit (if any) it earns. To compute the organisation's profit, and hence its tax liability, we need to prepare accounts.

1.6 Other people too have an interest in the accounts of an organisation. For example, a supplier may wish to ensure that a potential customer is financially stable before he agrees to supply goods on credit terms. A bank may equally be interested, especially if the organisation has requested a loan or overdraft. A buyer will want to know that a potential supplier is financially stable before relying on him for security of supply.

1.7 Finally, the owners of a business will wish to ensure that the business is being managed profitably. This is not a great problem in a small business, where the owner is probably the manager as well. But it is a problem in large companies where there may be many owners ('shareholders') who take no part in running the business. Instead they appoint managers ('directors') to act on their behalf. The annual accounts provide evidence of how well the directors have carried out this function.

Financial accounting and management accounting

1.8 To satisfy the information needs of all these interested parties, organisations prepare accounts at least annually and make them publicly available. Typically – as in the case of limited companies already mentioned – these accounts are prepared in a defined format and include details specified by the relevant legislation. The process of doing this is referred to as *financial accounting*.

1.9 This is all fine so far as it goes. However, the annual published accounts do not satisfy all possible information needs. In particular, they are quite inadequate as a basis for managers in the organisation to take financial decisions.

1.10 There are three main reasons for this.

- The financial accounts are published only infrequently – usually every twelve months. In a fast-moving business environment managers cannot afford to wait that long for financial information.
- The financial accounts are historical in outlook. They record how well the business has done over the period just ended. They do not include estimated information relating to the future, and yet that is precisely what managers need when making decisions.

- The form and content of the accounts are dictated by external regulations. They may not be at all in the form that best suits the information needs of managers.

1.11 For these reasons, the management of an organisation will prepare all kinds of accounting statements and analyses in addition to those required by law. They do so to help in taking decisions and running the business.

1.12 This process is called, appropriately, *management accounting*. Management accounts are not regulated by law: managers can prepare whatever accounting statements they think best, with whatever information content they think they need, and at whatever intervals they choose. Such accounts are internal documents, and there is no requirement to make them publicly available. Indeed, commercial secrecy ensures that management accounts are mostly kept confidential.

The buyer's interest in financial analysis

1.13 How does all this relate to purchasing professionals? The simple answer is that buyers need accounting information for similar reasons to those we have already discussed.

- Buyers wish to deal with suppliers who are financially stable. A supplier in financial difficulties cannot be counted on to provide a secure and continuous stream of supply.

- Buyers should seek to obtain prices which are fair to their own organisations and also fair to their suppliers. Often negotiation will revolve around the costs that a supplier must incur in providing the goods required.

- Buyers are involved with accounts even within their own organisations. For example, most organisations will establish budgets for each operational function, including the purchasing department.

2   The regulatory framework

Legal rules

2.1 We have already mentioned that the preparation of financial accounts is to some extent regulated. (Note that we are discussing *financial accounts*; regulation does not apply to *management accounts*, which managers are free to prepare in any way that they find helpful to themselves.)

2.2 The two main sources of regulation are legal rules embodied in Acts of Parliament and best practice embodied in statements issued by the accountancy profession.

2.3 The main source of legal rules affects the accounts of limited companies. Although other types of organisation are also affected by legal regulations on accounts, it is limited companies that you will mainly be dealing with in your professional work and in the examination.

2.4 The accounts of limited companies in the UK are very tightly regulated by the Companies Acts, and in particular by the Companies Act 1985, as amended by the Companies Act 1989. Requirements of these Acts include the following.

- The information must be prepared following certain accounting principles.
- Prescribed formats must be adopted for the profit and loss account and balance sheet.

- Detailed disclosures of information are required. For example, amounts paid to directors as remuneration must be disclosed.

- The financial statements must show a 'true and fair view'.

- The accounts must be audited by a qualified expert from outside the company. (This requirement does not apply to very small companies.)

Financial reporting and accounting standards

2.5 The requirements of the Companies Acts (and similar legislation relating to the accounts of other organisations) of course have legal force. However, in addition to these legal rules, the accountancy profession has laid down guidelines for the preparation of accounts. The main aim has been to standardise practice in areas where a variety of accounting methods would be theoretically possible.

2.6 From the early 1970s the Accounting Standards Committee (representing the principal accountancy bodies in the UK and Ireland) issued a series of *statements of standard accounting practice* (SSAPs) which have covered many important areas. SSAPs are applicable to all financial accounts intended to give a true and fair view, and in particular to the accounts of limited companies.

2.7 In 1990 the functions of the Accounting Standards Committee were taken over by the Accounting Standards Board, which was given wider powers than the Committee. The ASB issues *Financial Reporting Standards* (FRSs) which will eventually replace the SSAPs. Both FRSs and SSAPs are often referred to as 'accounting standards'.

2.8 Although accounting standards do not have legal force, the members of most UK accountancy bodies are required to comply with them, which means in practice that most limited companies will invariably follow the rules. If a company insists on preparing accounts that violate the rules of an accounting standard, then the independent auditor (if there is one) will comment on the fact in his report (unless the matter is a trivial one).

International accounting standards and convergence

2.9 In the paragraphs above we have described the accounting standards published in the UK by the ASC and the ASB. These have applied to UK companies, whereas other countries have established their own accounting standards. In many cases, this has led to a lack of comparability between accounts prepared under different regulatory regimes. For those involved in purchasing (and particularly international purchasing), this gives rise to problems.

- It is difficult to make valid comparisons between different companies on the basis of their published accounts.

- Anyone wishing to interpret accounts must become familiar with different sets of rules and regulations.

2.10 In an age when international trading is increasingly the norm, standard setters have tried to address these problems. An international body – the International Accounting Standards Board, or IASB – publishes standards that are meant to apply worldwide. These *international financial reporting standards* (IFRSs) are now the subject of EU regulation, under which European companies will be required to prepare their financial accounts in line with the IFRSs rather than their own national standards.

2.11 This is the culmination of a long period during which regulators have sought *convergence* between the standards applying in different countries. The new regime took effect in 2005, with limited exceptions stretching to 2007. At the same time, US regulators have introduced stringent new requirements (the Sarbanes-Oxley Act) on financial and accounting disclosure which have a major impact on any company with US links.

2.12 The differences between IFRSs and national standards are in many cases very significant. Adoption of the new uniform regime will therefore lead to major changes in the way that European companies report their financial transactions. The advantage of this is the increasing ability to perform valid comparisons between the accounts of companies in different countries. However, this should not be exaggerated: in particular, US companies will continue to operate under a different accounting regime. Efforts to reduce the differences between US standards and IFRSs will continue in the hope of extending the convergence already achieved in Europe.

Putting information into the public domain

2.13 We have already seen that companies are required to make their annual financial accounts open to public inspection by lodging them with the Registrar of Companies. And in Chapter 2 we saw that companies are also required to file a Memorandum of Association and Articles of Association with the same government official. Other information too must be made public in the same way.

- Each year a company must file an annual return, giving details of shareholders, directors, company secretary and any share transfers that have taken place during the year.

- A form must be submitted any time that a director or company secretary steps down from office or is appointed to office.

2.14 If you are asked for a list of documents that companies are required to make public the ones mentioned in the previous paragraph should suffice. If – as in the November 2008 exam – you are asked for a list of such documents specifically related to publication of accounts you could mention balance sheet, profit and loss account, cashflow statement, five year summary and chairman's report. As we will see in the next chapter, these statements are typically included in the annual accounts. The examiner's comment on the November 2008 question suggests that he regards these as separate documents, even though they are all filed together in the form of a single document.

3 *Sources of finance*

3.1 All organisations must generate funds to finance their operations. In this section we look at the possible sources of finance, beginning with funds of a short-term nature and moving on to longer-term finance.

Bank overdraft

3.2 Perhaps the most obvious way of solving a short-term cashflow problem is to request overdraft facilities from the bank. This procedure is familiar to most people in a personal context, and is even more common for businesses. In simple terms, the bank allows the business to spend more cash than it actually owns, the bank itself making up the shortfall. Of course, the bank requires something in return for this service. It will usually charge an arrangement fee for setting up the overdraft facility. And it will charge interest on the amount of cash that has been 'overspent' by the business.

3.3   The rates of interest charged on bank overdrafts are high, and there are other disadvantages of this form of finance. One such disadvantage is that the bank will take a close interest in the affairs of the business until the overdraft is repaid. Before even granting the overdraft the bank will probably insist that the business produces forecasts and budgets. And the bank manager will require these forecasts to be monitored and updated regularly.

3.4   Another disadvantage is that an overdraft is, technically, repayable on demand. In other words, the bank can withdraw the facility at a moment's notice and require the business to pay the amount owing. In practice, some businesses manage to run an overdraft for very long periods, but this possibility of immediate withdrawal always remains present.

3.5   A bank overdraft is an example of *debt finance* or simply *debt*. Other examples of debt finance include loans and debentures (which we discuss later). An important feature of debt finance is that any interest payable by the organisation is an allowable deduction from taxable profits. This means that by paying interest we at least reduce our tax bill. The effect is that debt capital is cheaper than the quoted interest rate might suggest.

Credit from suppliers

3.6   Another short-term method of improving cashflow is simply not to pay bills. If a business purchases goods and services on credit terms there will usually be an agreed date by which payment must be made. However, many businesses fail to comply with this agreement: they pay their bills late. Their suppliers have in effect – probably unwillingly – 'loaned' goods to the business, which is equivalent to loaning money.

3.7   This is likely to have a very bad effect on relations with the suppliers concerned. Although suppliers are of course anxious to win business, their patience will wear thin if they find that payment is regularly late. They can take serious action against the business in default: for example, they can sue for payment of the debt, and they can refuse to supply goods on credit in the future. All of this can have a damaging effect on the business and is not recommended.

3.8   However, there are cases where suppliers agree to this situation. In other words, the business might persuade a supplier to agree on payment several months after the goods or services change hands. The supplier might agree to this if he sees a chance of doing good business into the future by showing patience now.

Controlling working capital

3.9   In most businesses, working capital consists of stock, debtors and cash/bank balances, less any creditors. We have already seen how a short-term cashflow advantage can be obtained by withholding payment from creditors. Careful management of stock and debtors can provide a similar boost.

3.10   A company that holds stock must obviously pay for it. The more stock that is held, the more money is tied up. A company that holds high levels of stock will be that much less liquid in terms of cash balances, because some cash must have been expended in order to purchase or to manufacture the stock. High stock levels may be necessary to cope with customer demand, but holding more stock than necessary is a waste of cash resources. For this reason, a company should monitor its stock levels carefully and not hold more stock than it needs.

3.11 A similar pattern applies to debtors. Companies may need to offer credit terms to their customers in order to attract business. But until the customers pay up, cash resources are lower than they might be. A business should have in place efficient procedures for chasing debtors. An unduly high level of debtor balances suggests inefficient working capital management, which can lead to cash shortages.

Factoring and invoice discounting

3.12 These are methods of addressing the point made above about debtors. Suppose a company has high levels of debtor balances because its customers are slow to pay. One remedy might be to install efficient debt collection procedures, but an alternative solution is to hand the problem over to someone else: a specialist finance company.

3.13 Installing and maintaining debt collection systems may be difficult, and in any event business circumstances may make it difficult to insist on prompt payment. For example, in an industry where long credit periods are the norm, a business which refuses to grant extended credit may find it difficult to attract customers.

3.14 The basic problem is that a business wants cash immediately on selling its products, whereas commercial considerations may require the business to grant credit to its customers. Ways have been found to overcome this problem. In particular, financial institutions (such as banks) offer services such as invoice discounting and factoring. In essence, the business receives cash from the bank and in return transfers to the bank the right to receive cash owed by its debtors. Naturally, the bank charges a fee for this service.

Sale of assets

3.15 Another way of raising funds is to sell off unwanted assets. For example, a company that has experienced a downturn in trade may find itself with factory premises surplus to requirements. Or a company may want to focus on certain core activities and divest itself of peripheral activities.

3.16 Naturally, this kind of occurrence will be infrequent. But the amounts of cash involved could well be large and businesses should be alert to the possibility of selling assets no longer required. If the long-term strategy of the business suggests that there will be no further need of such assets, then disposal is a sensible move in order to realise cash.

Sale and leaseback

3.17 Rather than simply selling off surplus assets, a company may enter into a sale and leaseback agreement. A fixed asset, often a freehold property such as office premises, is sold to a leasing company and then immediately leased back. The advantage to the business is that it can continue to occupy the premises (paying rent to the leasing company) while at the same time raising cash from the sale.

3.18 The disadvantage to the business is that it will have an ongoing commitment to make regular payments to the leasing company, under the terms of the lease agreement. Furthermore, the business will forgo any potential future gain in the value of the premises. At the end of the lease agreement the business will need to renew the lease or find alternative premises.

Ordinary share capital

3.19 When a business's cashflow problems are short-term in nature, then short-term solutions are adequate. But managers must also look to the long term. They must ensure that adequate finance is available to permit investment and development of the business. Addressing these long-term needs by means of short-term finance is poor management strategy. Long-term finance must be found instead.

3.20 The simplest form of long-term finance is the capital provided by the owner(s) of a business. Normally, initial capital will have been injected into the business at its commencement. Further sums may be invested in the business at later stages by the owner(s).

3.21 A limited company may be owned by numerous individuals, each claiming a share in the profits and assets of the business. For that reason they are called *shareholders* of the company, and the company is said to be funded by share capital. Shareholders do not necessarily play any part in the running of a business, though in small companies the shareholders and the managers of the business may happen to be the same people.

3.22 By opening up the business to large numbers of shareholders, the original owners can potentially find far more capital than would be available from their own resources. The price they pay for this is that they are no longer the sole owners of the business: the assets and profits of the business are now owned by the shareholders in agreed proportions that depend on the amount that each shareholder has invested. The reward expected by shareholders is the receipt of dividends (a 'division' of the profits). Dividends are not tax-deductible. This contrasts with debt finance, where interest payable *does* attract tax relief.

Retained profits

3.23 When a business makes profits the value of its assets increases. The owner(s) may decide to withdraw the extra assets (usually in the form of cash) and spend it on personal living expenses. However, the owner(s) may instead decide to leave the money in the business. Any profits earned by the business and not withdrawn by the owner(s) are called *retained profits*.

3.24 In practice, a business owner needs cash to fund his personal living expenses, and so some of the business profits will invariably be withdrawn for this purpose. However, if he is keen for the business to grow and expand he will certainly aim to retain at least some of the profit within the business. (The phrase 'ploughing profits back into the business' is sometimes used to describe this.)

3.25 Although profits may be retained within the business they belong to the owner(s) and may at some stage be withdrawn. Usually, though, they remain in the business for the long term.

3.26 The advantage of this form of capital is that, in effect, it is 'free'. The retained profits belong to the owners (usually the ordinary shareholders in a limited company), and provided that the owners do not actually need to withdraw the money it can simply remain in the business at no cost.

Loan capital

3.27   A business may finance its long-term development by taking out a loan with a bank or other financial institution, to be repaid over a long period of time. This can be an effective way to meet large one-off expenditure (such as the purchase of a capital asset), or generally to provide a basis for long-term growth.

3.28   The terms on which the loan is agreed will vary from one case to another. The lender will take account of various factors, such as:

*   the purpose of the loan

*   the financial forecasts supporting the application

*   the financial strength of the applicant

*   the nature and value of any security for the loan (in which case it would be a loan backed by a mortgage)

*   the riskiness of the venture.

3.29   On the basis of this assessment the bank will decide the terms, if any, on which it is prepared to lend. A key factor in the decision will be the existence of security for the loan. If the business has assets which can be mortgaged to the bank in the event of the loan not being repaid the bank will be much more inclined to do business. If there are no assets valuable enough to cover the loan the proposition becomes much more risky, and less attractive, for a lender.

3.30   If a loan is granted, the borrower will be required to pay interest on the amount owing, usually at a risk-adjusted variable rate related to the base rate. When the base rate is low, interest payments will be comparatively low. The borrower will also be required to repay the loan according to agreed terms, whether the loan is secured by a mortgage or charge, or unsecured. This may mean a single repayment when the term of the loan has expired. Or there may be a schedule of repayment by instalments over the period of the loan.

Debentures

3.31   Another form of loan finance is a debenture. This is a loan taken out by a company and secured either on its fixed assets (a fixed charge) or on its current assets (a floating charge). Interest is payable at defined intervals, and the principal sum must be repaid on or before a specified date. Both forms of repayment are a major commitment; the firm must have the cash available to repay the capital and pay interest according to the agreed terms, otherwise it is in default. This would have significant consequences, including the possible sale of mortgaged or charged assets.

3.32   Interest on bank loans and debentures is an allowable deduction from a company's taxable profits, so although the interest has to be paid, at least a reduction in the tax bill will partly compensate.

Leasing and hire purchase

3.33   A frequent reason for seeking long-term finance is to purchase long-term assets. Leasing and hire purchase offer ways of achieving this without making a single lump-sum payment at the time of the purchase. Instead, the buyer in effect pays instalments over an agreed period, and legal ownership of the asset does not pass until the payments are complete. (On some variations of these schemes, ownership never passes to the buyer.)

3.34 There are many advantages to using lease or HP finance. The problem of finding a large amount of cash at once is avoided, while the agreement can also include repair and maintenance costs or even frequent options to replace the asset with a more up-to-date model. At all times the amount of expenditure in relation to the asset is known, as the regular payments are fixed, and the payments are (usually) completely tax-deductible.

3.35 However, there can be disadvantages. In many cases the asset never becomes the property of the business, and the interest rate charged can be quite high. If the entity wants to continue using the asset the payments must continue, so a lease agreement is as long-term a commitment as a loan, usually without the benefit of ownership.

Finance for the public sector

3.36 In the UK, as we saw in earlier chapters, the primary funding for public sector services – schools, hospitals, the police force, the armed forces etc – comes from local government and central government. Each of these must raise funds to finance the projects and services for which it is responsible, and must account to the public for their use of funds.

3.37 By far the largest element of public finance is raised from taxation. The central government raises tax revenue from both direct taxes (income tax, national insurance contributions, corporation tax, capital gains tax, etc) and indirect taxes (such as VAT and excise duties). Local governments raise revenue from council tax charged on householders and business rates charged on non-domestic occupiers of premises. Local governments also receive revenue from central government.

Government investment products and securities

3.38 Another way in which central government raises funds is by the issue of investment products. Members of the public are encouraged to purchase such investments. In most cases the investors are entitled to recover the sums they have paid according to the terms of the investment concerned. In the meantime, the government usually pays them interest for the use of the funds.

3.39 Many types of investment product are offered to the public under the banner of National Savings. For example, it is possible to pay money into a National Savings investment account which, just like a bank account, offers interest on the sum invested. Also under this heading, investors can purchase Premium Bonds. No interest is paid on Premium Bonds, but investors can hope to win cash prizes in a monthly draw.

3.40 National Savings provides the government with a source of long-term finance via products sold to the general public such as ISAs, National Savings certificates and Children's Bonds. Another source of long-term finance is government stocks and securities. For historical reasons, these are often called 'gilt-edged securities' or simply gilts. Gilts are effectively a form of borrowing by the government, and are the most secure form of investment for the people lending the money to the government, since they are guaranteed repayment.

3.41 An advantage for the government of using gilts is that the government retains control (which it might not do if the funds came from outside investors). A drawback arises if the availability of government funds leads to slack budgetary procedures; this could in turn lead to overspending.

Public–private partnerships

3.42 So far we have looked at direct financing of services by government. However, this does not exhaust the possibilities. An alternative that has been explored in recent years is the financing of public services by a mixture of private and public enterprise, often involving some kind of partnership between a public sector organisation and a commercial private sector firm. These arrangements were discussed in Chapter 5.

4 Costs and cost analysis

Fixed and variable costs

4.1 Cost behaviour is the way in which costs of output are affected by fluctuations in the level of activity. The level of activity usually refers to the volume of production in a period, though in some contexts another level of activity might be relevant (eg the level of sales).

4.2 To illustrate how total costs are affected as production levels vary we use a simple example. Suppose that when 10,000 widgets are produced in a period, a company's total production costs are £9,000, but when 20,000 units are produced total costs are £13,000.

4.3 Total costs have increased by less than 50 per cent although production has doubled. This is because some costs will not rise in relation to the increase in volume. For example, the production costs may include simply the following two elements.

- Rental of a fully equipped factory, £5,000 for the period
- Raw materials, £0.40 per widget

4.4 When production doubles, the raw materials cost increases from £4,000 to £8,000. We say that this is a **variable cost**. However, the factory rental is unchanged at £5,000. We say that this is a **fixed cost**.

4.5 The way in which costs behave as production output changes is a key element in the way prices are set by suppliers. Consider Figure 11.1.

4.6 The first diagram shows the behaviour of a fixed cost. An example already cited is that of factory rental: no matter how much production output is achieved the rental remains fixed at £5,000 (per year, say).

4.7 As with many cost behaviour patterns, this assumption might break down in extreme cases. For example, if production expanded massively it might be necessary to rent a second factory and rental payments would double. But the descriptions given here are adequate for most purposes, and certainly within what is called a 'relevant range of activity'.

Figure 11.1 *Patterns of cost behaviour*

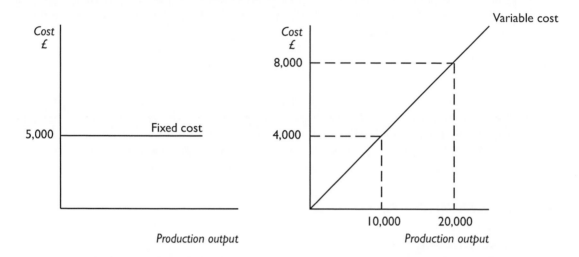

4.8 The second diagram shows a cost which is strictly variable with the level of production. An example might be the cost of raw materials used in producing widgets. If no widgets are produced, the cost of raw materials is zero; if 10,000 are produced, the total cost of raw materials is £4,000 (ie 40p per unit). And this unit cost remains constant: if production expands to 20,000 units, the total cost of raw materials rises to £8,000. Again, we are simplifying slightly by ignoring the possibility of bulk discounts.

Contribution

4.9 Contribution is the selling price less the variable cost of sales. Suppose that the unit selling price of a widget is £1. We know that its variable costs are £0.40. Its contribution is therefore £0.60. What this means is that every time we sell a widget we earn a contribution of £0.60 towards covering fixed costs and making a profit.

- If we sell only a few widgets, our total contribution will not be sufficient to cover fixed costs and we will make a loss.
- If we sell very many widgets our total contribution will more than cover fixed costs and we will make a profit.
- Somewhere in between there is a sales level such that our total contribution exactly matches our fixed costs. In this case we make neither profit nor loss: we break even.

How to account for fixed costs?

4.10 It is fairly easy to account for variable costs. When we work out the cost of a unit of output we include all the variable costs in the total, because it is clear that an additional unit produced leads to an additional variable cost incurred. This in turn means that the variable cost is clearly part of the cost of that additional unit.

4.11 Accounting for fixed costs is different. If our factory rental is £5,000 for the period, and we produce 10,000 units in that period, we might say that the fixed cost is £0.50 per unit. What then happens in the next period if we produce 20,000 units? Do we say that the true fixed cost per unit is £0.25, or do we say that the additional 10,000 units are 'free' as far as fixed costs are concerned, or what?

4.12 The problem of accounting for fixed costs has given rise to essentially two different approaches. These are called marginal costing and absorption costing.

Marginal costing and absorption costing

4.13 Marginal cost is the cost of one unit of product or service which would be avoided if that unit were not produced or provided. Under a system of marginal costing only variable costs are included in the cost of a unit of production. Fixed costs for a period are deducted in total from total contribution; we do not try to split them up so as to share them among cost units.

4.14 This contrasts with absorption costing. In absorption costing we attempt to allocate a 'fair' proportion of fixed costs to each unit of output (as with the rental cost above where we calculated a fixed cost per unit of £0.50).

Traditional absorption costing

4.15 As explained already, the distinction between marginal costing and absorption costing lies in the treatment of fixed overhead costs.

- Under marginal costing, we regard the cost of a product as comprising the *variable* production costs only. We do not attempt to attribute any proportion of *fixed* overheads to individual products. Instead, we deal with such costs as a single total to be deducted at the bottom of our profit and loss account.

- Under absorption costing, we attempt to absorb a 'fair' proportion of the total fixed overheads into each unit we produce. The problem under this method is deciding on a fair method of absorption.

4.16 Historically, the approach to this problem has been to calculate the amount of some measurable resource consumed in a production period, and to relate the fixed overhead to this resource. For example, we might expect to require 5,000 labour hours in our assembly department during a particular production period, while expected fixed overhead costs during the same period are £4,000. We might therefore conclude that for every labour hour worked we clock up £0.80 of fixed overhead. We would refer to an *overhead absorption rate* of £0.80 per direct labour hour.

4.17 Pursuing this logic, for any unit of product that is worked on in the assembly department for 30 minutes an amount of £0.40 of fixed overhead is incurred. This would be added to the direct costs incurred by the same unit of product, and by this means we could eventually determine all the costs – both variable and fixed – relating to that unit of product.

4.18 In practice there are three main problems associated with this kind of calculation. We need to estimate total overheads to be incurred, select a measurement unit (eg labour hours, machine hours) and estimate the level of activity (eg the total labour hours that will be worked). Any one of these three could lead to a discrepancy: we could wrongly estimate the total overheads; we could select an inappropriate measurement unit; or we could wrongly estimate the level of activity. The result is that total product costs calculated under absorption costing may well be incorrect.

4.19 In earlier decades this was less important than it has recently become. In a factory 30 years ago most costs were direct variable costs of labour and materials. As a proportion of the total, fixed overheads did not amount to much, and any inaccuracy in attributing such costs to product units would not make too much difference to the overall picture.

4.20 This situation has now changed dramatically. In most industries there has been a tremendous spurt of automation. Production workforces have been reduced, leading to a decrease in direct labour costs. In their place, expensive machines have been installed, leading to a massive increase in overhead costs. Inaccuracies in attributing such costs to product units can completely distort the information provided by the costing system.

Activity based costing

4.21 In response to this, new methods of absorption costing have been developed. One such method that has enjoyed great success in recent years is *activity based costing* (ABC).

4.22 This is not a textbook on costing techniques, and it would not be appropriate to delve too deeply into ABC. However, you may be expected to know some general principles, and these are explained below.

4.23 As the name suggests, ABC is based on the idea that activities cause costs. The first stage of setting up an ABC system is therefore to identify all the activities undertaken by the enterprise, and to analyse them into those that add value (primary activities) and those that are non-value-adding (secondary activities). All primary activities have some form of output that can be identified, and this is called the activity's *cost driver*. For example, an activity is the placing of a purchase order; the cost driver of the activity is the purchase order itself.

4.24 Another key feature of ABC is the use of *cost pools*. For example, all of the overhead costs associated with running the purchasing department might be regarded as a cost pool. The overheads associated with setting up machines for a production run might be another cost pool. When an overhead cost is incurred, it must be attributed to one or other of the available cost pools.

4.25 Once we have built up a cost pool (eg we have a total for the fixed overhead costs incurred in running the purchasing department) and determined an appropriate cost driver (eg the raising of a purchase order) we can calculate a *cost driver rate*. This is simply the total overheads divided by the number of purchase orders. It is equivalent to the overhead absorption rate used in traditional absorption costing, but the method of calculating it is believed to lead to more accurate costing information.

4.26 Remember that all of this relates just to the fixed overheads included in total cost. If we are interested in the total cost of placing a purchase order we must also include the direct variable costs.

4.27 Absorption costing and activity-based costing can give very different results. Nowadays, activity based costing is widely believed to present a more accurate picture and is regarded as more useful information for managers.

Chapter summary

Key learning points include the following.

- Preparing accounts is a requirement for most organisations in order to satisfy the information needs of stakeholders.

- Managers need more information, and different information, than that provided in the financial accounts. For this reason they prepare management accounts as well.

- The form and content of financial accounts are regulated by statute and accounting standards.

- All organisations require funds to finance their operations. Sources of funds may be short-term or long-term in nature.

- Fixed costs are those that do not vary with the level of activity. Variable costs increase in total as activity levels increase.

- In a marginal costing system, the cost of a unit of output includes only its variable costs. In an absorption costing system, the cost will additionally include a 'fair' share of fixed costs.

- Traditional absorption costing may not give accurate product costs. New systems – such as activity based costing – have been devised to deal with this problem.

Self-test questions

Numbers in brackets refer to paragraphs where you can check your answers

1   Distinguish between shareholders and directors of a limited company. (1.7)

2   Why are the annual financial accounts inadequate for managers? (1.10)

3   List requirements of the Companies Acts in relation to financial accounts. (2.4)

4   What is meant by convergence in the context of accounting standards? (2.11)

5   Interest on debt finance is an allowable deduction from taxable profits. True or false? (3.5)

6   Explain what is meant by invoice discounting. (3.12–3.14)

7   What factors will a lender consider when deciding on the terms of a loan? (3.28)

8   What are the main sources of finance for the public sector? (3.36ff)

9   Sketch the behaviour of a fixed cost and a variable cost. (Figure 11.1)

10   In the context of activity based costing, what is a cost driver? (4.23)

CHAPTER 12

Financial Analysis

Learning objectives and indicative content

3.2   Use a range of basic ratio analysis tools for assessing financial data on suppliers and competitors active in the purchasing environment, including:

- Gross profit ratio
- Net profit ratio
- Current ratio
- Acid test ratio

Chapter headings

1   The balance sheet

2   The profit and loss account

3   Ratio analysis

4   Profitability ratios

5   Liquidity ratios

6   Efficiency ratios

Introduction

Buyers are interested in financial information because they need to draw conclusions which will form the basis for decisions in the future. Much of this information will be gathered by calculating accounting ratios and making comparisons with:

- the performance of the business in previous years
- the budgeted or planned performance in the current year
- the performance of similar businesses.

The ratios themselves do not tell users what to do, but they do help to point in the right direction. Ratios should, therefore, make it easier to make better decisions. In this chapter we begin by describing the main financial statements published by organisations. We then show how the main accounting ratios are calculated from these statements and interpreted.

In the version of the syllabus published in 2007 you were specifically required to understand the principles of balance sheets and profit and loss accounts. In the revised (2009) version of the syllabus this requirement has been removed. However, you are still required to be able to calculate and interpret accounting ratios, which you cannot possibly do unless you know your way around a balance sheet and profit and loss account. For this reason we retain our coverage of these financial statements in this edition of the Course Book.

1   *The balance sheet*

The balance sheet and the profit and loss account

1.1   There are two main financial accounting statements.

- The balance sheet is a statement of assets and liabilities at a point in time (the balance sheet date). We will look at balance sheets in this section of the chapter.

- The profit and loss account summarises income earned and expenditure incurred over a period of time. If income exceeds expenditure there is a profit for the accounting period; if expenditure exceeds income there is a loss. We will look at profit and loss accounts in Section 2 of this chapter.

1.2   Note that the balance sheet is a 'position statement'. It describes the financial position of the organisation at a point in time. On the other hand, the profit and loss account is a 'period statement', summarising what has happened over the accounting period.

An example of a balance sheet

1.3   We begin by giving an example of a balance sheet. X plc is a retailer, buying goods from wholesalers for resale to its own customers. The company's balance sheet is on the next page.

1.4   This illustration is not as difficult as it looks. First of all, consider what information the balance sheet conveys. Note that all figures in the balance sheet are expressed in millions of pounds (£m). And note also that the corresponding figures from the previous year are also displayed by way of comparison.

1.5   The assets used in the business amount to £204m. This consists of **fixed assets** (£130m) plus **current assets** (£74m).

1.6   As regards the listing of assets in the balance sheet, the least liquid assets are dealt with first, followed by the more liquid assets. The term **liquid assets** refers to cash and those assets which will soon be converted into cash.

- A fixed asset is any asset acquired for retention by an entity for the purpose of providing a service to the business, and not held for resale in the normal course of trading. It is not the intention of the company to convert these assets into cash by selling them, so these are the least liquid of the assets. This category might include land and buildings, office equipment etc.

- Stock comes next, in this case consisting of goods held for resale. When the goods are eventually sold, the business will receive cash in exchange.

- If the goods are not paid for immediately (ie if the company grants credit to its customers) there will be an asset described as debtors. This term describes amounts owing from customers which will eventually result in the receipt of cash.

- The bank balance refers to the balance on the company's current account at the bank.

X PLC – SUMMARISED BALANCE SHEETS AT 30 JUNE

	20X7		20X6	
	£m	£m	£m	£m
Fixed assets		130		139
Current assets				
Stock	42		49	
Debtors	29		23	
Bank	3		5	
	74		77	
Creditors: amounts falling due within one year				
Trade creditors	36		55	
Taxation	10		10	
	46		65	
Net current assets		28		12
Total assets less current liabilities		158		151
Creditors: amounts falling due after more than one year				
5% secured loan		40		40
		118		111
Capital and reserves				
Ordinary share capital (£1 shares)		35		35
Retained profits		83		76
		118		111

1.7 **Liabilities** are claims on the business by outsiders. **Current liabilities** are those liabilities which are payable within twelve months of the balance sheet date. Some businesses might also have **long-term liabilities**, ie liabilities payable more than one year after the balance sheet date. For example, a business might borrow money from its bank repayable over a period of five years. In the case of X plc, long-term liabilities comprise £40m in the form of a 5% secured loan, evidently repayable more than twelve months after the balance sheet date.

1.8 In the case of X plc, the current liabilities include trade creditors. These are amounts owing to suppliers in respect of goods and services previously received. Current liabilities also include amounts of taxation owed to the tax authorities.

1.9 Notice that the total of current liabilities is deducted from the total of current assets to arrive at a subtotal referred to as **net current assets**. It is important that current assets exceed current liabilities. This means that the company has sufficient liquid assets to pay its creditors. If current liabilities exceeded current assets (a position of **net current liabilities**) the company might be in difficulties: it would not have enough liquid assets to pay its bills.

1.10 The link between the various forms of current assets, and the current liabilities, is sometimes shown in diagrammatic form: see Figure 12.1.

Figure 12.1 *The working capital cycle*

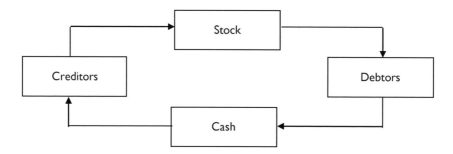

1.11 What this means is that stock is sold to customers, who then owe the company money (ie they are debtors of the company). Eventually they pay what they owe, so the debtors are converted into cash. Cash can be used to pay off creditors, who in turn supply more goods into stock. The cycle then repeats. A company's net total of stock, debtors and cash, less creditors, is often referred to as its **working capital**.

1.12 The top half of the balance sheet shows the net assets of the company, ie its total assets (fixed and current), less its liabilities. In this case the net assets total £118m. This is the balance sheet value of the business to the shareholders.

1.13 The shareholders provide the finance that pays for these net assets, ie they provide an investment of £118m. The way in which they provide this finance is shown in the bottom half of the balance sheet.

1.14 This indicates that the shareholders have injected £35m into the company as payment for the shares they own. The remaining finance (£83m) is provided by retained profits. This means the accumulated profits that the company has earned over the years and which have been ploughed back into the business. Of course, not all profits earned by the business are reinvested in this way. Some profits are paid out to the shareholders in the form of dividend. The balance sheet figure of retained profit measures only the profits that have been retained within the business.

1.15 In summary, the balance sheet shows the position of the business at one point in time – in this case at close of business on 30 June 20X7. At that point, the shareholders' investment in the company stands at £118m, and this investment is represented by the net assets listed in the top half of the balance sheet.

2 The profit and loss account

Calculating gross profit

2.1 We have stated that X plc has earned retained profits over the years of £83m. Some of this will have arisen in the current year, while the remainder will have been accumulated and brought forward from earlier years. The profit and loss account shows this in more detail: see next page.

2.2 Notice that, unlike the balance sheet, the profit and loss account summarises the trading activities of a business over a period of time, usually twelve months. Once again, all figures are expressed in millions of pounds (£m).

2.3 The figure of £209m for turnover (ie sales revenue) relates to goods sold during the year, whether or not the cash was actually received during the year.

2.4 Having arrived at a figure for sales, we must deduct the cost of buying the goods sold. In this case the cost of goods sold (often called the *cost of sales*) is £157m. This means that the gross profit – the difference between the sales value of the goods and their cost to X plc – amounts to £52m.

Calculating net profit

2.5 We have already calculated the company's gross profit as £52m. We next deduct the various expenses incurred by the business, in this case grouped under the two headings of administration expenses, and sales and distribution expenses. This leaves us with a figure for operating profit (or profit before interest and taxation). In this case, the figure is £27m.

2.6 It is usual to show loan interest as a separate deduction from operating profit. In this case, X plc has incurred loan interest for the year of £2m. In addition, a company has to pay tax (known as corporation tax) on its profits. In this case the tax bill amounts to £10m, leaving a profit after interest and tax of £15m. This amount can theoretically be paid out to the shareholders, since all expenses have now been covered.

2.7 In practice, the directors of the company have decided to retain some of the year's profit within the business, and the amount paid out to shareholders in the form of dividends is just £8m. That leaves £7m that can be ploughed back into the business just from the current year's profits. Added to retained profits from previous years (£76) that means the company has a total figure of retained profits at 30 June 20X7 of £83m. This ties in with the balance sheet presented earlier. The total amount of retained profits is sometimes known as the *profit and loss reserve*.

X PLC – SUMMARISED PROFIT AND LOSS ACCOUNT FOR THE YEAR ENDED 30 JUNE

| | 20X7 | | 20X6 | |
	£m	£m	£m	£m
Sales turnover		209		196
Cost of sales		157		151
Gross profit		52		45
Administration expenses	11		11	
Sales and distribution expenses	14		11	
		25		22
Operating profit (profit before interest and taxation)		27		23
Interest on 5% loan		2		2
Profit before taxation		25		21
Taxation		10		10
Profit after taxation		15		11
Dividends		8		7
Retained profit for the year		7		4
Retained profits brought forward		76		72
Retained profits carried forward		83		76

Other statements contained in the published accounts

2.8   The financial accounts published by a limited company are usually a bulky document. Apart from the balance sheet and profit and loss account they will typically contain a number of other statements relating to the company's financial position. Here are some examples.

- A **cashflow statement**. This is designed to identify the sources of cash coming into the business and the ways in which it has been spent. The statement ends by showing the overall cash surplus or deficit at the beginning of the year, during the year, and at the end of the year.

- A **five year summary**. This shows key accounting statistics and ratios from the current year and from the four previous years. The idea is to highlight trends in the company's financial performance.

- A **chairman's statement**. This is a high-level overview of key developments during the year, presented mostly in narrative format rather than tables of numbers.

3   *Ratio analysis*

Types of ratio

3.1   A buyer has access to the published financial information of suppliers and potential suppliers. He can use this to analyse financial standing and profitability. A key tool in this process is the analysis of accounting ratios. For example, a buyer may well be interested in the ratio of gross profit to sales turnover – this gives an indication of the profit margin being earned by his suppliers.

3.2   Ratios fall into several groups, the relevance of particular ratios depending on the purpose for which they are required. The groups we consider below are as follows.

- Profitability ratios – measuring the extent to which the business has traded profitably
- Liquidity ratios – measuring the extent to which the business has liquid assets sufficient to meet its short-term and long-term liabilities
- Efficiency ratios – measuring the efficiency with which the business is managing its assets

3.3   The number of ratios that can be calculated may easily lead to confusion. Try to organise your thoughts in this area by mentally dividing them into the categories above. This will help you to give structure to the solutions you write in the examination.

3.4   Remember above all that the ratios are not an end in themselves. The examiner is interested in your ability to draw conclusions from accounts. Calculating a ratio is not the same as drawing a conclusion, but it can point you towards a conclusion.

3.5   In practice, the small amount of detail disclosed in a set of published accounts places limits on the analysis that you can perform. However, in the present case we will assume that fairly full information is available. We will use the accounts of X plc displayed earlier in the chapter.

Possible drawbacks of ratio analysis

3.6   Ratios may highlight significant trends, but they do not in themselves provide reasons for the trends. To do this effectively, the interested party may need more information and a deeper insight into the affairs of the business. Often this may be difficult to obtain, because the amount of information available is limited unless the user is a manager within the organisation.

3.7   Another problem is the date at which the accounts are drawn up. Accurate information can only be obtained with any degree of certainty from up-to-date figures. Furthermore, seasonal variations in the particular trade should be taken into account.

3.8   Finally, accounting is not an exact science. Despite efforts by the accountancy profession to standardise accounting practice there is still room for a variety of methods in particular cases. This may affect the comparability of different accounts.

4   *Profitability ratios*

Gross profit percentage

4.1   Many ratios are expressed as a relation between a particular item and the level of sales turnover. Placing items in the context of turnover is a useful technique, because turnover tends to be a good guide to the overall size of a business.

4.2   The first ratio we look at is the gross profit percentage. This expresses the gross profit as a percentage of turnover. The ratio is in very common use, and is calculated as follows.

$$\frac{\text{Gross profit}}{\text{Sales}} \times 100$$

4.3   Using our example of X plc, the ratios for the two years are as follows.

20X7: $\dfrac{52}{209} \times 100 = 24.9\%$

20X6: $\dfrac{45}{196} \times 100 = 23.0\%$

4.4   What can be learned from these figures? Clearly, the gross profit percentage has improved but it is not known why. Nor is it obvious whether these figures are better or worse than those which would be expected in a similar type of business. Before coming to definite conclusions one would need further information.

4.5   For example, most businesses sell a wide range of products, usually with different gross profit percentages (or profit margins). It may be that in 20X7 the sales mix changed and that a larger proportion of items with a high profit percentage were sold, thus increasing the overall gross profit percentage of the business.

Net profit percentage

4.6   As the name suggests, this ratio relates the amount of net profit to the amount of sales turnover. It is calculated as

$$\frac{\text{Profit before taxation}}{\text{Sales}} \times 100$$

4.7   In the example of X plc, the ratios for the two years are as follows.

20X7: $\dfrac{25}{209} \times 100 = 12.0\%$

20X7: $\dfrac{21}{196} \times 100 = 10.7\%$

4.8 Note that when analysing the accounts of a limited company it is usual to use the profit before taxation in calculating this ratio, as we have done here. However, where a company has significant loans (**gearing**), it is often also useful to calculate this ratio based on operating profit, also known as 'profit before interest and tax'. For 20X6 this would be 23/196 = 11.7%; for 20X7 it would be 27/209 = 12.9%. The difference between these ratios calculated on these alternative bases reflects the effect of gearing on the company's profits.

4.9 What conclusions can be drawn from this apparent improvement between 20X6 and 20X7? Very few! Since operating profit equals gross profit less expenses, it would be useful to tabulate the various expenses for each of the two years, and to express them as a percentage of sales. These are known as **costs to sales ratios**. A suitable tabulation might be as follows.

	20X7		20X6	
	£m	%	£m	%
Sales	209	100.0	196	100.0
Cost of sales	157	75.1	151	77.0
Gross profit	52	24.9	45	23.0
Administration expenses	(11)	(5.3)	(11)	(5.6)
Sales and distribution expenses	(14)	(6.7)	(11)	(5.6)
Operating profit	27	12.9	23	11.7

4.10 Given a detailed trading and profit and loss account, the above type of summary could be very useful. Care must be taken in interpreting the results, particularly since sales (£) are used as the denominator. An increase in sales (£) could be due to a combination of price and quantity effects.

Return on capital employed (ROCE)

4.11 This is an important ratio as it relates profit to the capital invested in a business. Finance for a business is only available at a cost. For example, loan finance requires interest payments, and further finance from shareholders requires either the immediate payment of dividends or the expectation of higher dividends in the future. Therefore a business needs to maximise the profits per £ of capital employed.

4.12 Owing to its importance the ROCE is sometimes referred to as the **primary ratio**.

4.13 There are several ways of measuring ROCE, but the essential point is to relate the profit figure used to its capital base. A sensible formula is as follows.

$$\frac{\text{Profit before interest and tax (operating profit)}}{\text{Average capital employed}} \times 100$$

In the case of X plc for 20X7 we have:

$$\text{ROCE} = \frac{27}{(158+151)/2} \times 100 = 17.5\%$$

4.14 Average capital employed in this case includes long-term finance but does not include short-term finance such as bank overdrafts.

4.15 Note the following points about this ratio.

- The interest referred to is the interest payable on the long-term liabilities. Any interest on short-term liabilities, such as a bank overdraft, is deducted from the profit. This ensures that the numerator and the denominator are computed on a consistent basis.

- The denominator could alternatively be calculated as total assets less current liabilities (to give the same figure as above).

- The calculation is based on the average capital employed during the accounting period. This is computed by averaging the capital employed in the opening and closing balance sheets. In an exam question, if you are not given the capital figure for the previous year, just use the figure for the current year.

- Profit before interest and tax (or operating profit) may also be called **earnings before interest and tax** (abbreviated to EBIT).

5 *Liquidity ratios*

Short-term liquidity (or stability) ratios

5.1 In order to prosper, a business must ensure that it has plenty of cash and other liquid assets, as well as being profitable. This will enable the business to pay short-term liabilities which would otherwise endanger its survival.

5.2 The two main ratios relating to short-term liquidity are the **current ratio** (also called the **working capital ratio**) and the **quick ratio** (also called the **acid test ratio** or **liquidity ratio**). Both ratios measure the relationship between the organisation's liquid assets and its current liabilities. Liquid assets means cash plus other assets that can quickly be converted into cash, for example amounts owing from debtors or stocks of finished goods which can be sold.

5.3 The current ratio is calculated as follows.

$$\frac{\text{Current assets}}{\text{Current liabilities}}$$

5.4 In the case of X plc the ratio for 20X7 is calculated as:

$$\frac{74}{46} = 1.61$$

5.5 The quick ratio (or acid test ratio, or liquidity ratio) is calculated as follows.

$$\frac{\text{Current assets - stock}}{\text{Current liabilities}}$$

5.6 The point of this is to emphasise that stock, though a current asset, is the least liquid of such assets. Before stock can be converted to cash it must be sold. Even when it is sold the customer may enjoy credit terms, which means that cash may not be received for some time. The quick ratio therefore focuses only on current assets (mainly cash and debtors) that can be used quickly to pay off liabilities.

5.7   In the case of X plc, the ratio for 20X7 is calculated as:

$$\frac{32}{46} = 0.7$$

5.8   The current ratio and quick ratio in 20X6 were 1.2 and 0.43. Both of these ratios show a strengthening from 20X6 to 20X7. The extent of the change between the two years seems surprising and would require further investigation. It would also be useful to know how these ratios compare with those of a similar business, since typical ratios for supermarkets, say, are quite different from those for heavy engineering firms.

5.9   What can be said is that in 20X7 the current liabilities were well covered by current assets. Liabilities payable in the near future (creditors), however, are only partly covered by cash and debtors.

5.10   Conventional wisdom suggests that an ideal current ratio is 2 and an ideal quick ratio is 1. It is very tempting to draw definite conclusions from limited information or to say that the current ratio should be 2, or that the liquidity ratio should be 1. However, this is not very meaningful without taking into account the type of ratio expected in a similar business.

Medium- and long-term solvency ratios

5.11   Being able to pay immediate liabilities is important, but a business must also be concerned about liquidity into the long term. Our next group of ratios help to assess this.

5.12   **Gearing** is relevant to the long-term financial stability of a business. There are different ways of calculating a gearing ratio, but always the idea is to consider the relationship between:

•   Ordinary shareholders' funds (or equity interest); and
•   Fixed-return capital – in simple terms, debt capital.

5.13   Having to meet the demands of fixed-return investors may place strain on a company if times are lean. For this reason it is advisable to restrict the proportion of such finance in the total financial structure of the company. In other words, fixed-return capital must be balanced with a good measure of equity capital.

5.14   The gearing ratio measures the proportions in which these two different types of capital are present. A high gearing ratio means that there is a lot of fixed-return capital in the overall mix, and may be a danger signal in the long term. A low ratio means that the company is relying mainly on equity capital and should have less difficulty in weathering difficult years.

5.15   In this text we calculate the gearing ratio as follows.

$$\frac{\text{Fixed - return capital}}{\text{Ordinary share capital and reserves}}$$

5.16   In this formulation, the top line is the fixed-return capital and the bottom line is the equity capital. (Remember that reserves belong to the ordinary shareholders.) The total of ordinary share capital and reserves is sometimes referred to as the **net worth** of a company. For X plc in 20X7 the gearing calculation is as follows.

$$\frac{40}{118} \times 100 = 33.9\%$$

In 20X6, the figure was 36.0%.

6 *Efficiency ratios*

Asset turnover

6.1   Asset turnover is a measure of how well the assets of a business are being used to generate sales. A business that 'turns over' its assets frequently is getting good value from them, so high turnover ratios suggest efficient management, though there are dangers in taking this idea too far.

6.2   The meaning of asset turnover will be clearer after we have shown how to calculate the ratio. Looking at all of the operating assets within a business, asset turnover is calculated as follows.

$$\frac{Sales}{Operating\ assets} = times\ per\ year$$

6.3   Operating assets can be defined in various ways but the most sensible approach is to use the same amount as computed for capital employed. In the case of X plc this was £154.5m, the average of the 20X6 and 20X7 figures. Asset turnover for 20X7 is then computed as follows.

$$\frac{209}{154.5} = 1.35$$

6.4   The meaning of the ratio may now be clearer: for every £1 of assets employed in the business X plc is generating £1.35 in sales revenue. Clearly it is desirable to generate as much sales revenue as possible for as little investment as possible, so a higher ratio is preferable to a lower one. A ratio of 1.35 does not seem particularly impressive.

Elements of working capital

6.5   We do not need to include all of the operating assets of a business in calculating turnover ratios. Similar calculations are often applied to individual asset categories to focus attention on particular areas where asset management could be improved.

6.6   We will look at three areas in particular: stock, debtors and creditors. Note that stock plus debtors plus cash less creditors is often referred to as the working capital of a business, so that the ratios we are about to explain may be referred to as working capital ratios. Creditors of course are a liability, not an asset, so we will find that ratios relating to creditors are interpreted in a way that is a mirror image of the interpretation relating to stocks and debtors.

6.7   We begin with stock. Companies have to strike a balance between being able to satisfy customers' requirements out of stock (which suggests a need for high stock levels) and the cost of having too much capital tied up in stock (which suggests that stock levels should be kept low).

6.8   By calculating a **stock turnover ratio**, and monitoring it from one period to the next, managers can assess how successfully they are balancing these conflicting needs. The calculation is as follows.

$$\frac{\text{Cost of sales}}{\text{Average stock in period}} = \text{times per year}$$

6.9   Notice that in this case the relevant benchmark is cost of sales rather than sales. The bottom line of the fraction is average stock, but often it is convenient to use closing stock. In some cases (especially in exam questions) the closing figure may be the only one available. However, if you have access to the opening figure as well it is preferable to base the calculation on the average of opening and closing stock.

6.10   In the example of X plc the calculation for 20X7, based on average stock value, is as follows.

$$\frac{157}{\frac{1}{2}(49 + 42)} = 3.6 \text{ times per year}$$

6.11   An alternative calculation of the stock turnover ratio is to show the result in days. The calculation is as follows.

$$\frac{\text{Average stock during the accounting period}}{\text{Cost of sales}} \times 365 \text{ (ie length of accounting period)}$$

$$\frac{\frac{1}{2}(49 + 42)}{157} \times 365 = 106 \text{ days}$$

6.12   This means that the stock held by the company is on average sufficient to last for 106 days of business activity, which seems a high level of stock. However, much depends on the nature of the business. A jeweller would stock items that might well remain in stock for 106 days, or even much longer. At the other extreme, a fishmonger's stocks would obviously turn over much more quickly.

6.13   Next we look at debtors. Businesses which sell goods on credit terms specify a credit period. Failure to send out invoices on time or to follow up late payers will have an adverse effect on the cashflow of the business. In general, a business will try to ensure that customers take as few days credit as possible.

6.14   The **debt collection period** relates closing trade debts to the average daily credit sales. It indicates how many days' sales are represented by the debtors figure – in other words, how many days worth of sales we still have not been paid for.

6.15   For X plc in 20X7 we assume that all sales were credit sales and calculate as follows.

Credit sales per day $\dfrac{£209\text{m}}{365} = £573,000$

Closing trade debtors = £29m

Debt collection period $\dfrac{£29m}{£573,000}$ = 50.6 days

6.16 This indicates that customers pay for goods about 51 days after purchasing them. This should be compared with:

- the credit period actually offered by X plc. If the company usually offers 60 days credit, then collecting debts within 50 days on average is very efficient; on the other hand if the usual credit period offered is 30 days, then most customers appear to be taking more credit than they are entitled to

- the similar ratio for the previous year, to indicate whether matters are improving or worsening.

6.17 A quicker way to compute the debt collection period is to use the following formula.

$\dfrac{\text{Closing trade debtors}}{\text{Credit sales for the year}} \times 365$

6.18 Finally we perform a similar calculation for creditors (the **creditor payment period**). In this case we relate closing creditors to average daily credit purchases. In the case of X plc in 20X7 the calculation is as follows.

Credit purchases per day $\dfrac{£157m}{365}$ = £430,000

Closing trade creditors = £36m

Average period of credit
allowed by suppliers = 83.7 days

6.19 The quicker method of calculation is as follows.

$\dfrac{\text{Closing trade creditors}}{\text{Credit purchases for the year}} \times 365$

$\dfrac{36m}{157m} \times 365 = 83.7 \text{ days}$

6.20 Often, suppliers request payment within thirty days. X plc is taking nearly three months to pay for its supplies. Trade creditors are thus financing much of the working capital requirements of the business which is beneficial to the company.

6.21 However, there are three potential disadvantages of extending the credit period.

- Future supplies may be endangered.
- The possibility of discounts for prompt payment is lost.
- Suppliers may quote a higher price for the goods knowing the extended credit taken by the company.

ROCE revisited

6.22 In the light of our calculations on working capital ratios it is useful to take another look at the primary accounting ratio: return on capital employed. There are two factors that affect ROCE.

- Profitability of sales.
- Rate of asset utilisation.

6.23 Note that multiplying the ratios for these two factors gives the return on capital employed.

$$\frac{\text{Operating profit}}{\text{Sales}} \times \frac{\text{Sales}}{\text{Operating assets}} = \frac{\text{Operating profit}}{\text{Operating assets}} = \text{ROCE}$$

6.24 In the example of X plc for 20X7:

$$\frac{\text{Operating profit}}{\text{Sales}} = \frac{£27m}{£209m} = 12.9\%$$

$$\frac{\text{Sales}}{\text{Operating assets}} = \frac{£209m}{£154.5m} = 1.35$$

$$12.9\% \times 1.35 = 17.4\%$$

6.25 Allowing for a small rounding difference, this is the ROCE we calculated earlier. It follows that to improve the primary measure of accounting success one must either increase the profit margin achieved on sales or increase the rate of asset turnover.

Chapter summary

- A balance sheet is a 'position statement': it shows the financial position of the organisation (its assets and liabilities) at a point in time.

- A profit and loss account is a 'period statement': it shows the results of the organisation's activities, including its profit or loss, over a period of time (typically one year).

- Ratios are a useful method of assessing the performance of a business, especially when used in comparison with similar ratios from other businesses or from earlier years.

- Profitability ratios measure the extent to which the business has traded profitably. They include gross profit percentage, net profit percentage and return on capital employed (ROCE), the primary accounting ratio.

- Liquidity ratios measure the extent to which the business has liquid assets sufficient to meet its short-term and long-term liabilities. They include current ratio, quick ratio, and gearing ratio.

- Efficiency ratios measure the efficiency with which the business is managing its assets. They include operating assets turnover, stock turnover, debtors collection period and creditors payment period.

Self-test questions

Numbers in brackets refer to paragraphs where you can check your answers

1   Describe the order in which assets are listed in a balance sheet. (1.6)

2   What is meant by 'net current assets'? (1.9)

3   How is gross profit calculated? (2.4)

4   List three categories of accounting ratios. (3.2)

5   How is the gross profit percentage calculated? (4.2)

6   How is ROCE calculated? (4.13)

7   How is the acid test ratio calculated? (5.5)

8   How is gearing calculated? (5.15)

9   How is the stock turnover period calculated? (6.8)

10   How is the creditor payment period calculated? (6.18)

CHAPTER 13

Mock Exam

THE MAY 2007 PAPER

The exam paper below was set in May 2007. If you are able to make a good attempt at this you should be very well prepared for the live examination.

Instructions for Candidates

This examination is in two sections.

Section A has two compulsory questions, worth 25 marks each.

Section B has four questions: answer two. Each question is worth 25 marks.

Note that full solutions are provided in the next chapter for Questions 1–4 (ie we choose Questions 3 and 4 from the four optional questions), while brief guidance is given in relation to Questions 5 and 6.

SECTION A

You are strongly advised to carefully read and analyse the information in the case study before attempting to answer Questions 1 and 2.

Wessex Manufacturing and Construction plc

Wessex Manufacturing and Construction plc (WMC) is a major employer in the southwest of England. It consists of three divisions:

I. Wessex Timber Products Ltd

Wessex Timber Products Ltd operates in a monopolistic competitive market. It manufactures a wide range of products to supply to house builders. Examples include doors, window frames and staircases. To minimise costs, most of its timber inputs are purchased from European countries, which use the euro (€) as their currency.

2. Somervale Building Company Ltd

Somervale Building Company Ltd operates in an oligopolistic market. It specialises in building private high-quality houses. It has five competitors within the region in which it operates. It does not compete on price, but rather on the quality of the houses it builds.

3.   Helius Heating Systems Ltd

Helius Heating Systems Ltd operates in a monopoly market. It manufactures and supplies a unique under floor heating system for new houses, using wind turbines to generate the power for the heating systems. It has no competitors in the UK because of the unique nature of its products, which it manufactures and sells under licence from a company based in the United States.

The WMC group balance sheet at 31 December 2006 contained the following information.

Current assets:	£
Stock	840,000
Debtors	2,350,000
Cash	120,000
Total	3,310,000

Current liabilities:	£
Creditors	3,460,000
Bank overdraft	2,000,000
Total	5,460,000

The WMC group's profit and loss account for 2006 contained the following information.

	£
Sales	84,000,000
Cost of sales	12,000,000
Gross profit	72,000,000
Expenses	59,680,000
Operating profit before tax	12,320,000

At the beginning of 2007, WMC approached a firm of management consultants, AB Business Services Ltd and asked it to produce a report forecasting changes in the external environment which would be likely to take place during the year. The report highlighted the following changes:

- The Bank of England's Monetary Policy Committee would be likely to raise the base rate by 0.75% during the year
- The level of unemployment was likely to rise from 1 million to 1.8 million
- The Great Britain Pound (£GBP) is likely to weaken against the euro (€) from €1.45 = £1 to €1.30 = £1

- New government legislation is expected to encourage house building in the south-west of England
- The national life expectancy rate is likely to continue to rise.

The information in this case study is purely fictitious and has been prepared for assessment purposes only.

Any resemblance to any organisation or person is purely coincidental.

Questions

Questions 1 and 2 relate to the case study and should be answered in the context of the information provided.

Question 1

(a)   From the WMC group financial information calculate and comment on:

     (i)   the gross profit percentage

     (ii) the operating profit before tax ratio

     (iii) the current ratio

     (iv) the acid test ratio.   **(8 marks)**

(b)   Discuss TWO advantages and TWO disadvantages for Wessex Manufacturing and Construction plc (WMC) of using share capital.   **(8 marks)**

(c)   Describe the features of the market types that each of the three divisions of WMC is operating in.   **(9 marks)**

SECTION B

You are strongly advised to spend 10 minutes carefully reading the questions in Section B before selecting TWO questions to answer. It is recommended that you spend approximately 35 minutes answering each question from this section.

Question 3

(a)   Identify THREE examples of natural environmental concern at a local level and THREE examples at an international level.   **(6 marks)**

(b)   Explain the main contents of an environmental policy.   **(10 marks)**

(c)   Discuss the aims of the Kyoto agreement.   **(9 marks)**

Question 4

(a)   Explain, using examples, THREE sources of English law.   **(9 marks)**

(b)   Describe FOUR of the main provisions of the UK Sale of Goods Act 1979. **(8 marks)**

(c)   Identify the FOUR criteria that must be satisfied to protect employees when there is a transfer of a business under the Transfer of Undertakings (Protection of Employment) (TUPE) Regulations of 1981.   **(8 marks)**

Question 5

(a)   Describe the characteristics of organisations in the public and private sectors.
(8 marks)

(b)   Explain how purchasing for an organisation in the public sector differs from purchasing for an organisation in the private sector.   **(8 marks)**

(c)   Outline the technological factors that affect purchasing operations.   **(9 marks)**

Question 6

(a)   Describe the nature of a public-private partnership.   **(8 marks)**

(b)   Explain the roles of the European Commission and the European Union Council of Ministers.   **(9 marks)**

(c)   Identify the main aims of the World Trade Organisation.   **(8 marks)**

CHAPTER 14

Mock Exam: Suggested Solutions

THE MAY 2007 PAPER

Some general observations

Make sure that you have read the 'Instructions for Candidates' section at the front of the Mock Exam, in order to be quite clear as to what is required.

Please bear in mind that our solutions are lengthier than you would attempt in an exam, in order to cover the wide range of points that might be included – and to reflect the suggestions given in the CIPS Answer Guidance.

SUGGESTED SOLUTIONS

SECTION A

Solution 1

Part (a)

Part of this question is pure calculation, but you are also required to comment on what these ratios and figures tell you about the organisation's performance/success, etc.

(i)   £72m/£84m = 85.71%

(ii)   £12,320,000/£84,000,000 = 14.67%

These two profitability ratios measure how well the company is performing and the higher they are, the better. WMC has a very high gross profit percentage and a reasonably good operating profit percentage.

(iii) £3,310,000/£5,460,000 = 0.61

The current ratio measures whether a company is in a position to settle its debts to creditors and the bank. Ideally, it should be at least 1.0 and WMC's current ratio is below this giving cause for concern although such concern is not great.

(iv)   (£3,310,000 – £840,000)/£5,460,000 = 0.45

The acid test ratio measures whether a company is in a position to settle its debts after stock has been taken away. Again, the ideal ratio is about 1.0 and WMC's is well below this, which could cause liquidity problems.

Part (b)

Advantages include:

*   No fixed interest charges to pay

*   The money need not be repaid, as would be the case for loan capital.

Disadvantages include:

*   Shareholders may not be prepared to invest in the company

*   Shareholders will demand dividends.

Part (c)

Here, you should describe the key features of each type of market in terms of the number of competitors, ease of entry into the industry and the methods used by companies to compete. This would be as follows.

*   Monopolistic competition: there is usually a fairly large number of competitors and competition might take the form of price-based competition or differentiation of many kinds. Such markets are reasonably easy to enter.

- Oligopoly: here, there are a few competitors and sometimes these will collude to fix prices (or at least ensure that they are all close). Price differentiation is rare. Instead, companies tend to use product differentiation as the main means of competing. Such markets are quite difficult to enter because huge advertising is often necessary for a would-be entrant with the drawback of there probably being only a small market share to gain.

- Monopoly: here, there are no competitors and therefore, no competition. Market entry is virtually impossible because of the amount and cost of product development required by a would-be entrant with little prospect of gaining any market share to speak of.

Solution 2

Part (a)

There is not much scope for discussion with questions such as this. You should identify that the fall in the GBP against the euro would lead to higher import prices. In the light of this, the purchasing department of WMC would have to address the fall in the value of GBP and decide whether to accept the higher prices or implement change, such as:

• Buying before the fall in the GBP although this would demand good forecasting of requirements

• Sourcing in the UK if this is possible

• Sourcing from another country which doesn't have the euro as its currency, again, if this is possible.

Part (b)

Here, you should identify and explain the negative impact on companies in the building industry of the forecast economic changes, which specifically are rising interest rates and higher unemployment. You should also explain the positive changes for building, in terms of longer life expectancy and government policy to encourage more house building. There is no need to divide answers between the three divisions because these likely changes would affect all of them. A detailed answer should state that:

• A rising interest rate would mean that the cost of borrowing (in the case of the building industry: mortgages) would increase, meaning that fewer people would be inclined or able to take out mortgages, which would mean the demand for houses falling.

• Similarly, a rise in unemployment would mean that fewer people are able to take out mortgages with the same effect as above.

On the other hand, increased life expectancy is likely to mean more people wanting houses of their own because there will be more people of house-owning age and government policy to encourage house building should, of course, have a positive effect for WMC because it will be easier/more profitable (we are not told exactly what the government policy is) to build houses.

Part (c)

This is a fairly straightforward question and you should note that the command word 'identify' means that no explanation is required.

• **Internal stakeholders** are: employees, managers, directors and shareholders

• **External stakeholders** are: customers, suppliers, banks and government agencies

Solution 3

Part (a)

You should note here that the command word is 'identify' and so no explanation of the points you make is required.

- Natural environmental concerns at local level are: noise, dirt, vibration (usually caused by heavy vehicles and/or factories with 'heavy'/violent processes such as drop forges) which can damage surrounding property, and water or air pollution. Any three of these would suffice

- International level concerns are: the destruction of the ozone layer, global warming and deforestation.

Part (b)

Some care is required here because your answer should focus on policy which is likely to affect purchasing departments, although more 'general' suggestions would not lose marks. Specific suggestions could include:

- Using suppliers who conform to environmental standards such as ISO 9000 (an organisation cannot claim to be environmentally friendly if its suppliers, particularly major suppliers, are not)

- Using inputs which are environmentally friendly

- Ensuring that all departments in the organisation operate in an environmentally friendly manner. This would focus on aspects of operations such as:

  - Production and disposal of waste – producing as little as possible and disposing of it in an environmentally friendly manner such as recycling
  - Reducing air pollution to the smallest amount possible
  - Eliminating water pollution by not disposing of waste water into rivers, streams, etc.

Part (c)

A good starting point here would be to explain briefly that the Kyoto Protocol is an international agreement that many countries including the UK (but not the USA) signed up to. Its basic aim is that the signatory countries will strive to reduce greenhouse gas emissions. The implications of this for the signatory countries and on organisations in these countries would be as follows.

- The investment required by both central governments and individual organisations to meet this target. Investment would be needed by organisations to contribute to meeting government targets and although government aid to organisations is likely, it would almost certainly not cover all costs.

- Changes in technology needed to achieve the aims. Again, these would require investment and development by organisations in support of government targets. This would involve technological developments in trying to improve the environmental impact of, for example, production processes and transport, these being the largest sources of greenhouse gas emissions.

Solution 4

Part (a)

Here you should identify the following sources of English law:

- **Statute law**: examples might include the Unfair Contract Terms Act (1977) and the Sale of Goods Act (1979) or the Supply of Goods and Services Act (1982).

- **Case law**: examples might include *Butler Machine Tool Corporation Ltd v Ex-Cell-O Corporation* (1979), *Carlill v The Carbolic Smoke Ball Co.* (1893) and *Atlas Express Ltd v Kafco* (1989).

- **European law**: examples of European law would be regulations and directives. These must be enacted into UK law unless subject to one of the exemptions that apply to the UK.

The Senior Assessor's report states that 1 mark was awarded for each of the three sources and 2 marks for examples in each of the three categories, meaning that 2 examples per source of law were required although the question does not make this clear.

Part (b)

Here, you are required to identify any four of the implied terms introduced by the UK Sale of Goods Act (1979) and then briefly describe them and their implications. The main implied terms of this Act are as follows.

- **Section 12: Title:** The Act states that there is an implied condition that the seller has the right to sell the goods. This is important because, if the seller did not have that right, the buyer would not acquire the rights of ownership of the goods once they had been purchased.

- **Section 13: Description:** The Act states that, when goods are sold by description (eg in a catalogue), there is an implied condition that the goods shall correspond with the description. This can also apply to goods that are sold against a specification.

- **Section 14(2): Satisfactory quality:** The 1979 Act referred to 'merchantable quality' but this has subsequently been amended to 'satisfactory quality'. This is an implied condition that, where the seller sells goods in the course of a business, goods supplied will be of satisfactory quality. The Act defines 'satisfactory quality' as 'meeting the standard that a reasonable person would regard as satisfactory taking into account any description of the goods, the price and all other relevant circumstances'.

- **Section 14(3): Fitness for purpose:** where the seller sells goods in the course of a business and the buyer, expressly or by implication, makes known to the seller any particular purpose for which the goods are being bought, there is an implied condition that the goods supplied are reasonably fit for that purpose whether or not that is a purpose for which such goods are commonly supplied, except where the circumstances show that the buyer does not rely, or that it is unreasonable for him/her to rely, on the skill or judgement of the seller.

- **Section 15: Sale by sample:** in any sale by sample there are implied conditions that:

  - The bulk of the items shall correspond with the sample
  - The buyer shall have a reasonable opportunity of comparing bulk with the sample
  - The goods shall be free of any defect rendering them unsatisfactory which would not be apparent on a reasonable examination of the samples

In all of these terms, there is considerably more detail but use of something similar to the above descriptions should gain high marks.

Part (c)

You should start this answer by stating that the Transfer of Undertakings (Protection of Employment) (TUPE) Regulations of 1981 were designed to protect employees if there is a transfer of a business. You should then explain that, for an employee to benefit from this protection, the following four criteria must be fulfilled.

- There must have been a transfer of an economic activity. An example here might be where an activity previously performed 'in-house' is outsourced to an external service provider.

- The employee concerned must have been employed by the old employer immediately before the transfer. Using the example above where an external service provider takes on an outsourced activity: an employee previously working 'in-house' is transferred to the new service provider.

- The employment must have been in the economic activity transferred. In other words, using the above example, the employee must have been doing the same job for the previous employer as for the new service provider.

- The employee must have been in a situation where their contract would have been terminated by the transfer. In other words, again using the example above, where the employee would have been made redundant because the activity was outsourced had they not been taken on by the new service provider.

Solution 5

A solution to parts (a) and (b) can easily be compiled from Chapter 2 of this text. For part (c) the answer comes from Chapter 8.

Solution 6

All parts of this question are covered by the material in Chapter 5 of the text.

Subject Index

5 forces model 52

Absorption costing 172
Accounting standards 164
Acid test ratio 186
Activity based costing 174
Age structure 107
Aggregate demand 88
Articles of Association 29
Asset turnover 188
Audit Commission 33

Balance of payments 93
Balance sheet 178
Bank overdraft 165
Barriers to entry and exit 44
Barriers to international trade 58
Biodiversity 134
'Boom and bust' 91
Business cycle 91
Business ethics 108
Business sectors 19
Buyer power 53

Cartels 50, 158
Case law 146
Cashflow statement 182
Chairman's statement 182
Circular flow of income 88
Civil law 147
Climate change 136
Closed systems 5
Collusion in oligopoly markets 50
Commission for Equality and Human Rights 153
Common law 146
Common markets 94
Competition law 158
Competitive forces 52
Competitor analysis 56
Complementary goods 40
Concentrated industries 54
Conflicting stakeholder goals 69
Connected stakeholders 64
Consumer preferences 41
Consumer trends 102
Contract law 147
Contribution, in cost accounting 172
Convergence of accounting standards 164
Corporate social responsibility 65, 108
Cost analysis 171
Costs to sales ratios 185
Council of Ministers 80
Council of the European Union 80
Credit from suppliers 166
Creditor payment period 190
Criminal law 147

Culture 102, 103
Current assets 178
Current liabilities 180
Current ratio 186
Cyclical unemployment 91

DBFO projects 79
Debentures 169
Debt collection period 189
Demand and supply 40
Demand curves 41
Demographics 102, 106
Developed and developing economies 22
Direct discrimination 153
Disability Discrimination Act 153
Disposable income 41
Diversity 112

Earnings before interest and tax 186
E-auctions 125
EC law 147
E-commerce 124
Economic factors in the environment 10, 85
Economic growth 88
Economic integration 94
Efficiency ratios 183, 188
Electronic catalogues 125
Electronic data interchange 123
Employer associations 78
Employment Act 2002 154
Employment Equality (Age) Regulations 153
Employment law 151
Employment policy 90
English law, sources of 146
Environmental analysis 8
Environmental change 6
Environmental damage 135
Environmental factors 131
Environmental law and regulation 137
Environmental monitoring 9
Environmental policy 139
E-procurement 125
Equal opportunity law 153
Equal Pay Act 153
Equity, as a source of law 146
E-sourcing 125
E-tendering 125
Ethical factors in the environment 12
Ethics 102, 108
Ethnicity 107
EU procurement directives 33
European Commission 80
European Court of Justice 81
European Parliament 81
European Union 80
Exchange rates 95
External stakeholders 64

Externalities 65, 109

Factoring of invoices 167
Fair Trading Act 158
Feedback 5
Finance for the public sector 170
Finance, sources of 165
Financial accounting and management accounting 162
Financial analysis 15, 177
Financial concepts 161
Financial reporting standards 164
Five forces model 52
Five year summary 182
Fixed assets 178
Fixed costs 171
Flexible working hours 154
Forward exchange contracts 96
Fragmented industries 54
Free-trade areas 94
Frictional unemployment 90
Funding for national government 79

Gearing, in accounts 185, 187
General Agreement on Tariffs and Trade 81
Globalisation 3, 58
Government departments 32
Government influence on business 78
Government investment products 170
'Green' business 141
'Green' consumerism 138
Gross domestic product 22
Gross national product 88
Gross profit 181
Gross profit percentage 184
Group of Eight 82

Harassment 153
Health and safety at work 155
Hire purchase 169
Hofstede, Geert 111
Human resource management 102

Impact assessment grid 14
Indirect discrimination 153
Industry structure 54
Inflation 89
Intensity of rivalry 54
Interest groups 77
Interest rates 89
Internal stakeholders 64
International accounting standards 164
International economics 93
International politics 80
International sourcing 97
International trading 56, 110
Internet, intranet, extranet 124
Invoice discounting 167

Knowledge transfer networks 120

Kyoto Protocol 137

Leasing and hire purchase 169
Legal factors in the environment 12, 145
Liabilities in the balance sheet 180
Limited companies 28
Liquid assets 178
Liquidity ratios 183, 186
Loan capital 169
Local government authorities 32, 75
Local politics 75
Local/national/international environment 2
Long-term liabilities 180

Macro-economic factors 86
Management accounting 162
Management information systems 123
Marginal costing 172
Market economy 24, 40
Market mechanism 40
Market structure 40, 43
Markets, types of 39
Memorandum of Association 29
Mendelow's matrix 67
Micro/macro environment 1
Mixed economy 25
Monetary policy 89
Monopolistic competition 43, 48
Monopoly 43, 46
Monopoly regulation 47
Multinational corporations 20
Municipal enterprises 32

National Audit Office 33
National debt 92
National economic policy 86
National politics 76
National Savings 170
Natural environment 132
Net current assets 180
Net profit 181
Net profit percentage 184
Net worth 187
NFP sector regulation 35
Not-for-profit organisations 34

Oligopoly 43, 49
Open systems 5
Organisation as an open system 5
Organisation culture 104
Organisation for Economic Co-operation and Development 82

Partnership 28
Perfect competition 43, 44
PESTLE framework 9
Point of sale systems 122
Political factors in the environment 10, 73
Political parties 77
Population size 106

Porter's five forces.................................... 52
Potential new entrants to a market................ 53
Power/interest matrix................................ 67
Pressure groups 77, 138
Price cartels.................................... 50, 158
Price discrimination................................ 46
Primary industries................................. 20
Primary ratio...................................... 185
Private and public sectors 23
Private Finance Initiative......................... 79
Private limited company.......................... 28
Private sector organisations...................... 27
Private sector regulation......................... 31
Privatised firms................................... 31
Procurement directives............................ 33
Product lifecycle.................................. 118
Product markets................................... 40
Profit and loss account........................... 181
Profitability ratios...................... 182, 184
Public Contracts Regulations.................... 158
Public corporations............................... 32
Public limited company.......................... 28
Public sector borrowing requirement.............. 92
Public-private partnerships 79, 171
Public sector finance............................. 170
Public sector organisations...................... 32
Public sector procurement........................ 158
Public sector regulation.......................... 33
Purchasing environment 1

Quangos... 32
Quick ratio 186
Quotas as a barrier to trade..................... 94

Race Relations Act............................... 153
Radio frequency identification.................. 122
Ratio analysis............................... 16, 183
Redundancy....................................... 151
Regional distribution............................ 107
Regional trading blocs....................... 81, 94
Regulation of monopoly........................... 47
Regulation of the NFP sector.................... 35
Regulation of the private sector................ 31
Regulation of the public sector................. 33
Regulatory framework of accounting............. 163
Resource depletion and management.............. 134
Retail buying..................................... 21
Retained profits................................. 168
Return on capital employed.............. 185, 191
Reverse auctions................................. 125

Sale and leaseback............................... 167
Sale of goods law................................ 147
Schumpeter, Joseph.............................. 119
Scottish Parliament.............................. 75
Seasonal unemployment........................... 90
Secondary industries............................ 20
Sectors of the economy........................... 20
Services, characteristics of..................... 22
Sex Discrimination Act.......................... 153

Share capital.................................... 168
Silent stakeholders.............................. 67
Single European currency......................... 96
Single European Market.......................... 80
Small and medium enterprises 20, 29
Social factors in the environment........... 11, 101
Social infrastructure........................... 102
Socio-economic class....................... 102, 108
Sole trader...................................... 27
Stakeholders................................ 3, 63
Stakeholder management.......................... 68
Statute law...................................... 146
Stock turnover ratio............................. 189
Structural unemployment.......................... 90
Subscription paid sector......................... 34
Substitute goods........................... 40, 53
Supplier power................................... 54
Supply and demand............................... 40
Supply curves.................................... 42
Supply markets................................... 40
Sustainable procurement.......................... 75
SWOT analysis.................................... 14
Synergy.. 71
Systems theory.................................... 5

Tariff barriers to trade......................... 94
Taxation as a source of funds.................... 79
Technological factors in the environment.... 11, 115
Technology development........................... 117
Technology transfer.............................. 120
Tertiary industries.............................. 20
Theory of comparative advantage.................. 57
Third sector..................................... 34
Tools of environmental analysis.................. 13
Tracking systems................................ 122
Trade associations............................... 78
Trade unions 78
Treaty of Rome............................. 80, 158
Trompenaars, Fons............................... 103
TUPE regulations................................ 151
Turbulent change.................................. 7

Unemployment, types of........................... 90
Unfair contract terms........................... 150

Variable costs................................... 171
Virtual teams................................... 123
Voluntary sector................................. 34

Welsh Assembly................................... 75
Working capital ratio............................ 186
Working capital................... 166, 180, 188
World Trade Organisation.......................... 81